S0-BFF-110

EXECUTIVE'S GUIDE TO ONLINE INFORMATION SERVICES

by Ryan E. Hoover

Knowledge Industry Publications, Inc.

*Information and Communications
Management Guides*

The Executive's Guide to Online Information Services

Library of Congress Cataloging in Publication Data

Hoover, Ryan E.
  The executive's guide to online information services.

  Bibliography: p.
  Includes index.
  1. Management—Information services. 2. Information
storage and retrieval systems—Management. 3. Informa-
tion storage and retrieval systems—Business. I. Title.
HD30.35.H66 1984   025′.04′024658   84-15427
ISBN 0-86729-090-0
ISBN 0-86729-089-7 (pbk.)

HD
30
.35
.H66
1984

Printed in the United States of America

Copyright © 1984 by Knowledge Industry Publications, Inc., 701 Westchester Ave.,
White Plains, NY 10604. Not to be reproduced in any form whatever without
written permission from the publisher.

10   9   8   7   6   5   4   3   2   1

Table of Contents

List of Tables

List of Figures

TRADEMARK ACKNOWLEDGMENTS

The following names, described in the text and/or illustrations, are trademarks or service marks of the companies as listed.

ABI/Inform (Data Courier, Inc.); Accountants Index (American Institute of Certified Public Accountants); Academic American Encyclopedia (Grolier Electronic Publishing); ADP, ADP Network Services, Autonet, Datapath (Automated Data Processing, Inc.); Adtrack (Corporate Intelligence, Inc.); AP Videotex (Associated Press, Inc.); Apilit, Apipat (American Petroleum Institute); Apple (Apple Computer, Inc.); AT&T (American Telephone & Telegraph Co.); BI/Data Forecasts, BI/Data (Business International Corp.); Biography Master Index, Encyclopedia of Associations (Gale Research Co.); BIOSIS Previews (BioSciences Information Service); Books in Print, Ulrich's International Periodicals Directory (R.R. Bowker Co.); BRS, BRS/After Dark; BRS/Medical Colleague (Bibliographic Retrieval Services, Inc.); Business Information Wire (Canadian Press, Ltd.); CA Search (Chemical Abstracts Service); Citibase (Citibank Corp.); Compendex (Engineering Information, Inc.); CompuServe (CompuServe, Inc.); Compustat, Standard & Poor's News (Standard & Poor's Corp.); Comp-U-Store (Comp-U-Card International, Inc.); Conference Papers Index (Cambridge Scientific Abstracts, Inc.); Congressional Record Abstracts, Federal Register Abstracts (Capitol Services, Inc.); D&B, Million Dollar Directory, Dunsprint, Dunsplus, Dun's Market Identifiers 10+, Principal International Businesses (Dun & Bradstreet, Inc.); Dialog, Knowledge Index (Dialog Information Services, Inc.); Disclosure II, Disclosure/Spectrum Ownership, microDisclosure (Disclosure, Inc.); Dow Jones News/Retrieval Service, Dow Jones, Wall Street Journal, Barron's, Market Microscope, Spreadsheet Link, Market Manager, Market Analyzer (Dow Jones & Co., Inc.); EIS Industrial Plants, EIS Nonmanufacturing Establishments (Economic Information Systems, Inc.); Electronic Yellow Pages (Market Data Retrieval, Inc.); Forbes Directory (Forbes, Inc.); GTE Telenet, Telenet, Telemail (General Telephone & Electronics Corp.); Harvard Business Review (John Wiley & Sons, Inc.); IBM, IBM Personal Computer, IBM PC (International Business Machines Corp.); Industry Data Sources, Legal Resource Index, Magazine ASAP, Magazine Index, National Newspaper Index, Newsearch, Search Helper, Trade & Industry ASAP, Trade & Industry Index (Information Access Co.); InSearch (Menlo Corp.); I.P. Sharp, Infomagic, Micromagic (I.P. Sharp Associates, Ltd.); Lexis, Lexpat, Nexis, UBIQ (Mead Data Central); Management Contents, The Computer Database (Management Contents, Inc.); Marquis Who's Who (Marquis Who's Who, Inc.); Media General Database, Stockvue (Media General Financial Services, Inc.); Microcomputer Index (Database Services); NaturalLink (Texas Instruments, Inc.); NewsNet, NewsFlash (NewsNet, Inc.); NTIS (National Technical Information Service); OAG, OAG Electronic Edition (Official Airline Guides, Inc.); Orbit, SDC Information Services, SearchMaster (System Development Corp.); PC/NetLink (Informatics General Corp.); PCTalk (Headlands Press, Inc.); PTS Annual Reports Abstracts, PTS Defense Markets & Technology, PTS PROMT (Predicasts, Inc.); Radio Shack (Tandy Corp.); SciMate, SciSearch (Institute for Scientific Information); Smartcom II, Smartmodem (Hayes Microcomputer Products, Inc.); The Source, Bizdate, Bizdex (Source Telecomputing Corp.); Trademark-scan (Thompson & Thompson); Tymnet, OnTyme (Tymnet, Inc.); Uninet (Uninet, Inc.); UPI, Stockcheck (United Press International, Inc.); Value Line Data Base II (Arnold Bernhard & Co., Inc.); Viewtron (Knight-Ridder Newspapers, Inc.); Vu/Text (Vu-Text Information Service, Inc.); World Patents Index (Derwent Publications, Ltd.).

Online data and information records and their display formats are copyrighted by their publishers, producers and vendors and may not be reproduced without their permission.

ACKNOWLEDGMENTS

The author wishes to thank the various online information service vendors and database and software publishers, particularly David Keith of I.P. Sharp Associates Ltd., for their information and assistance in preparing this book. The author also wishes to express his gratitude to Adrienne Hickey, senior book editor of Knowledge Industry Publications, Inc., without whose support and assistance this book would not have been possible.

This book is dedicated to Rosalie, my wife,
whose patience, understanding and encouragement
helped make it a reality.

Preface

How often have you needed a particular item of information to help you make an important business decision? Of course, you want that information immediately. Timely information about a competitor, a product, an invention, research and development, or financial and economic trends can help you make important daily decisions if you are an executive, manager or entrepreneur.

That information is probably available for immediate retrieval at your desk, at reasonable cost, if you have a telephone and a personal computer or other data terminal. A local phone call is all you need in most cases to get information stored in computer systems around the world — through online information services.

WHAT ARE ONLINE SERVICES?

The term "online" means that, with the proper terminal equipment, you have access over telephone lines to databases of computerized electronic information on remote computer systems. Thus, you are "on the line," communicating with a computer system that may be next door or halfway around the world.

As of spring 1984, approximately 250 commercial electronic online information services provided access to more than 2000 databases covering virtually any topic you can imagine. In 1983 online electronic publishing revenues were more than $1.5 billion, and the growth of this industry is accelerating.

Most online information services are reasonably priced. Generally, you pay only for the information you actually use and the time required to get it. Online requests for information seldom take more than 10 or 15 minutes. When you compare the time and cost of an online request with that of tracking down the same information in traditional ways, the advantages soon become apparent.

THE STRUCTURE OF THIS BOOK

Online information services have many applications. This book will tell you what those services are, how to use them, what they cost and what they can mean for you.

The many illustrations included show you specific kinds of information available and how the data actually appear on your terminal screen or paper printout.

Chapter 1 presents an introduction to online services: how they developed, how they work, the kinds of information available and how you can retrieve that information. Some general applications of online services to business are discussed. Chapter 2 tells you how to decide if online services are for you, what they cost and what you will need to go online. You also will learn how you can take advantage of online services without going online yourself. In Chapter 3, you will learn about the commercial data communications networks, which permit telephone access to online services at low cost. Other types of access are also discussed.

Chapters 4-9 describe the various types of databases and information that you have available to you online and that you are most likely to use in your business.

Chapter 4 is an overview of major services and databases. These include Dow Jones News/Retrieval Service, CompuServe Information Service, The Source, Mead Data Central, NewsNet, Dialog Information Services, Bibliographic Retrieval Services (BRS), SDC Orbit Search Service, ADP Network Services and I.P. Sharp Associates. Costs, ease of use and types of business information offered are described. Chapter 5 looks at databases that contain general news about the business world. Many of these databases are available from major online services, such as Dow Jones, The Source, CompuServe and Dialog. More specialized services such as NewsNet and Nexis are also described.

In the next two chapters we describe the wealth of information that is available online about specific companies and corporations, both public and private and of all sizes. Chapter 6 looks at databases that provide such information as company descriptions, officers and directors, annual reports and corporate rankings. Among the publishers of these databases are Disclosure, Predicasts, Inc., Dun & Bradstreet, Standard & Poor's and the U.S. Department of Commerce. Chapter 7 discusses databases that offer numeric information—corporate financial data, stock quotes and other securities data about specific companies, as well as general economic statistics and forecasts. These databases are provided by Disclosure, Standard & Poor's, the Value Line, Dow Jones, Citibank and others.

Bibliographic citations and other reference data are the largest category of online information. Through the library research services, you can have access to index, abstract and full-text records of nearly all of the world's major business and technical publications over the last 10 years or more. Chapter 8 looks at several of the major bibliographic and reference databases in business, industry, law, government, scientific and technical research and development, and general reference.

Most of the online services described in this book are general rather than specific, in that they offer large numbers of databases on a wide variety of topics. In Chapter 9, however, you will learn about some specialized information services that provide airline schedules and fares; legal, medical and marketing information; and electronic shopping.

Chapter 10 tells you about some of the ways in which a personal computer can help you take increased advantage of online information. Special interfaces simplify the process of searching databases. Inexpensive software packages allow you to download, manipulate and reformat information you retrieve online. With standard business software such as spreadsheet and word processing programs, you can then incorporate information into your daily work. Several of these packages are described in this chapter.

Chapter 11 offers an overview of some types of current online services besides information, and an evaluation of some of the barriers to wider use of online services. The chapter also reviews the problems and promise of multipurpose online services known as videotex (which offers both text and color graphics).

Appendixes include a glossary of terms commonly used in computer communications; sources of additional information, including articles, books, journals, directories, online databases and annual conferences; and a directory of the online services and networks discussed in this book.

THE ONLINE "BOOM"

Since the online information industry is growing so rapidly, it is inevitable that some of the material in this book will be outdated or irrelevant by the time you read it. Every effort has been made to be certain that the information was current and accurate as of mid-1984. Readers are advised to contact the service provider for the latest information about a particular database or service.

The online electronic publishing industry is still young. Industry giants like IBM, Burroughs, Boeing, General Electric, Dow Jones, General Telephone and Electronics, McGraw-Hill, Times Mirror, Knight-Ridder, The New York Times Co. and Lockheed are already in the business or are preparing to enter it. By the turn of the century, the data processing industries, including electronic publishing and related services, will be a driving force in the world economy. You can take advantage of the online world now by getting an information edge on your competitors. This book will show you how.

Ryan Hoover
July 1984

1

Online Information: an Introduction

No successful business person operates in a vacuum. The most critical resource for an effective manager is *information*—of many kinds and from many sources.

How do you, as a busy executive, get the information you need? You probably read *The Wall Street Journal,* business sections of other newspapers, trade magazines and journals, and specialized newsletters to keep abreast of general economic trends and new developments in your own field. No doubt you and your business associates exchange news about major competitors, corporate finance, and research and development. In addition, you and your colleagues may spend a lot of time on the telephone tracking down the latest information about various companies: their products and services, their mergers and acquisitions, their executives and officers, their headquarters and branch locations.

Online information services can give you all this information—and dramatically reduce the time you must spend to acquire it by traditional means. Online services provide current and constantly updated information on virtually every business topic, including accounting, law, technology and market research.

Online information is available in five basic forms:

- Bibliographic: citations and abstracts of magazine, newspaper and journal articles, technical reports, proposals, patents, annual reports, books, theses, dissertations and other publications.

- Reference: directories of companies, professional and trade associations, people, educational institutions, research in progress and research facilities.

- Full text: complete or abridged newspaper, magazine and journal articles, law cases, patents and reviews.

- Numeric: securities and commodities price quotations, balance sheets, income statements, econometric time series and forecasts, and statistical representations of all of the above.

- Specialized: entries integrating two or more of the above forms, including air schedules and fares, chemical and physical properties, job placement services, corporate annual reports with text and numbers, compilations of drugs (pharmacopoeias) and more.

Although databases include information on every conceivable subject, this book will emphasize those database services that are important to business and professional people.

Online information services can help you keep up with what's happening in the business world almost as it occurs. News and stock exchange wires, for example, appear online within 15 to 90 minutes. If your competitor is a public company, you can be among the first to know how that company's stock is performing, what patents it has applied for, what lucrative contracts it has been awarded, what new articles have been published about it, what its quarterly income statements are, and more.

Online services can give you a competitive edge not only on the job, but also in your personal business and investments. For example, you can manage your personal investment portfolio, shop at home and check airline fares and schedules.

In short, online information services can be a significant enhancement to your current information sources. With the proper terminal equipment, all you need to gain access to online information is the telephone.

This book will explain what online services are, how you can select the ones most appropriate to your needs, and how they can make you a more productive manager.

THE MICROCOMPUTER AND THE "INFORMATION AGE"

We are witnessing the decline of the industrial age and the emergence of the information age. Central to this change is the computer, which has revolutionized our ability to collect, store and retrieve information.

Computers have developed from massive, extremely expensive machines in the 1950s and 1960s to much smaller, less costly, yet more powerful devices. Early computers used vacuum tubes, transistors and wire in their circuits; they generated a lot of heat and required specially air-conditioned rooms, along with small armies of technicians, to keep them running. None but the largest corporations and government agencies could afford computer systems through the 1960s. But semiconductors and integrated microprocessor chips, perfected about 1970, have made smaller and much more powerful computers affordable for almost anyone.

The microcomputer, or personal computer, has put computing power within the reach of the average person. Coupled with data communications devices, microcomputers can tap the growing world of online databases of information on every topic. The information in these systems comes from traditional print publishers using computers to electronically phototypeset their publications, from news and stock exchange wire services, and from government agencies, educational institutions and research organizations that use computers to compile massive amounts of statistics.

It is estimated by various sources that at least 5 million personal computers were bought in 1983 and that 300,000 to 500,000 of these purchasers will sign up to use online services by the end of 1984. That will bring the total number of people using online services to between 500,000 and 1 million. Most of these online users will use personal computers as their terminals.

THE TECHNOLOGY OF ONLINE SERVICES

Online services are relatively easy to use. They require little expertise in computer or telecommunications technologies. But to use them most effectively you should have a basic understanding of how they work. The remainder of this chapter will explain the technology of online services, then briefly discuss their development and current status.

Components of Online Services

Online information services consist of the following components:

- electronic data compilation

- computer timesharing

- random-access storage devices

- interactive information retrieval software

- data telecommunications

- computer terminals

Continuing developments in these technologies, coupled with growing demands for timely information, make online services increasingly attractive. Each of these components will be discussed briefly below.

Electronic Data Compilation

A database is a collection or compilation of information in a form that can be "read" by a computer. Databases provide the information content of online service systems. Often they are the product of electronic publishing, which is many times faster and—potentially—much less costly than manual type-setting methods.

In electronic publishing computers are used to create, organize and store electronic information for use in various computerized processes. The typical storage medium is reels of magnetic tape. The most common use of database tapes by publishers is for electronic phototypesetting of printed publications. Thus, many electronic databases have printed counterparts. The magnetic tapes resulting from the typesetting operation can be formatted by online service vendors and transferred to magnetic disks for interactive searching.

An increasing number of databases are being created for online retrieval and display *only* and have no printed counterparts. News and stock exchange wires and tapes of financial or economic statistics, already in electronic form, are also sources for online databases. Since the 1970s, publishers have been moving away from traditional typesetting and have even abandoned some print publications altogether in favor of electronic publishing. This trend will continue for the remainder of the century.

Computer Timesharing

A central computer is the primary component of an online information system. The powerful mainframe computers used by corporations, govern-ment agencies and other organizations often have more than enough capacity to handle the data-processing needs of their owners. Most are most active only during the work week between 8 a.m. and 6 p.m. Even then they are rarely used to full capacity, because they can handle hundreds of thousands of computer-processing transactions each second. On evenings, weekends and holidays, many remain relatively idle.

In the early 1960s, when only the largest corporations and government agencies could afford computer systems, companies with large computer system capacity and idle time began to sell that time to other organizations that wanted to take advantage of the benefits of data processing. Thus, the computer timesharing services industry was born. Timesharing means that many users can share the processing time and resources of a single computer simultaneously. In recent years there has been a proliferation of computer timesharing service companies that do nothing but buy large computers and sell shared processing time to their customers through data telecommunications networks.

Random-access Storage Devices

Data storage devices provide a place to store computer-readable data and information outside of the computer itself. In the early days of computers, reels of magnetic tape were the primary storage device. Magnetic tape does not lend itself to fast retrieval of specific items of information, however, since it must be scanned from beginning to end to find the desired information. Using reels of magnetic tape to find specific information is much like trying to find a specific song on a stereo music tape—it is difficult to pinpoint.

To permit immediate retrieval of random pieces of data, magnetic disks and drives were developed. They work a lot like stereo phonograph records. Just as you can place the stylus of a record player on the particular song you want, you can retrieve precise items of information stored on magnetic disks by scanning them with a magnetic pickup at very high speed.

The computer matches your online request against all of the databases stored on magnetic disks until it finds the items that correspond to your query. This random access occurs in fractions of seconds and is why all online service companies use magnetic disks to store their databases.

Interactive Information Retrieval Software

Computer programs, or software, are the instructions that tell the computer what to do. Sophisticated information search and retrieval software is the link between the computer's processing center and the databases in storage on disks. Many retrieval programs are extremely powerful. Most incorporate search logic that permits you to ask the computer to find two words next to each other in the same sentence, in the same paragraph or in the same article. Other systems let you choose items from "menus," or lists of items contained in the databases. (A basic introduction to these search techniques is given below.) Numeric database services give you access to powerful computing programs that permit you to manipulate and reformat the numeric data retrieved.

Interactive information retrieval programs allow you to actively communicate with the databases. You enter commands that instruct the computer to retrieve information from the databases, and the results are immediately displayed. You may then ask more specific questions about the data retrieved or modify your search strategy by typing in additional commands.

Data Telecommunications

Since most users of timesharing computer systems are some distance from the central, or host, systems they are using, there must be a way to transmit computer data between the user's terminal and the host computer. The telephone network has become the primary means for communicating with remote data systems. Since telephone systems were designed originally for audio, or voice, communications, digital data signals must be converted to sound signals to be transmitted over phone lines. A modem (modulator/demodulator) is the device that does this. Both the host computer and the user's terminal must be connected to modems to pass information back and forth by telephone. (Chapter 2 has more information on modems.)

Early timesharing computer systems leased special phone lines and formed "data access arrangements" with the telephone companies. These lines were dedicated to computer data communications. However, dedicated data lines are very expensive. In the 1970s special networks for data communications were established to facilitate remote access to and between computers, using ordinary voice telephone lines. These computer communications networks, called packet-switching networks (PSNs) because of the way they transmit data signals, permit low-cost access to remote computer systems; the caller simply dials a local telephone number to reach a computer in the same or virtually any other city. The interactive communication between computers and terminals over telephone lines is what makes these computerized services "online." (Chapter 3 discusses packet-switching networks in more detail.)

Computer Terminals

A computer terminal is a device for sending and receiving data and information to and from the computer. Computer terminals consist of a typewriter-like keyboard and a means of displaying data—typically a video screen, a printer or both. A terminal can be one of three types:

- a personal computer

- a communicating word processor or electronic typewriter

- a dedicated data terminal without any computing capability (known as a "dumb" terminal)

As noted above, for use with online information services, terminals must be used with a modem. In addition, most personal computers and word processors need to have communications software on diskettes or plug-in cartridges for use as online terminals. (Terminal equipment will be discussed in more detail in Chapter 2.)

How Online Services Work

Figure 1.1 illustrates how the various elements of an online information system are combined. As shown in the figure, the online service operator (also called a database vendor) maintains databases from various information providers on magnetic disks of a central host computer system. Special programs are used to design the databases in a consistent format and to update and load them into the system on a frequent basis. Special interactive retrieval programs permit you to get information from the databases. Connections to data telecommunications networks make it possible to dial the central computer from almost anywhere, at low cost, to retrieve the information.

To use a typical online service, you sit down at your terminal and dial a local data communications access number on your telephone. The phone answers with a shrill whistling sound when it has connected with the data communications network. You type in the address or code for the online service vendor you wish to use, and the network connects you with that service's host computer. You are greeted by the online service and asked to enter your personal ID and password. Thus authorized, or logged in, you then use the interactive retrieval program to request specific information.

Online systems can be described as being either *menu-driven* or *command-driven*. In general, menu-driven services are designed for novices without computer experience and are easier to use. You just enter a number, letter or other symbol from a displayed menu to get the information you want.

Command-driven services require that you enter a keyword (a significant word that indicates the topic on which you want information) or a string of keywords, connected by logical "operators" ("and," "or," "not," "adjacent," etc.), to form keyword phrases to get what you need. These services usually require complex command protocols and were designed for professional information or data processing managers. Some services combine elements of both menu-driven and command-driven systems.

Figure 1.1: A Typical Online Information Service System

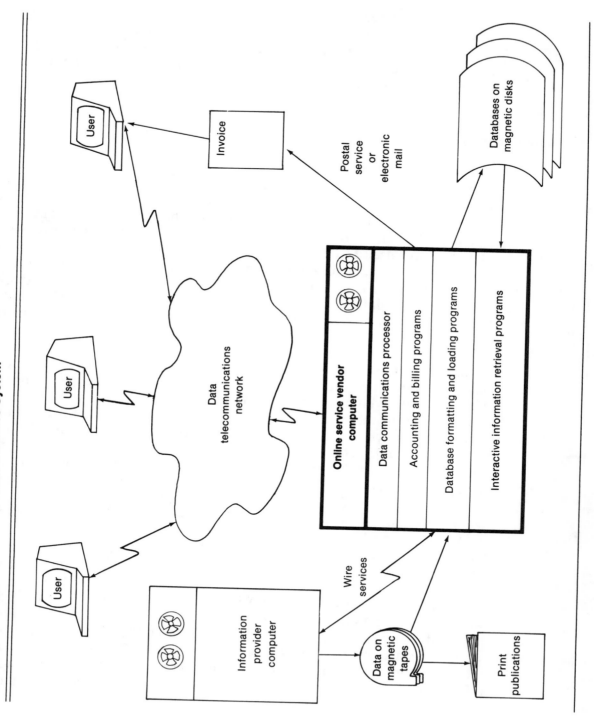

Figure 1.2 shows a sample menu-driven online session. A service combining both menu-driven and command-driven retrieval is illustrated in Figure 1.3. Figure 1.4 contains a command-driven online session; you can see in this figure that the user is assumed to be familiar with the system.

Figure 1.2: A Typical Online Session on CompuServe Information Service, A Menu-driven Retrieval System

```
COMPUSERVE  INFORMATION  SERVICE

20:51 CDT   WEDNESDAY 04-JUL-84


WHAT'S NEW THIS WEEK:

* JULY HOLIDAY HOURS ANNOUNCED
* NETWORK SURCHARGES REMINDER

FOR MORE DETAILS, TYPE GO NEW
FROM ANY PROMPT.

[% % % % % % % % % % % % % % %]
[   FOR NEW & NOTEWORTHY IN THE   ]
[     ELECTRONIC MALL, GO NNW     ]
[% % % % % % % % % % % % % % %]

KEY S OR <ENTER> TO CONTINUE!


COMPUSERVE              PAGE CIS-1

COMPUSERVE  INFORMATION  SERVICE

1 HOME SERVICES
2 BUSINESS & FINANCIAL
3 PERSONAL COMPUTING
4 SERVICES FOR PROFESSIONALS
5 THE ELECTRONIC MALL (TM)
6 USER INFORMATION
7 INDEX

ENTER YOUR SELECTION NUMBER,
OR H FOR MORE INFORMATION.
!1
```

```
COMPUSERVE              PAGE HOM-1

HOME SERVICES

 1 NEWS/WEATHER/SPORTS
 2 REFERENCE LIBRARY
 3 COMMUNICATIONS
 4 HOME SHOPPING/BANKING
 5 DISCUSSION FORUMS
 6 GAMES
 7 EDUCATION
 8 HOME MANAGEMENT
 9 TRAVEL
10 ENTERTAINMENT

LAST MENU PAGE. KEY DIGIT
OR M FOR PREVIOUS MENU.
!1


COMPUSERVE             PAGE HOM-10

        NEWS/WEATHER/SPORTS

NEWS SERVICES
 1 THE WASHINGTON POST ($)
 2 ST. LOUIS POST-DISPATCH
 3 AP VIDEOTEX WIRE
 4 NOAA WEATHER WIRE
 5 OFFICIAL PGA TOUR GUIDE
 6 HOLLYWOOD HOTLINE ($)
 7 AMERICAN SKI ASSOCIATION
 $ INDICATES SURCHARGED SERVICE

LAST MENU PAGE. KEY DIGIT
OR M FOR PREVIOUS MENU.
!3
```

(continued on next page)

Figure 1.2: A Typical Online Session on CompuServe Information Service, a Menu-driven Retrieval System (cont.)

```
REQUEST RECORDED,
ONE MOMENT, PLEASE
THANK YOU FOR WAITING

AP VIDEOTEX          PAGE APV-1

ASSOCIATED PRESS NEWS HIGHLIGHTS

1 LATEST NEWS-    7 ENTERTAINMENT
  UPDATE HOURLY
2 WEATHER         8 BUSINESS NEWS
3 NATIONAL        9 WALL STREET
4 WASHINGTON     10 DOW JONES AVG
5 WORLD          11 FEATURE NEWS
6 POLITICAL      12 HISTORY

ENTER YOUR SELECTION NUMBER
OR KEY <ENTER> FOR SPORTS

!8


AP VIDEOTEX         PAGE APV-1342

1 DOLLAR TRADES UP, GOLD DOWN
2 CLOSING MARKETS AT A GLANCE
3 MONDAY'S WORLD GOLD PRICES
4 COMMODITY FUTURES TRADE MIXED
5 WARNER SELLS ATARI TO TRAMIEL
6 CHRYSLER CREDIT CONFIRMED
7 MONDAY'S WORLD GOLD PRICES
8 MAY'S GAINS TOP APRIL DECLINE
9 JOINT CAR MAKING DEAL DELAYED
0 ROYAL CROWN GOES PRIVATE

INPUT A NUMBER OR KEY
<ENTER> FOR MORE CHOICES
!5
```

```
AP VIDEOTEX          PAGE APV-1490

AP 07/02 11:57 EDT V0947
WARNER SELLS ATARI TO TRAMIEL

   NEW YORK (AP) -- WARNER
COMMUNICATIONS INC. SAID TODAY
IT SOLD THE MAIN PARTS OF ITS
LOSS-PLAGUED ATARI INC. CONSUMER
ELECTRONICS UNIT TO A COMPANY
LED BY JACK TRAMIEL, THE FORMER
HEAD OF COMMODORE INTERNATIONAL
LTD.
   AS A RESULT OF THE SALE,
WARNER SAID IT EXPECTS TO POST A
$425 MILLION LOSS FOR THE SECOND
QUARTER.
   WARNER SOLD THE HOME-COMPUTER
AND HOME-VIDEO SEGMENTS OF
ATARI, BUT RETAINED ITS
COIN-OPERATED GAMES UNIT AND
OTHER ASSETS.
   WARNER SAID TRAMIEL AND HIS
ASSOCIATES HAD INVESTED $75
MILLION IN THEIR NEW COMPANY,
WHICH ACQUIRED WARRANTS GIVING

KEY S OR <ENTER> TO CONTINUE
!BYE

OFF AT
host: call cleared (c  0,d  0):
dte originated
```

Figure 1.3: A Typical Online Session on Dow Jones News/Retrieval Service, a System with Both Menu- and Command-driven Retrieval

```
     DOW JONES NEWS/RETRIEVAL
         COPYRIGHT (C) 1984
     DOW JONES & COMPANY, INC.
        ALL RIGHTS RESERVED.

WARNER SELLS ATARI ASSETS
TO COMPANY HEADED BY FORMER
COMMODORE CHIEF, SEE //NEWS.
DATA-BASE LIST IN //MENU.
ENTER QUERY
      //menu

         Master Menu
      Copyright (C) 1984
    Dow Jones & Company, Inc.

PRESS    FOR
   A    Dow Jones Business And
           Economic News Services
   B    Dow Jones Quotes
   C    Dow Jones Text-Search
           Services
   D    Financial And Investment
           Services
   E    General News And
           Information Services
   F    Mail Service and
           Free Customer Newsletter

        a

        Dow Jones Business
    And Economic News Services

For help, type code and HELP.
   (Example: //DJNEWS HELP)

   TYPE      FOR

//DJNEWS   90-Day News From The
           Broadtape, Selections
           From Barron's And The
           Wall Street Journal

   -PRESS RETURN FOR MORE-
      //djnews
```

```
DOW JONES NEWS IS BEING ACCESSED

ENTER QUERY
      .txn

   N   TXN       01/03 BD 1/4
   /TXN   ROK   CAT   F   /      /DEF
     06/29 TEXAS INSTRUMENTS, ROCKWELL,
   (DW) FORD, OTHERS GET DEFENSE PACTS
     WASHN -DJ- TEXAS INSTRUMENTS INC.
   RECEIVED A $7.1 MILLION ARMY CONTRACT
   FOR HEAD ASSEMBLIES FOR TANK THERMAL
   SIGHTS.
     CATERPILLAR TRACTOR CO. GOT A $6.5
   MILLION ARMY CONTRACT FOR ENGINES.
     FORD AEROSPACE & COMMUNICATION CORP.
   RECEIVED A $6.4 MILLION ARMY CONTRACT
   FOR SPARE PARTS FOR THE SERGEANT YORK
   AIR DEFENSE GUN.
     ROCKWELL INTERNATIONAL CORP. GOT A
   $6.4 MILLION NAVY CONTRACT FOR TESTING
   AND REFURBISHING OF SHIP INERTIAL
   NAVIGATION SYSTEMS.
     HAMILTON TECHNOLOGY INC. RECEIVED A
   $5.8 MILLION ARMY CONTRACT FOR FUSES.
     GENERAL DYNAMICS LAND SYSTEMS
   DIVISION RECEIVED A $5.6 MILLION ARMY
   CONTRACT FOR EXTENSION OF ENGINEERING
   DEVELOPMENT OF THE ADVANCED M-1E1 TANK.
      //text

        DOW JONES TEXT-SEARCH SERVICES
             COPYRIGHT (C) 1984
          DOW JONES & COMPANY, INC.

   PRESS    FOR

     1       THE WALL STREET JOURNAL:
               FULL-TEXT VERSION
               FROM JANUARY 1984
             * * A NEW SERVICE * *

     2       DOW JONES NEWS:
               BROADTAPE, AND SELECTED
               STORIES FROM BARRON'S AND
               THE WALL STREET JOURNAL
               FROM JUNE 1979
        2
```

(continued on next page)

Figure 1.3: A Typical Online Session on Dow Jones News/Retrieval Service, a System with Both Menu- and Command-driven Retrieval (cont.)

```
DJ/NRS  - SEARCH MODE - ENTER QUERY
   1_:            texas adj instruments

RESULT      581 DOCUMENTS

   2_:            1 and professional adj computer

RESULT       12 DOCUMENTS

   3_:            ..print 2 all/doc=1

               DOCUMENT=      1 OF      12    PAGE =     1 OF      2

AN         120314-0487.
HL         TEXAS INSTRUMENTS TO MARKET PHASER SYSTEMS INC. PRODUCT
DD         03/13/84
SO         DOW JONES NEWS WIRE (T)
CO         TXN   PHAS
TX            SAN FRAN -DJ- PHASER SYSTEMS INC.  SAID TEXAS INSTRUMENTS
           WILL BE DISTRIBUTING PHASER'S MICRO-SPF PRODUCT A PROGRAMMING
           TOOL  FOR THE TEXAS INSTRUMENTS PROFESSIONAL COMPUTER.
              4 39 PM

               DOCUMENT=      1 OF      12    PAGE =     2 OF      2

             END OF DOCUMENT

     ..off

PLEASE SIGN ON TO TEXT-SEARCH SERVICE

     disc

LOG ON: 13 33  LOG OFF: 13 35  EASTERN TIME       JULY 09, 1984
   609 42 DISCONNECTED 00 40
```

Figure 1.4: A Typical Online Session on Dialog Information Services, a Command-driven Retrieval System

```
XXXXXXXX  LOGON Filel Mon 9jul84 9:21:00 Port0A6

DIALOG News (Enter ?NEWS for details):
  Available July 1:
    MOODY'S CORPORATE PROFILES (File
      555)
    STANDARD & POOR'S CORPORATE
      DESCRIPTIONS (File 133)
  Free time in July:
    FOOD SCIENCE AND TECHNOLOGY
      ABSTRACTS (File 51)--$37.50
      combined connect time and
      TYPEs/DISPLAYs.
  Announcements:
   Price change on TRIS (File 63) now
   in effect.
   Price change on METADEX (File 32)
   now in effect.
? begin 75

         9jul84 9:21:41 User32424
   $0.33  0.013 Hrs Filel*
   $0.10  Telenet
   $0.43  Estimated Total Cost


File75:Management Contents - 74-84/Jun
(Copr. Management Contents Inc.)
         Set Items Description
         --- ----- -----------


? select ibm (w) personal (w) computer

         1      4 IBM (W) PERSONAL (W)  COMPUTER
? type 1/5/1-2

    1/5/1
     279687   DAB84A0013
     Creating Winners.
     Doesher, W.F.
     Dun & Bradstreet Reports, Vol.22, No.1, Jan./Feb. 1984, P. 13-15.,
   Journal.
     The Information Industry Association awarded its annual Hall of Fame
   award jointly to: Philip D. Estridge, president of IBM's Entry Systems
   Division and Daniel H. Fylstra, chief executive officer of VisiCorp, a
```

(continued on next page)

Figure 1.4: A Typical Online Session on Dialog Information Services, a Command-driven Retrieval System (cont.)

software company. Estridge is head of the team which created the IBM personal computer. VisiCorp engineers developed the VisiOn system, which enables the user to view several different programs simultaneously. Flystra predicts that business information previously available to only large companies will become accessible to small businesses through computers.
   Descriptors: Microcomputer; Computer Industry; Computer Services; Research and Development; Achievements and Awards; 0497; 0896; 0122; 0446; 1037

```
1/5/2
   266991    BWE83J3195
   Is 'The Real Revolution' in Personal Computers Just Beginning?
   Anon
   Business Week, No.2814, Oct. 31, 1983, P. 95,99+., Journal.
```
   The IBM Personal Computer introduced in 1981 may mark the real beginning not the end of the computer revolution. More powerful than their earlier PCs, IBM has allowed more applications and became indispensable in the office. Now more powerful machines easier to operate are entering the market and desktops are expected to boom as applications increase even more.
   Descriptors: Computer; Information Processing; Office; Sales; Market; Computer System; 0497; 0495; 0822; 0557; 0604; 1299

```
? print 2/5/1-4

Printed2/5/1-4  Estimated Cost: $1.72 (To cancel, enter PR-)
? logoff


          9jul84 9:24:00 User32424
   $3.36   0.040 Hrs File75 5 Descriptors
   $0.32   Telenet
   $0.56   2 Types
   $1.72   4 prints
   $4.24   Estimated Total Cost

LOGOFF  9:24:04

213 236 DISCONNECTED 00 00
```

Figures 1.5 through 1.8 illustrate several of the forms of information listed earlier in this chapter. Figure 1.5 shows activity on the New York Stock Exchange, available on The Source. Figure 1.6 contains a partial printout of a full-text newsletter article from NewsNet. A printout of a bibliographic citation and abstract from SDC Information Services, Inc. Orbit Search Service is given in Figure 1.7. Figure 1.8 shows airline information from the Official Airline Guide Electronic Edition.

Figure 1.5: Market Data from The Source

```
MARKET AT 1630 ON MONDAY, SEPT.19

DOW JONES CLOSING AVERAGES

    Stock   Open     High     Low      Close    Change
30 Indus  1227.64  1242.68  1221.24  1233.94  up   8.23
20 Trans   574.23   588.02   571.86   582.84  up  10.11
15 Utils   131.45   132.32   130.64   131.45  off  0.44
65 stock   489.90   469.90   487.04   493.17  up   4.29
Transactions in stocks used in averages:
                Monday           Friday
Indus        7,784,400        7,307,400
Trans        3,048,000        3,349,900
Utils        2,729,200        1,682,000
65 Stock    13,561,600       12,339,300
     .
     .
     .

15 MOST ACTIVE STOCKS IN NYSE COMPOSITE TRADING

    Stock            Sales        Close     Net Change
    Cmwlth Ed      x-1,017,500    26 1/2     off 1/8
    Chrysler Cp      974,000      29 5/8      -
    ATT Co           968,800      67         off 1/8
    LTV Corp         956,400      18         up 1/2
    IBM Corp         911,500     123 3/4     up 5/8
    Pfizer Inc       900,000      38 1/8     up 1/8
    Kmart Cp         830,900      37 3/8     up 1 1/4
    Genl Motors      822,000      73 1/4     up 1 7/8
    Ford Motor       743,300      63         up 2
    Merrl Lynch      733,500      37 5/8     up 3/4
    Dow Chem         637,000      36 3/8     up 3/8
    G Wst Fncl       623,600      24         up 5/8
    Fed Ntl Mtg      622,200      26 7/8     up 1 3/8
    Pan Am Air       603,800       7 3/8     up 1/8
    Sears Roeb       590,000      37 3/4     up 5/8
    X-Ex-Dividend.

United Press International via THE SOURCE

--END--
```

Figure 1.6: A Partial Printout of a Full-text Newsletter Article from NewsNet

```
1)
                    CONTROL DATA TO BUY A STAKE IN THE SOURCE;
         BRIDGE BETWEEN "VIDEOTEX" AND "MAINSTREAM" SERVICES EXPECTED

            The Reader's Digest Association and Control Data Corp. have
         announced the signing of a letter of intent for Control Data to
         make an investment in RD's Source Telecomputing Corp (STC)
         subsidiary.  The letter is expected to lead to a formal agreement
         under which RD will maintain a controlling interest in the company.

            Currently, Reader's Digest owns 80% of STC; 20% is held by
         investor Jack Taub, and is not involved in the announced agreement.
         LINK sources indicate  that Control Data plans to acquire about
         30% of The Source for about $5 million -- which is also roughly
         the Source's expected operating loss for 1983.

            The announcement, the culmination of extended negotiations
         between Source CEO George Grune and CDC Senior Vice President of
         Data Services Walter Bruning, is striking in its verisimilitude to
         the objectives voiced by Grune in the July 1982 issue of this
         newsletter: "From the very beginning," Grune stated then, "...we
         made it clear that we would entertain a partnership with an
         appropriate organization that had the technical resources,
         specifically in computers, networking capabilities, etc., to
         enhance the future delivery of our services to increasing numbers
         of subscribers."

            The intent of that declaration has now been realized, and
         although other combinations might have had their own logic (with
         GTE Telenet, Tymshare, ADP, Dialog or BRS -- fill in your own
         candidate), Control Data brings a powerful set of potential
         synergies to its new partner.

            Overall, it brings its status as one of the largest suppliers
         of commercial and scientific timesharing services in the world,
         with a large collection of IBM mainframes and CDC Cyber
         "supercomputers" and an extensive international leased-line
         network at its disposal.  More specifically, CDC brings an
         established line of specialized data services for which The Source
         is likely to be tested as a distribution channel or ancillary
         service.

            Ticketron, for one.  The Source could provide added value to
         the ticket-ordering service successfully developed by Control Data
              .
              .
              .
```

Figure 1.7: A Bibliographic Citation and Abstract from SDC Orbit Search Service

ACCESSION NUMBER	83-21399
TITLE	Electronic Publishing Moves Off the Drawing Boards
AUTHORS	Anonymous
SOURCE	Business Week (BUWEA3,BWE), n2802, PP.54-593, PAGES, ISSN 0007-7135, Aug 8, 1983
AVAILABILITY	ABI/INFORM
DOCUMENT TYPE	J (Journal Paper)
LANGUAGE	English
INDEX TERMS	Electronic; Publishing industry; Videotex; Newspapers; Online (DP); Data bases
ABSTRACT	Electronic publishing is a topic causing growing excitement in the publishing world. Knight-Ridder Newspapers Inc. and Times Mirror Co. are among the firms who now believe it is becoming economical and viabie to distribute information electronically instead of using printing presses. This vote of confidence is the result of the explosive growth in the number of personal computers in the US, since the desktop machine can be easily modified to get information through the telephone or cable television. While the lion's share of electronic publishing is delivered on dedicated terminals, the growth in the market will now stem from the delivery of information to personal computers in homes and offices. Thus, publishers are hurrying to develop new products for personal computers that offer both innovation and variety. They are watching closely the success of Knight-Ridder in signing up customers for its Viewtron service in southern Florida. Knight-Ridder has signed up 150 advertisers to keep costs to consumers low. The industry is already looking to create new market definitions. Many publishers, to get in the market quickly, are exploring joint ventures. Graph. Illustrations.

Figure 1.8: Airline Schedule and Fair Information from the Official Airline Guide Electronic Edition

```
              DIRECT FLIGHTS        TUE-03 JUL
FROM-DALLAS;FT.WORTH,TX,USA
# TO-CHICAGO,IL,USA
 NO EARLIER DIRECT FLIGHT SERVICE
1   630A   DFW   830A   MDW  ML 304 D9S S 0
2   706A   DFW   921A   ORD  AA 242 M80 B 0
3   820A   DFW  1020A   ORD  BN  30 72S B 0
4   831A   DFW  1035A   ORD  UA 204 72S B 0
5   840A   DFW  1052A   ORD  AA 470 767 B 0
6   915A   DFW  1125A   ORD  DL1190 73S B 0
ENTER +,CX,X#,F#,RS       (#=LINE NUMBER)
      f1


FARES IN US DOLLARS           TUE-03 JUL
SELECTED FOR DFW-ML 304 MDW

# ONE-WAY  RND-TRP  ARLN/CLASS FARECODE
 NO LOWER FARES IN CATEGORY
1*          269.00    ML/B      BE7
2  180.00   360.00    ML/Y      Y
 NO HIGHER FARES IN CATEGORY
 * ENTER L# TO VIEW LIMITATIONS
ENTER L#,X#,S,RS         (#=LINE NUMBER)
      l1


LIMITATIONS DISPLAY           TUE-03 JUL
DFW-CHI      CLASS:B  FARECODE:BE7
MIDWAY AIRLINES
FARE DESCRIPTION: ADVANCE PURCHASE
 EXCURSION FARES
BOOKING CODE: B.

MAXIMUM STAY ALLOWED IS 60 DAYS.

PURCHASE TICKET FOR TRAVEL NO LATER
 THAN 7 DAYS BEFORE DEPARTURE.
 * END OF LIMITATIONS DISPLAY *
ENTER F TO RETURN TO FARE DISPLAY
ENTER S TO RETURN TO SCHEDULE DISPLAY
```

After receiving the information you requested, you sign off of the system with a simple command like "bye" and are disconnected. The system shows you how much time you used; some also indicate how much money you spent for the session. Chapter 2 will discuss in greater detail how online services work.

THE EVOLUTION OF ONLINE SERVICES

Government agencies in the 1960s were the first to see the advantages of electronic publishing for handling the large numbers of articles, reports, dissertations and patents created by the scientific and technical "information explosion" of the time. Researchers saw a use for excess computer resources in organizing and storing databases of information for later search and retrieval. Private computer system companies, under contract to the federal government, led the development of software and systems to permit interactive searches of computerized databases and to display results on a printer or a video screen. The designers of these information systems soon realized they had commercial potential for use by information seekers everywhere.

Library Research Services

The library research, or bibliographic, services that evolved from these government-sponsored projects were the pioneers of the commercial online information services industry. Designed to simplify and vastly reduce the time required for library research, these services index and identify published literature in every form on every topic. Many bibliographic databases also provide abstracts, or summaries, of the publications indexed. The major library services are Dialog Information Services, Inc., SDC Information Services, Inc. Orbit Search Service and Bibliographic Retrieval Services, Inc. (BRS).

Numeric Database Services

In the 1960s and 1970s several computer timesharing companies began to make available online various financial, economic and demographic time series and statistics compiled electronically by public corporations, the federal government and other organizations. The numeric databases include economic time series and forecasts, financial balance sheets and income statements, and other number series. Major companies offering numeric database services include ADP Network Services, Inc., I.P. Sharp Associates, Data Resources, Inc. and Chase Econometrics/Interactive Data Corp.

The early library research and numeric database services were designed primarily for professionals—librarians, technical information specialists, economists, financial analysts and market researchers—and required considerable training and the mastering of extensive command languages to be used effectively. However, as the number of personal computer users grows, library research and numeric database services are trying to make their services more attractive to business people by providing their databases in easier to use formats, by developing special microcomputer software to facilitate use and by lowering the costs of using their systems during non-prime-time hours.

Popular Information Utilities

Since the personal computer became popular, new online services have been started by communications and information utilities and by electronic publishers. Designed specifically for personal computer users, the popular information utilities are much easier to use than the early library research and numeric database services.

CompuServe Information Service and The Source are utilities that were originally oriented to computer hobbyists. They offered electronic mail, bulletin boards for exchange of hobby information and computer programming online. As business and professional people began using personal computers, these utilities added databases of news and business information.

Dow Jones, publisher of *The Wall Street Journal* and *Barron's* financial weekly, got into the online information service business as a result of its publishing activities and the increasing popularity of personal computers among business people and private investors. Dow Jones was an early user of electronic phototypesetting in publishing its newspapers. It also provided the Dow Jones News wire to other newspapers and used the wire services of the New York, American and over-the-counter stock exchanges to publish their stock quotes. The Dow Jones News/Retrieval Service provides up-to-the-minute stock quotes and business and financial news from these sources.

New Developments In Online Services

New online information services oriented to personal computer users are being established that emphasize full-text databases. NewsNet, for example, makes available online the full text of specialized business newsletters from various publishers.

In addition to new and easier-to-use databases of information, we are beginning to see the emergence of related online services—e.g., remote shopping, banking, electronic mail and computer conferencing—which, to some extent, are the outgrowths of the same industries and technologies that made online information possible. Figure 1.9 illustrates this evolution.

Figure 1.9: The Evolution and Interrelationship of Online Services

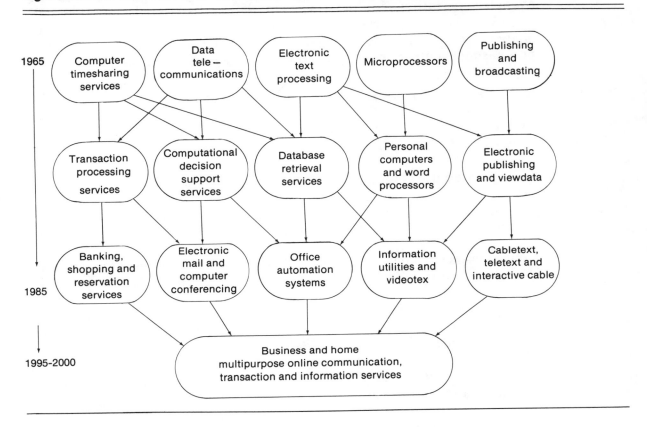

BUSINESS USES OF ONLINE SERVICES

As of spring 1984, there were more than 2000 online databases offered for public use by about 275 online commercial retrieval services worldwide, both private and government. A decade ago there were approximately 35 databases on four or five online services, most of them government systems.

Yet despite the rapid growth of the online information industry, the total number of users of online information services is probably fewer than 500,000. The market for online information services among business people is still largely untapped.

Current Use

In a study by Link Resources Inc. of New York of electronic information users and department heads in more than 1000 major U.S. companies, the average penetration of online services in 1982 was estimated at between 10% and 15%.* The study surveyed accountants, brokers, economists, investment analysts, lawyers, marketing managers, media researchers, planners and purchasing agents in the manufacturing, service and financial industries.

Some key findings of the study include the following:

- Of the users, 53% reported that their personal use of online services increased 37% in 1982.

- The greatest use of online services is among lawyers and securities brokers.

- System reliability, constantly improving, is considered to be the most important aspect of online database services among lawyers and brokers.

- Other users consider quality of information the most important aspect of online services.

- Other features of service in descending order of importance are: timeliness, database availability, ease of use, scope and depth of coverage, and system response time.

- The most sensitive issue among users is price. Cost-saving query methods rather than value-added features are recommended.

- The largest void in current online offerings is considered to be information on companies—47% of users surveyed mentioned an unfulfilled need in this area.

- Typical business customers use only one database or service—30.8% of those surveyed use more than one service.

- About two-thirds of those surveyed reported that they typically stay online to review and manipulate information rather than download it into a personal computer.

Online Business Information

New databases and information services are being made available online every month, so any voids that now exist probably won't in the near future.

---

*1983 press release, International Data Corp., Framingham, MA.

In fact, the amount of information available online can be overwhelming until you identify your information needs and the specific service or services that can fulfill them.

Figure 1.10 shows the basic types of online information service and their targeted markets.

Figure 1.10: Types of Online Services and Their Markets

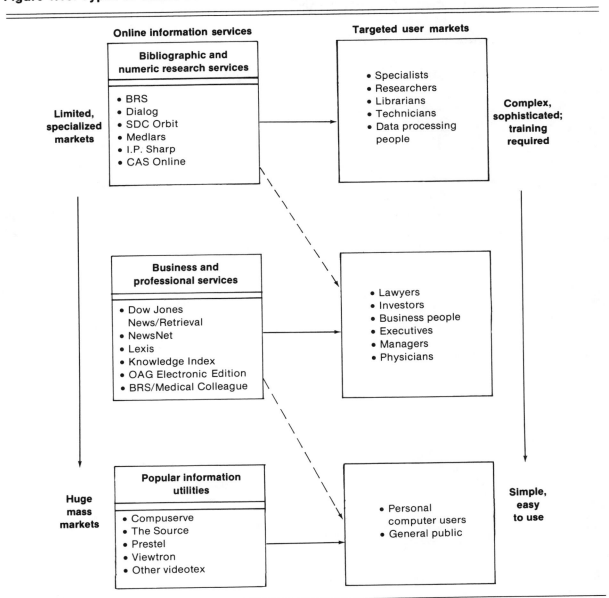

Among the more than 2000 databases commercially available online, there are many that can supply information for business users. The remainder of this book investigates online information in the following broad business and professional categories:

• business and industry news

• information about companies

• financial, investment and economic data

• bibliographic research and development data

• specialized information on such subjects as law, medicine, business travel and recruiting

A chapter will be devoted to each of the above business categories, showing you what online information services are available and how you can use them. First, however, we will discuss the time and money involved in learning about and using online services and the data communications networks that give you access to them. These are the subjects of Chapters 2 and 3.

2

Making the Online Connection

There are several factors to consider in determining whether or not online services are right for you. Among the questions to ask yourself are:

- Do you have a need for "instant information" on a frequent basis?

- Do you make a lot of phone calls to get this information?

- Do you frequently ask your secretary or subordinates to track down some important item of information?

- Do you try to read a lot of business publications on a regular basis, looking for items important to your business?

- Do you subscribe to a number of costly business newsletters?

- Are you a frequent user of a corporate library or information center?

- Are you frustrated by having to make frequent requests of your data-processing department for company information?

- Are you a frequent business traveler trying to find the least expensive and most convenient flights?

- Do you have considerable personal investments and spend a lot of time on the telephone with your broker or financial analyst?

- Do you use a personal computer for financial planning, budgeting or other applications?

- Are you comfortable with computers and other office equipment?

- Are you an advocate of office automation?

- Are you intrigued by new technology?

- Do you and your family use a personal computer at home?

If the answer to many of these questions is "yes," then online information services can be an efficient and cost-effective answer to many of your information-related problems.

PLANNING CONSIDERATIONS

If you have decided to explore the use of online information services, the next step is planning. Your planning considerations should include the following:

- Determine what equipment you will need to use online services and how much it will cost.

- Find out how you can learn to use various online services effectively.

- Find out how much it will cost to subscribe to and use online services.

- Determine what alternatives are available for using online services without acquiring the equipment and investing the time and money yourself.

This chapter will discuss these considerations.

EQUIPMENT REQUIREMENTS

The telephone on your desk is the electronic link to the universe of online information. In addition to your telephone, you will need the following equipment to gain access to online services:

- a terminal

- a modem

- communications software

In addition, a printer, though not essential, is recommended for using online services.

Let's discuss each of these items in more detail.

Terminals

A terminal is simply a device that connects people to computers. As noted in

Chapter 1, there are three basic types of terminals that are commonly used with online services:

- personal computers

- communicating word processors or electronic typewriters

- dedicated data terminals

You may already have one of these terminals available at work or at home. If you don't, consider the following points before making a purchase.

Personal Computers

The personal computer is hailed by many as the most useful single tool you can buy. Figure 2.1 shows the main components of a typical personal computer system. Personal computers can be used for many business-related applications, such as financial spreadsheets and analysis, budgeting, business planning, database management (organizing letters, customer records, mailing lists and other business documents for easy filing and retrieval) and word processing.

With the addition of communications equipment and software, the same personal computer can be used as a terminal to connect you with online information services. The computing power of the personal computer also makes it easy to download, or capture, information from online services, manipulate and reformat it "offline" at your leisure and even incorporate it into documents and reports. These are things that most other terminals cannot do.

Because personal computers are so versatile and so reasonable in cost, if you must make a purchase for terminal equipment, it is recommended that you buy a personal computer. (On the other hand, if the primary use for your equipment is to be word processing, you may prefer to purchase a dedicated word processor. This option is discussed below.)

You will spend between $2500 and $6000 for a basic desktop personal computer system adequate for most business applications. When used primarily for your business, some of the purchase price of the system is tax deductible, according to new IRS rules (see your tax accountant for details).

There are several portable computers and terminals—some will fit in a briefcase—that enable you to do computing and use online services away

Figure 2.1: Main Components of a Typical Personal Computer

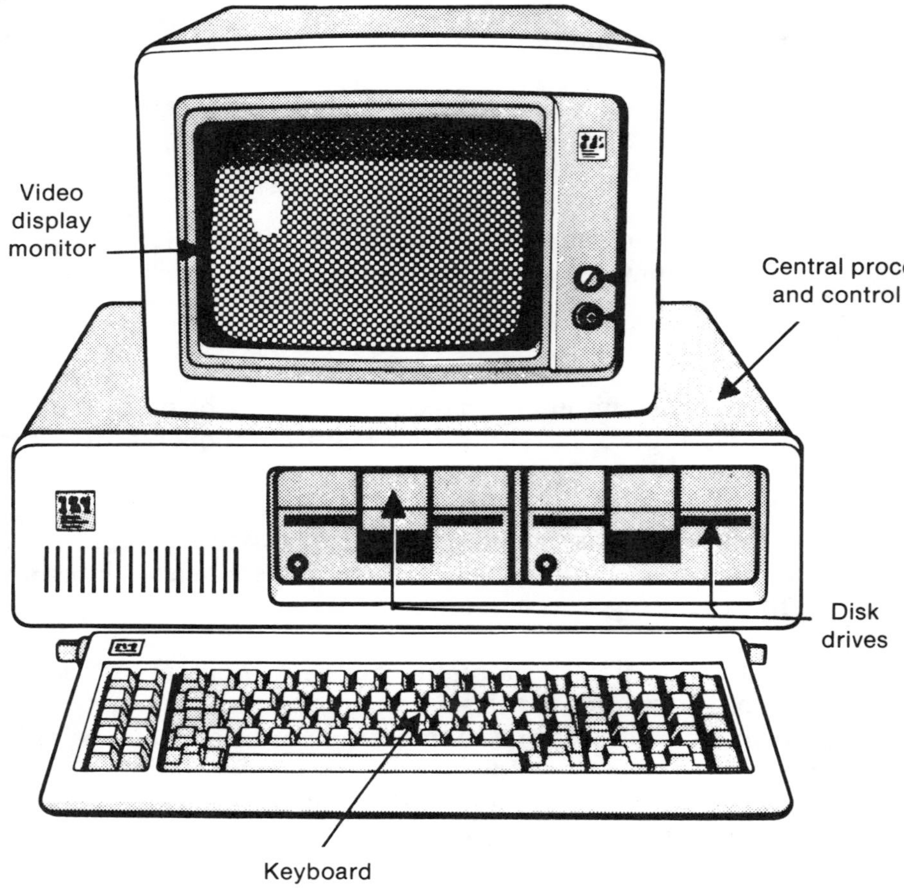

from the office, but, because of size constraints, they generally have more limited capabilities than desktop machines. Many of the less expensive "home" computers also have limited capabilities, as well as restricted screen width (40 characters or less) and the ability to display only upper-case letters.

Most online information services, however, require a screen display width of from 60 to 80 characters, and many display text in both upper- and lower-case letters. If you already own a home computer (such as an Apple II, Commodore 64, or Atari 400 or 800) that does not have a screen width of 80 characters (a standard typewritten 8½″ x 11″ page) or upper *and* lower case letters, you can buy software to modify these features.

If you have not yet bought a computer but are planning to, get one with an 80-character by 25-line screen display and at least 256 kilobytes (256K) of random-access memory (RAM), which is necessary for common business applications like financial spreadsheets and word processing. In addition, an MS-DOS (or PC-DOS) operating system or MS-DOS plus CP/M is recommended for widest software compatibility. Many other factors should be considered when purchasing a computer, but a discussion of these is beyond the scope of this book. There are many books and periodicals available that can help.

Table 2.1 lists some selected popular personal computers used for business purposes.

Communicating Word Processors and Electronic Typewriters

Dedicated word processors and electronic typewriters are specialized computers dedicated to one purpose—writing. Electronic typewriters (which are simply electric typewriters with small computer processors attached) can cost from $1500 to $3000. Word processors cost from $5000 to $15,000.

Many word processors and electronic typewriters are designed to double as data terminals. Listed below are some that can communicate with online information services:

- CompuCorp word processor

- IBM Displaywriter

- IBM electronic typewriter

- AM-Jacquard AMTEXT word processor

- Lanier word processing system

- Lexitron word processor

- Vydec word processor

- Wang word processing system

- Xerox Memorywriter

If you already have one of these machines available, see your dealer or service representative about adding modems and communications software.

Table 2.1: Selected Personal Computers Used for Business Applications and Suggested for Most Online Information Services

Make and Model	Processor Speed	Operating System	Memory (RAM) in Kilobytes	Screen Display (Characters x Lines)	List Price*
Apple III	8 bit	Apple DOS	48-256K	80 x 24	$4295
Columbia VP	8-16 bit	CP/M MS-DOS	128-256K	80 x 25	$2995
Commodore BX 256-80	8-16 bit	CP/M86 MS-DOS	256-960K	80 x 25	N.A.
COMPAQ (portable)	16 bit	MS-DOS	256K	80 x 25	$2995
DEC Professional 300	16 bit	DEC-DOS	256K	80/132 x 24	$5995
DEC Rainbow 100	8-16 bit	CP/M MS-DOS	256K	80/132 x 24	N.A.
Eagle PC or 1600	8-16 bit	CP/M86 MS-DOS	128-512K	80 x 24	N.A.
Heath-Zenith Model 100	8-16 bit	CP/M MS-DOS	128-768K	80 x 24	$2199
Hewlett-Packard HP-86	8 bit	CP/M HP-DOS	575K	80 x 24	$1795
IBM Personal Computer (PC)	8-16 bit	CP/M86 PC-DOS	64-640K	80 x 25	$2205
IBM PC Portable	8-16 bit	CP/M86 PC-DOS	64-640K	80 x 25	$3195
IBM PC XT	8-16 bit	CP/M86 PC-DOS	128-640K	80 x 25	$4995
IBM PC jr	16 bit	PC-DOS	64-128K	40 x 24	$ 995
KAYCOMP II Portable	8 bit	CP/M	64K	80 x 24	$1795
NEC APC (Advanced Personal Computer)	16 bit	CP/M86 MS-DOS	128-640K	80 x 24	N.A.
Radio Shack TRS-80, 16	8-16 bit	TRS-DOS	512K	40/80 x 24	N.A.
Texas Instruments Professional Computer	16 bit	CP/M86 MS-DOS	64-512K	80 x 25	$2595
Texas Instruments Professional Portable	16 bit	CP/M86 MS-DOS	64 x 256K	80 x 24	$2995
Xerox 16-8 Professional	8-16 bit	CP/M MS-DOS	64-256K	80 x 24	N.A.

*Suggested list price retail, 1984, for least memory. Cost can be more, depending on options, or less through discount outlets.
N.A. = not available.

Word processors have specialized keyboards with special functions for editing and formatting blocks of text. However, good word-processing software for a personal computer permits the same functions using a standard computer keyboard. Generally, a personal computer with word-processing software is a better buy for general business purposes because of its greater versatility at lower or comparable cost. Unless your primary business is writing, don't buy a word processor, especially if you want to gain access to online services.

Dedicated Data Terminals

If you do not yet have or need a personal computer or word processor in your business, you may have access to a dedicated data terminal through your company's data-processing department or corporate library or information center. A data terminal lets you communicate with remote computer systems; it is "dumb" in that it does not contain a microprocessor or computer chip and cannot manipulate data on its own.

Data terminals may display information on a video screen, print it on paper or both. Generally, a good data terminal costs as much as a personal computer. If you need an ordinary data terminal temporarily to use online services, rent or lease one until you feel justified in buying a computer. Some common video display data terminals are:

- ADDS Regent and Viewpoint

- Anderson-Jacobson 510

- Beehive Minibee and Superbee

- Digital Equipment DEC VT-100

- Hazeltine 2000

- Hewlett-Packard 2600

- Lear-Siegler ADM

- Northern Telecom DisplayPhone

- Tymshare Scanset

• Zenith Z19 and Z91

Some common printing data terminals are:

• Anderson-Jacobson 833 and 860

• Computer Devices Miniterm 1203

• CTSI Execuport 4000 and 4080

• Digital Equipment (DEC) LA34, LA36 and LA120

• GE Terminet 200, 300, 2030 and 2120

• Texas Instruments Silent 700 and 800 series

• 3M Whisperwriter 1000

• Xerox 1700 and 1800 series

Some of these printing terminals, like the Xerox 1700 and 1800, can double as letter-quality printers for personal computers.

Modems

As noted in Chapter 1, for use with online information services, terminals must be used with a modem. A modem changes the digital data signals generated by a computer to audio signals for transmission over voice-carrying telephone lines, then changes them back to digital signals to be understood by the receiving computer or terminal.

All dedicated data terminals and some personal computers and word processors have modems built in. They may be direct-connect modems, which snap into a modular telephone jack, or use acoustic couplers, devices with rubber cups that are designed to hold a standard telephone handset. Since there is wide variety in the shapes and sizes of handsets available and not all handsets can be used with acoustic couplers, direct-connect modems are preferable.

Telephone networks are designed to carry audio data signals at relatively low transmission speeds. The most common speeds are 30 characters per second and 120 characters per second, referred to as 300 baud and 1200 baud respectively. (Baud rate is a measure of transmission of electrical signals and is named after a Frenchman, Baudot, who was a pioneer in the development of the telegraph.) Available modems for personal computers and word processors, therefore, are rated at 300 baud, 1200 baud or both. Many fine modems are available at prices ranging from $150 to $1000, depending on transmission speed and other features. Generally, 1200-baud and dual-speed modems are more costly than 300-baud modems.

Among additional features available on modems, the most useful are what are commonly referred to as "smart" features. Smart modems have microprocessors in them that can be programmed to automatically listen for the telephone to ring, answer it and, if the "caller" is an online system, have your personal computer or terminal print out the data. They can also be programmed to automatically dial a data-access phone number, enter the online service address in the data network, enter your identification number and password, and begin your search—all with the push of a single key. These features are sometimes billed as "auto answer" and "auto dial" features (indicated in Table 2.2 as "smart" features). They also add to the cost of a modem, but are recommended as features that save time and reduce dialing errors. Table 2.2 lists some popular modems.

Communications Software

In addition to the modem, you will need data communications software to let your personal computer (or word processor) behave like an ordinary data terminal. There is a wide variety of communications software packages on the market; they fall into one of three general categories: communications programs, terminal-emulation programs and electronic-mail or bulletin board programs. Communications programs usually emulate the most common class of data terminal—TTY (also known as Teletype or ASCII); these will work for any service vendor. Terminal-emulation programs emulate a specific make or model of terminal, such as DEC VT-100, Tektronix 4010, IBM 3101 or IBM 3270; these are meant to "talk" with a single host computer. Electronic-mail or bulletin-board programs are designed specifically for online message-sending applications.

By far the most common data terminals in use are of the TTY (ASCII) type, and 90% of online service systems communicate in ASCII (American Standard Code for Information Exchange) code through TTY terminals. Because of the widespread adoption of TTY terminals and ASCII code as industry standards, it is recommended that you buy a general-purpose TTY communications software package. It is also recommended that you buy one

Table 2.2: Selected Popular Modems Permitting Online Communication with Personal Computers

Make and Model	Baud Rate	"Smart" Features	Computer Restrictions	List Price*
Hayes Micromodem 100	110-300	dial answer	—	$339
Hayes Smartmodem 300	300	dial answer	—	$289
Hayes Smartmodem 1200	1200	dial answer	—	$699
Microcom PCS 1200	300-1200	dial answer	—	$995
Microconnection R1A-RS232	300	dial answer	—	$199
Microconnection T1A-TRS-80	300	dial answer	Radio Shack computers	$259
Novation Apple-CAT II	300-1200	dial answer	Apple II computers	$389
Novation Auto-CAT	300	answer	—	$249
Novation Auto-CAT 212	300-1200	answer	—	$695
Novation D-CAT	300	—	—	$199
Novation J-CAT	300	dial answer	—	$249
Novation Smart-CAT 103	300	dial answer	—	$249
Novation Smart-CAT 212	1200	dial answer	—	$595
Radio Shack DC-1200	300-1200	answer	—	$699
U.S. Robotics Autodial 212A	300-1200	dial answer	—	$599
U.S. Robotics Autolink 1200	1200	answer	—	$499
U.S. Robotics Autolink 212A	300-1200	answer	—	$549
U.S. Robotics Autolink 300	300	answer	—	$269

(continued on next page)

Table 2.2: Selected Popular Modems Permitting Online Communication with Personal Computers (cont.)

Make and Model	Baud Rate	"Smart" Features	Computer Restrictions	List Price*
U.S. Robotics Courier	300–1200	dial	—	$519
U.S. Robotics Phonelink	300	—	—	$189
Universal Data Systems 1030ALP	300	—	—	$145
Universal Data Systems 103JLP	300	answer	—	$195
Universal Data Systems 212A	300–1200	answer	—	$675
Universal Data Systems 212LP	1200	—	—	$445

*Manufacturers suggested retail price as of April 1984. Cost may be less through discount outlets.

that will work with most 8- or 16-bit computers using the various CP/M or MS-DOS (PC-DOS) operating systems, as these are used by more makes and models of personal computers than any others. If you already have a computer with a proprietary operating system—e.g., Apple or Radio Shack TRS-80—buy a TTY communications package designed for these machines.

The more expensive communications software includes autodial directory capabilities that let you program data-communications network access phone numbers and sign-on protocols for up to 20 online vendors' services. You can then make completely automatic connections to online services with one or two keystrokes on your keyboard. Many packages include instructions for automatically dialing and signing on to the popular information utilities.

In addition to those features mentioned above, you will eventually want the following features in your communications software.

- An online directory that lists the phone numbers and log-on protocols of the online services you will use—this can be created by you.

- Online help menus and prompts, so you don't have to remember or look up how to use various commands and features of the software.

- File-transfer capability—i.e., the ability to download information online to your diskette for later use and to upload files online from your computer to someone else's.

A good software package that has all of the features described above will cost from $120 to $200, on the average. Table 2.3 lists some communications software for TTY or ASCII communications with some or all of these features.

Printers

If your computer system does not yet have a printer, or if you are using a video display data terminal and are planning to buy a computer, invest in a printer. If you intend to make frequent use of online information services, inevitably you will want to have a printout ("hard copy") of the data you retrieve. You can't keep a print record of your online information if you have only a video display screen.

Printers can be classified by the quality of their output. "Letter-quality" output is comparable to that of a high-quality electric typewriter. The characters in "dot-matrix" output consist of a pattern of small dots. You will want letter quality if you will use your system for business correspondence and reports. Dot-matrix printers are entirely adequate for most data purposes and have the advantage of being less costly and quieter than the letter-quality models.

The specifics of selecting printers are outside the scope of this book. Most books on selecting computers will also discuss buying accessories, including printers.

Figure 2.2 shows a modem, a printer and a diskette used for data communication and other software.

LEARNING TO USE ONLINE SERVICES

Many online services are designed for the so-called end user, the person with little or no familiarity with computers, data processing or interactive information retrieval.

In most cases the amount of time and money you must invest to use online information services is minimal. Probably you will want to spend a couple of hours and about $25 to $50 for user documentation—manuals and guides—

Table 2.3: Selected TTY Data Communications Software Designed for Use with Most Online Services and Most Popular Personal Computers

Vendor and Package	Online Phone Directory	Automatic Log-on	Online Help	File Upload and Download	List Price*
Cawthon Scientific Group Computer Phone Link	X	X	X	X	$165
Dynamic Microprocessor Associates ASCOM	X	X	X	X	$175
Ferox Microsystems, Inc. LogOn	X	X	X	X	$150
Frontier Technologies Corp. COMPAC	X	X	X	X	$125
Hayes Microcomputer Products Inc. Smartcom II	X	X	X	X	$119
Headlands Press, Inc. Freeware PC-Talk II	X	X	X	X	Free**
Link Systems DataLink PC	X	X	X	X	$199
Microstuf, Inc. Crosstalk IV	X	X	X	X	$195
Perfect Software, Inc. Perfect Link		X	X	X	$149
Pickles & Trout Lync 3.0		X	X	X	$155
The Software Store Softcom	X	X	X	X	$150
TeleVideo Systems, Inc. TeleAsync		X	X	X	$150
Transend Transend PC	X	X	X	X	$189
U.S. Robotics, Inc. Telpac 2.0	X	X	X	X	$ 79

*Suggested retail list price as of April 1984. May be less in wholesale outlets.
**Free, but $25 contribution suggested. This excellent program can be downloaded online by contacting Headlands Press or a known user.

Figure 2.2: Additional Microcomputer Components Required to Make Effective Use of Online Information Services

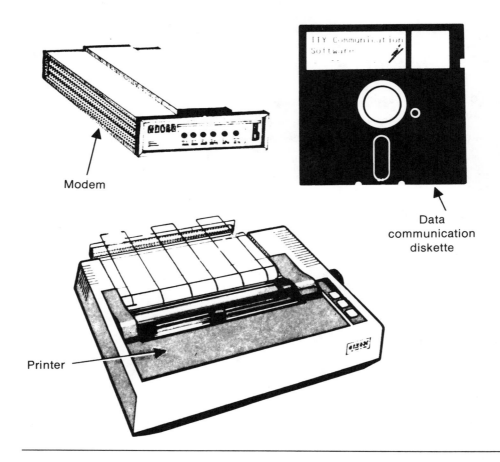

Modem

Data
communication
diskette

Printer

for each online service you subscribe to. To enable you to become familiar with finding and retrieving information, a majority of the commercial services give you one or two hours of system use at no charge when you subscribe. (Charges for this time are deducted from your first monthly invoice for system use.)

User manuals range in price from $5 to $50. A basic use guide is usually included in your subscription price. Additional manuals for special services and databases cost extra and may be billed to your monthly account in most cases. Your decision to purchase them depends on the extent to which you plan to use the services they describe.

Using the Popular Information Utilities

The popular information utility services like CompuServe, Dow Jones News/Retrieval or The Source are fairly self-explanatory. They provide online menus of choices and easy-to-understand prompts and messages. Most will also display helpful tutorial descriptions of how to proceed whenever you enter "help" or a similar command.

When you subscribe to CompuServe, Dow Jones News/Retrieval or The Source, a user manual or guide is usually provided free of charge or for a small fee. And if the self-tutorials and user manuals don't provide all of the answers to your questions about using the service, there is usually a toll-free customer-service "hot line" you can call.

Using the Library Research Services

Of the online information services that will be outlined in Chapter 4, the library research services—Dialog Information Services, Inc., Bibliographic Retrieval Services, Inc. (BRS) and SDC Information Services, Inc. Orbit Search Service—are the most complex. They contain huge amounts of information and provide extremely sophisticated retrieval techniques that you will seldom need to use. Although the library research services were designed for professional librarians and technical information specialists, end users can use them with relative ease for routine bibliographic research.

The library research services provide large, comprehensive system user manuals, as well as documentation describing the particulars of effectively using each of the databases they offer. Dialog maintains several online training and practice (Ontap) databases—subsets of major databases—on its system at very low cost, to help you learn to make effective use of them.

The bibliographic services also offer training courses at beginning, intermediate and advanced user levels on general system use, and special training courses aimed at using business, chemical, patent and other database groups. The training courses offered by the bibliographic services cost from $100 to $200. Depending on the level of expertise and the specialty, they are available from once to several times a year in major cities. However, unless you are a frequent and heavy user of these services, you probably won't need any but the beginning system use sessions. Further training is usually designed for and used by professional librarians and other information specialists.

There are software interface packages available for personal computers that simplify the use of the library research services. These are described in Chapter 10. As another alternative, both BRS and Dialog have less complex, less expensive, easier-to-use services designed especially for end users with personal computers. These services, BRS/After Dark and Knowledge Index, respectively, make available the major databases from their primary services. The simplified services are available only on evenings and weekends, however.

If you are not inclined to learn to use the library research services yourself, professional librarians and information specialists can help you take advantage of them. These services are frequently available in corporate, academic and public libraries. In major cities there are information brokerage services that have specialists who do research in the bibliographic services at your request.

Chapter 4 will discuss how easy specific online services are to use.

THE COST OF GOING ONLINE

As you have seen, small amounts of time and money are required to learn to use online information services. If you don't already have the equipment, you will make an additional investment in acquiring a personal computer, modem and communications software. There are also costs associated with subscribing to and actually using online services:

- subscription fees and monthly minimums

- connect-time charges

- display and print charges

- computer resource unit (CRU) charges

- telecommunications charges

Most of these charges are elements of your monthly invoices from the online services. These charges are tax deductible if you are using online services for business purposes.

Subscription Fees and Monthly Minimums

Most of the services charge a one-time subscription or sign-up fee, which varies from $25 to $100 and provides you with your user account, password and basic documentation on using the service. Sign-up packages may be purchased at many retail computer stores. Some of the numeric database vendors, such as Data Resources, Inc., require an annual subscription, ranging from $500 to several thousand dollars. These annual subscriptions are available directly from the vendor.

In addition to the sign-up or annual subscription fee, some vendors require a monthly minimum to cover billing and other costs associated with carrying your account. Monthly minimums range from $10 to $100.

Connect-time Charges

The costs incurred while connected to and interacting with an online service, usually called connect-time charges, vary from $3 to $300 per hour; the average cost is between $65 and $75 per hour. This cost is incurred as long as you are connected, whether or not you actually interact with the system. Most services will automatically sign you off after five to 15 minutes of inactivity, however. Connect costs depend upon the service you use, the database being accessed and the time of day you are connected. Connect charges are typically higher during the business day (commonly referred to as prime time) and lower during evenings, weekends and holidays.

Display and Print Charges

The costs associated with searching, displaying and reading most databases available through online services involve royalties to their producers or providers. A percentage of the fees collected by vendors for searching and displaying information is passed back to the publisher of the information, just as a percentage of a publisher's revenues from book sales is paid to the author as royalties.

Royalty payments are obtained from you, the user, through connect-time charges and sometimes through charges for displaying or printing records from the databases. Display or print charges for the library research services range from as little as 3 cents to as much as $55 dollars for a single record; average charges are about 10 cents to 25 cents. Extra display charges are usually not assessed by the popular information utilities.

Computer Resource Unit (CRU) Charges

Most numeric database services assess charges for computer resource units

(CRUs) used. Complex algorithms are used to calculate CRUs, which reflect total computer facility usage based on connect time, computational manipulation of numeric data and other factors. These costs range from .05 cents to 10 cents per CRU.

Telecommunications Charges

With some services you will also pay a small charge for using the data telecommunications network that links you to the online service's host computer. The networks used most often are GTE Telenet, Tymnet and Uninet. Charges are from $3 to $10 per hour and are collected by online service vendors. Frequently, these telecommunications charges will be hidden in the basic connect-hour rates for using a service. The popular information utilities include telecommunications charges in their standard connect rates. The library research services itemize telecommunications charges as a separate amount on your invoices. (Chapter 3 discusses telecommunications charges in greater detail.)

Cost of a Typical Online Session

A typical online session takes from 5 to 10 minutes, and its total cost is from $10 to $30. For more economical online searching, use CompuServe, The Source, Dow Jones News/Retrieval, Dialog's Knowledge Index and BRS/After Dark in the early morning, evening or on the weekend. At these times you seldom pay more than $5 to $10 per hour (less than 18 cents per minute) for connect time and telecommunications; display and print charges for Knowledge Index and BRS/After Dark are seldom more than 5 cents per item, and, as noted above, the popular information utilities do not assess extra display or print charges. Chapter 4 discusses the charges of specific online services in more detail.

The cost of using online services may seem like a lot compared to buying newspapers or using "free" libraries. Consider, however, that you are getting much more current information and getting it much faster than you could by more traditional methods. If you are researching a topic, you or someone you designate might take from a few hours to several days to track down the necessary information from libraries or other sources—with considerable telephone and transportation time involved in the process. The sophisticated library research services, which cover far more information than even the largest research libraries can accommodate, can save hours, days and sometimes weeks of exhaustive library research.

ALTERNATIVES TO GOING ONLINE YOURSELF

If you have both the equipment and the inclination to use online information services yourself, you will save time and money in your quest for information. But some people simply do not like to use computers. If you are one of them, there are alternatives that enable you to take advantage of online information services.

- Train a secretary or other person to be an online information specialist.

- Use your corporate information center's online services.

- Use an academic or public library's online service center.

- Use a private commercial information broker.

We will look at each alternative.

Train an Information Specialist

In this age of office automation, your personal or departmental secretary may already be using a word processor or a personal computer. She (or he) is also the person who most frequently makes telephone calls for you, tracks down people or information, makes business travel arrangements and does many other related tasks. It is sometimes a relatively easy step to put the secretary online to the electronic information world. She can be expected to spend as much time learning to use online services as you yourself would.

Some secretaries, of course, may resent having to learn what seems to them a new skill unrelated to their primary responsibilities. (These are also usually the people who are reluctant to give up typewriters for word processors and personal computers.) But others, who appreciate the time-saving rewards of computer technology, may welcome the opportunity to learn to use online services effectively. The new technical skills they gain will increase their employability and salary bargaining power for future jobs.

Use the Corporate Information Center

If you work for a large corporation, the easiest way for you to take advantage of the bibliographic services like BRS and Dialog may be your own company's technical library or information center. The biggest customers of the bibliographic search services are large corporate libraries with trained online searchers on their staffs. Corporate research and development divisions are also frequent users of online information services.

Information requests sent to the library can usually be fulfilled the same day. Individual departments of a corporation often have accounts to which these services can be charged.

Professional librarians, other information specialists, data processing personnel, and research scientists and engineers are the people who most frequently use online services in the corporate setting. Because these people are heavy users of online services, they can help you get the most out of the services in the least amount of time and at the lowest cost.

Use Academic and Public Libraries

Most libraries at large universities and many large municipal public libraries make online research services available to their clientele, and some also provide these services to the business community at cost plus a service fee. Check with libraries in your city for available services. The services most likely to be provided are the bibliographic search services.

Some people argue that since state universities and public libraries are tax supported, online information services should be entirely subsidized and provided free for the asking. But if that were the case, libraries might be swamped with frivolous requests. Besides, the price is trivial to a business person needing information, and seldom more than you would pay if you were doing your own online searching.

Use Information Brokers

Information brokers are entrepreneurs who have established businesses that provide information upon request. They use online information services very heavily. Most major cities have at least one information brokerage service. Many brokerage houses have been started or are managed by professional librarians or other information specialists who used online services extensively for their former employers.

Like libraries that offer online services, information brokers provide online information research for a fee. The cost of the online transaction plus service and consulting fees is generally higher than those charged by libraries. A broker provides you with the results of an online search request, along with interpretive information and rates for delivering copies of documents that you may want to read in full. A few major online information brokers are listed in Appendix C.

You may wish to use libraries and brokers as a partial alternative to doing all online searching yourself. As we have noted, the popular information utilities are generally less costly and easier to use than the bibliographic services. You may wish to use the former yourself and look to brokers and libraries for more exhaustive research in the bibliographic services.

BENEFITS OF ONLINE SERVICES

Regardless of which online information services you use, the benefits of using them can far outweigh their costs. To summarize the advantages of online services:

- They provide frequently updated information.

- They will save you time.

- They are cost effective.

- Many are easy to use.

- They may be accessed with most personal computers, word processors and data terminals.

- This terminal equipment can also be used for other computer-based services like electronic mail and access to your company data banks.

- Equipment and online service subscription and usage costs may be tax deductible when used for your business.

The next chapter describes the data telecommunications networks that will put you in touch with the online information world.

3

Data Communications Networks

The telephone is the key to using commercial online services. There are five ways you can use the telephone to gain access to online services:

- by low-cost packet-switching data communications networks

- by a local phone call

- by AT&T direct distance dialing

- by lower-priced long-distance services like GTE Sprint and MCI

- by dedicated digital leased land lines

Each of these will be discussed in this chapter. However, the data communications networks are generally the most inexpensive and widely used alternative. We will discuss them first and at greatest length.

PACKET-SWITCHING DATA COMMUNICATIONS NETWORKS

Several companies have established networks specifically designed for sending digital data from one computer to another using the telephone system. These networks are called packet-switching networks (PSNs).

PSNs use interconnected minicomputers, placed in cities throughout the nation, which serve as relay stations to get digital data from their origin to their destination. These minicomputer locations are called access nodes. Each node is given a phone number. Leased dedicated telephone lines connect all of the nodes in the system.

Whether you work in Los Angeles or Manhattan, all you need to communicate with, say, an online service in New Jersey is your terminal and a local telephone call. After you dial the local PSN access number, the network will ask for your terminal identifier code (so the PSN "knows" how best to transmit information between your terminal and the online host computer) and the address code of the online service you want. Figure 3.1 shows the elements of a typical PSN.

How PSNs Work

Data communications networks of this type are called packet-switching networks because they transmit data in "packets" of set length that can share phone channels with other packets. PSNs "switch" the data packets from one node to another, checking for errors and selecting the most efficient route. When the destination is reached, the packets are separated and sent to the designated computer or terminal address code. PSNs use a standard communications protocol, usually asynchronous or S.25 interfaces, for connecting user locations. This interfacing process is commonly called "handshaking."

Availability of PSNs

PSNs have been around since 1970 and have grown rapidly as the need for computer communications has increased, particularly with the recent proliferation of microcomputers. Virtually every medium to large city in the U.S. has at least one PSN node. Large metropolitan areas have several, some designated for transmission at 30 characters per second (cps), some at 120 cps and others at both speeds. If you happen to live in an area not served directly by a PSN node, thus requiring a long distance call, most PSNs provide WATS service to the nearest node, so you can still save money.

The four largest commercial public PSNs in the U.S. are Autonet, Telenet, Tymnet and Uninet. In most cities, you either have now or soon will have a choice of these four PSNs to access commercial online information services.

A few providers of online services (e.g., CompuServe, Data Resources Inc., and Mead Data Central) maintain private PSNs for their customers at lower rates than the public PSNs, through which they may also be available. But all of the larger online services covered in Chapter 4 use either Tymnet, Telenet or both, and many are adding Autonet and Uninet to give you the greatest possible choice of dial-in access methods.

In Canada, DataPac is the public PSN. Most other countries have PSNs that are controlled and operated by the national postal and telecommunications agencies. Most public PSNs can "talk" to each other across international borders, so you can also connect your computer terminal to public online services around the globe—at considerably less expense than the cost of an international phone call.

Figure 3.1: A Packet-switching Data Telecommunications Network

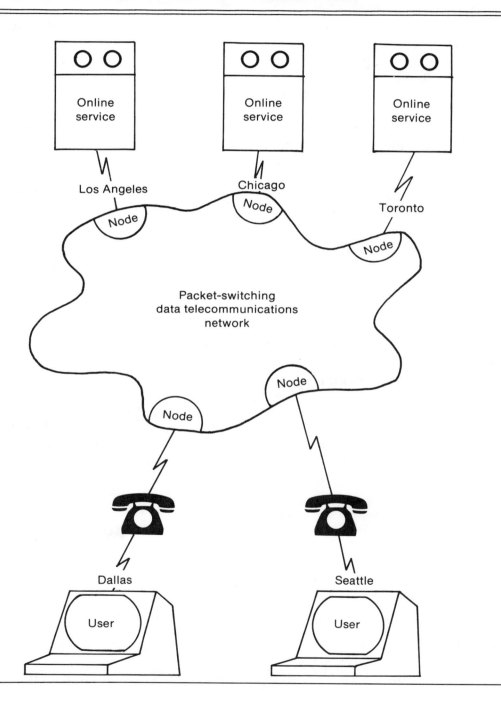

Data Communications Costs

The rates for using PSNs vary from $3 to $10 per hour—much less than WATS, Sprint, MCI or AT&T long-distance rates. PSN rates vary depending on the online service you are using, baud rate and node density (large metropolitan areas have high-density nodes, which accommodate high network usage at lower cost).

Charges for PSN use are collected from you by the online service vendors and may be either itemized on your monthly invoice as telecommunications charges or hidden as part of the vendor's basic connect-time charges. Some online services—Dialog, for example—differentiate PSN rates depending on which network is used. Others—like NewsNet— charge the same rate for telecommunications regardless of the network used.

Since the deregulation of the telecommunications industry and the breakup of AT&T, telephone service companies are increasing their rates and will continue to do so. Since the PSNs utilize the local and long-distance telephone systems, they also will raise rates to keep pace.

Table 3.1 lists the approximate number of cities (nodes) served and the range of hourly rates of Autonet, Telenet, Tymnet and Uninet.

Customer Service Information

Autonet, Telenet, Tymnet and Uninet all provide free customer-service information online, including information about the services they offer and directories of their local access phone numbers. To find out how you can get online to view this information, call their toll-free customer service telephone numbers and ask for your terminal identifier code and nearest access phone number.

The PSN customer service departments will also mail you printed information about their services, and you can call them to find out about getting WATS service. (Customer service department addresses and phone numbers are listed in Appendix C.)

Let's take a closer look at the four major networks.

AUTONET

Autonet is owned and operated by ADP Network Services, Inc., a division of

Table 3.1: Four Commercial Packet-switching Data Communications Networks (PSNs)

Network	Parent Company	Number of Nodes	Hourly Connect Rate Range*	WATS Rate*
Autonet	ADP Network Services, Inc. (Automatic Data Processing, Inc.)	280+	$3.00-$5.00	$20
Telenet	GTE Telenet Communications, Inc. (GTE Corp.)	350+	$3.90-$6.90	$23
Tymnet	Tymnet, Inc. (Tymeshare, Inc.)	400+	$4.25-$9.75	$25
Uninet	Uninet, Inc. (United Telecom Computer Group, Inc.)	175+	$3.00-$5.00	$20

*As of May 1984. Rates are subject to increase with telecommunications industry deregulation. Rates vary depending on baud rate (transmission speed) and node density (usage volume).

Automated Data Processing, Inc., of Ann Arbor, MI. The newest of the commercial public PSNs, Autonet became a public service in 1982. Prior to that, Autonet was a private network used by customers and clients of ADP's computer timesharing and online database services. ADPs private online customers and its own commercial services are the primary users of Autonet.

Autonet has more than 280 nodes. In cities not served directly, Autonet has arrangements with the other public PSNs and with DataPac in Canada. Prime-time hourly rates for Autonet dial-in service are $3 per hour for 300-baud transmission and $5 for 1200-baud transmission, as of May 1984. (Of the four PSNs discussed here, Autonet is the only one whose rates do not vary according to node density.) AutoWATS (Autonet's Wide Area Terminal Service) rates are $20 per hour.

The Autonet Information Directory (AID) is Autonet's online interactive network user's guide. You can get updated lists of telephone access node numbers, news about Autonet, terminal identification codes, a glossary of Autonet communications terms, information about trouble-shooting procedures and a guide to using Autonet. Figure 3.2 shows the Autonet Service Key (ASK) information service main menu and terminal information.

Figure 3.2: ADP Autonet ASK Information Service Main Menu and Terminal Information

```
                         ***   ASK   ***

                    ADPNS/Autonet Service Key

To obtain a list of your options, please type 'HELP'.  'HELP' can
also be used at any prompt where you may need assistance.


OPTION:  help

    ACCESS          - Third party network access information
    ASK             - Lists how to use ASK
    BISYNC          - Lists bisync service setup procedures
    CONNECT         - Lists Autonet connection procedures
    DONE            - Exits from program
    FORMS           - Lists lineprinter forms descriptions
    HELP            - Lists this set of options
    INTERNATIONAL   - ADPNS/Autonet international access information
    PHONE           - Lists Autonet access phone numbers
    PLOT            - Lists how to use off-line plotters
    SERVICE         - Lists customer services
    TERMINAL        - Lists Autonet terminal identity codes
    TROUBLE         - Lists Autonet trouble reporting procedures

OPTION:  terminal

                                            Terminals
                            Last reviewed: August 1983
                            Last updated:   March 1983
                                             2 pages


AUTONET TERMINAL IDENTITY CODES

To optimize Autonet's treatment of your terminal, use the
identity code suggested for your terminal model.  Enter the code
by using the TERMINAL command during the Autonet connection
procedure.  Autonet will interpret the code and will
automatically establish the most effective parameters for
operating characteristics of your device.



In most cases, if you are using an intelligent asynchronous ASCII
CRT, you may use code D1.  Your Autonet Account Administrator,
the person in your organization who handles Autonet matters, can
advise you.  We will list new models as they become available.
An asterisk (*) indicates a new entry since:  March 1, 1983.
```

(continued on next page)

Figure 3.2: ADP Autonet ASK Information Service Main Menu and Terminal Information (cont.)

```
Code        Terminal Model

D1          ADDS CONSUL 520, 580, 980
D1          ADDS ENVOY 620, REGENT SERIES
A1          ALANTHUS DATA TERMINAL T-133
A8          ALANTHUS DATA TERMINAL T-300
A3          ALANTHUS DATA TERMINAL  T-1200
A2          ALANTHUS MINITERM
D1          AM-JACQUARD AMTEXT 425
D1          ANDERSON JACOBSEN 510
B1          ANDERSON JACOBSEN 630
B3          ANDERSON JACOBSEN 830, 832
B5          ANDERSON JACOBSEN 860, 880
D1          ANN ARBOR TERMINALS AMBASSADOR, 400S
D1          APPLE II, II+, IIe, III
D1          ATARI 400, 600, 800, 1200
D1          AT&T DATASPEED 40, 40/1. 40/2, 40/3
B3          AT&T DATASPEED 43
D1          BEEHIVE MINIBEE, MICROBEE, SUPERBEE
D1          BURROUGHS B20
A8          CENTRONICS 761
D1          COLUMBIA MPC, VP
D1          COMMODORE PET, VIC-20, 64
D1          COMPAQ
D1          COMPU-COLOR II
A2          COMPUTER DEVICES CDI 1030
A8          COMPUTER DEVICES TELETERM 1132
A2          COMPUTER DEVICES MINITERM 1200 SERIES
A2          COMPUTER TRANSCEIVER EXECUPORT 300, 380, 3000
A9          COMPUTER TRANSCEIVER EXECUPORT 1200
A8          COMPUTER TRANSCEIVER EXECUPORT 4000
D1          CPT 6000, 8000
```

GTE TELENET

GTE Telenet was established in the early 1970s and is the second largest public PSN. Telenet is owned and operated by GTE Telenet Communications Corp. in Vienna, VA. Telenet had more than 350 local nodes or access numbers as of May 4, 1983.

GTE Telenet's hourly rates range from $3.90 to $6.90, depending on baud rate and node density. WATS service on Telenet costs $23 per hour.

GTE Telenet also provides an electronic mail service (Telemail) over its PSN. Information about Telemail and other aspects of Telenet service is available from the GTE Telenet information service. Figure 3.3 shows a list of local access numbers for the 213 area code (Los Angeles area) obtained online.

On request, Telenet's customer service department will send you copies of *How to Use Telenet* and its *Directory of Computer-Based Services*.

TYMNET

Tymnet is the largest and oldest of the public PSNs. Owned and operated by Tymshare, Inc. of Cupertino, CA, it began operations in 1970. Tymnet had 60 nodes in 1975, 270 by 1980 and more than 400 in 1984. New nodes are being added continuously. Tymnet's hourly access rates vary from $4.25 to

Figure 3.3: GTE Telenet Access Phone Numbers

```
WELCOME TO THE TCO ACCESS LISTING.
THERE ARE SEVERAL WAYS YOU CAN GET INFORMATION ON OUR TCO'S. PLEASE
SPECIFY WHETHER YOU WANT INFORMATION ON A 'STATE', 'AREA.CODE', 'ALL'
OR 'SALES.OFFICE' LOCATIONS BY TYPING THE WORD THAT IS IN DELIMITERS.


LAST UPDATE:   06/28/84


* NEW TELENET CENTRAL OFFICE
# NEW 1200 BAUD ACCESS AVAILABLE
& NEW TELENET CENTRAL OFFICE ADDED CURRENT MONTH
$ NEW 1200 BAUD ACCESS AVAILABLE ADDED CURRENT MONTH
% NEW LEAD NUMBER/NUMBER CHANGED

     GTE/TELENET PROVIDES LOCAL NETWORK ACCESS IN THESE U.S.
CITIES OF 50,000 POPULATION OR MORE.  IN-WATS ACCESS IS AVAILABLE
IN OTHER LOCATIONS.  1200 BPS ACCESS NUMBERS REQUIRE THE USE OF
BELL 212- OR VADIC 3405- COMPATIBLE MODEMS, AS NOTED.
(B) = BELL 212, (V) = VADIC 3405, (B/V) = EITHER BELL 212 OR VADIC 3405.

     < > INDICATES THE ACTUAL LOCATION OF TELENET FACILITIES.  IN
SOME CASES, LOCAL ACCESS MAY REQUIRE EXTENDED METRO TELEPHONE SERVICE
OR INVOLVE MESSAGE UNIT CHARGES.
```

(continued on next page)

Figure 3.3: GTE Telenet Access Phone Numbers (cont.)

```
TELENET CUSTOMER SERVICE:
        CONTINENTAL USA --        800/336-0437
           IN VIRGINIA --         800/572-0408
        OUTSIDE CONTINENTAL USA -- 703/442-2200

TELEMAIL CUSTOMER SERVICE:
        CONTINENTAL USA --        800/368-3407
           IN VIRGINIA --         703/442-1900


STATE OR AREA.CODE OR ALL OR SALES.OFFICE:

area.code


PLEASE ENTER FIRST DIGIT OF AREA CODE.

2

PLEASE ENTER COMPLETE AREA CODE.

213
```

		300 BPS		1200 BPS
CA 213	ALHAMBRA	507-0909	<GLENDALE>	(B/V) 507-0909
CA 213	CANOGA PARK	306-2984	<MARINA DEL REY>	(B/V) 306-2984
CA 213	COMPTON	516-1007		(B/V) 516-1007
CA 213	COVINA	330-1630		(B/V) 330-1630
CA 213	EL MONTE	507-0909	<GLENDALE>	(B/V) 507-0909
CA%818	GLENDALE	507-0909		(B/V) 507-0909
CA 213	HOLLYWOOD	689-9040	<LOS ANGELES>	(B/V) 624-2251
CA 213	HOLLYWOOD	937-3580	<LOS ANGELES>	(B/V) 937-3580
CA 213	INGLEWOOD	689-9040	<LOS ANGELES>	(B/V) 624-2251
CA 213	INGLEWOOD	937-3580	<LOS ANGELES>	(B/V) 937-3580
CA 213	LONG BEACH	548-6141	<SAN PEDRO>	(B/V) 548-6141
CA 213	LOS ANGELES	689-9040		(B/V) 624-2251
CA 213	LOS ANGELES	937-3580		(B/V) 937-3580
CA 213	MARINA DEL REY	306-2984		(B/V) 306-2984
CA 213	NORWALK	404-2237		(B/V) 404-2237
CA 213	PASADENA	507-0909	<GLENDALE>	(B/V) 507-0909
CA 213	SAN PEDRO	548-6141		(B/V) 548-6141
CA 213	SANTA MONICA	306-2984	<MARINA DEL REY>	(B/V) 306-2984
CA 213	TORRANCE	548-6141	<SAN PEDRO>	(B/V) 548-6141
CA%818	WOODLAND HILLS	887-3160		(B/V) 887-3160

```
ANOTHER AREA CODE?   no

     This mail session is now complete.
```

$9.75. Tymnet's WATS service is $25 per hour to the nearest high-density node.

In addition to the data network service, Tymnet also offers electronic mail (OnTyme II), a free directory of commercial online services via Tymnet *(The Bluebook)* and a Tymnet User Group newsletter *(THUGS News).*

Various kinds of customer service information can be obtained online by using the Tymnet "information menu." (The other networks provide similar menus.) In Figure 3.4 we have selected item 6 from the general information menu and asked for a list of companies with personal computer products verified by Tymnet. You can also get lists of public access numbers for the U.S. and for international access. You can get instructions for reaching Canadian services using DataPac from the U.S. and U.S. services from Canada by connecting from DataPac to Tymnet.

UNINET

The Uninet PSN was started in 1981 by Uninet, Inc. of Kansas City, MO, and is a somewhat lower-priced alternative to Telenet and Tymnet. Uninet's standard hourly rates range from $3 to $5, and its WATS service costs $20 per hour. Uninet has more than 175 nodes and is rapidly adding nodes in most of the larger cities already served by either Tymnet or Telenet. Uninet is also "protocol sensing"—it automatically senses the terminal type and protocol you are using, making the entry of a special terminal identifier code unnecessary when signing on to the network. Figure 3.5 shows Uninet's information menu and information about sign-on and reporting trouble, obtained by selecting number 5 of the menu.

ALTERNATIVES TO USING PSNs

As noted above, although PSNs are the most commonly used method of gaining access to online services, there are other ways of using the telephone to connect to them. They are briefly discussed below.

Local Phone Calls

If you happen to live in the same city or area code region as an online service vendor's host computer facility, a local telephone call is the least expensive means of access. Since voice telephone systems are not designed for data communications, you may experience some online interference, however, and the chance of being disconnected may be greater than when using the data communications networks.

Figure 3.4: Tymnet Information Service Main Menu and Personal Computer Communications Information

```
                        TYMNET INFORMATION SERVICE
        Welcome to TYMNET's Information Service!  TYMNET is the world's
    largest Public Data Network, with local access in over 500 U.S. cities
    and access to and from over 50 foreign countries.  If you need more
    help, please don't hesitate to call one of our sales offices listed in
    the directory for more personal and extensive help with your applica-
    tion.  To exit this service, please type the word 'EXIT'.

    1.  HELP IN USING THE INFORMATION SERVICE
    2.  DIAL-UP ACCESS INFORMATION
    3.  DATA BASE AND TIMESHARING SERVICES AVAILABLE OVER TYMNET
    4.  INTERNATIONAL ACCESS INFORMATION
    5.  X.25 PRODUCTS CERTIFIED BY TYMNET
    6.  PERSONAL COMPUTER COMMUNICATION PRODUCTS VERIFIED BY TYMNET
    7.  HOST TYPES CURRENTLY INTERFACED ON TYMNET
    8.  TYMNET SALES OFFICE DIRECTORY
    TYPE THE NUMBER OF THE DESIRED MENU ITEM FOLLOWED BY A CARRIAGE RETURN:6


            PERSONAL COMPUTER PRODUCTS VERIFIED BY TYMNET

        TYMNET is the "PC Friendly Network."  To make it easier for you
    to use personal computers over our network we have been busy verifying
    P.C. communication products.  This is to ensure that they work ade-
    quately, particularly those that can be used to access 3270 applica-
    tions through our Character Mode Terminal support.  A list of products
    verified, and details about individual products are available below.
    To return to the main menu, type the word 'UP'.  To exit, type 'EXIT'.

    1.  LIST OF COMPANIES WITH PC PRODUCTS VERIFIED BY TYMNET
    2.  DETAILED INFORMATION ABOUT PRODUCTS VERIFIED BY TYMNET FOR A
            SPECIFIC COMPANY.
    3.  LIST OF CATEGORIES OF PC PRODUCTS VERIFIED BY TYMNET
    4.  LIST OF COMPANIES WITH PRODUCTS VERIFIED IN A SPECIFIC CATEGORY
    5.  BRIEF INFORMATION ABOUT PRODUCTS VERIFIED IN A SPECIFIC CATEGORY
    6.  DETAILED INFORMATION ABOUT PRODUCTS VERIFIED IN ONE CATEGORY


    TYPE THE NUMBER OF THE DESIRED MENU ITEM FOLLOWED BY A CARRIAGE RETURN:1
            COMPANIES WITH PERSONAL COMPUTER PRODUCTS VERIFIED BY TYMNET


    ADVANCED SOFTWARE PRODUCTS, INC.      APPLE, INC.
    COMMUNCATIONS RESEARCH                DIGITAL EQUIPMENT CORP.
    DIRECT INCORPORATED                   FORTE DATA SYSTEMS, INC.
    HEADLANDS PRESS                       ISC SYSTEMS CORPORATION
    MARK OF THE UNICORN, INC.             MICROCOM, INC.
    MICROSTUF                             P2/i
    PERSOFT, INC.                         POLYGON ASSOCIATES, INC.
    PRENTICE, INC.                        SATURN CONSULTING GROUP, INC.
    SOFTRONICS, INC.                      TECHLAND SYSTEM
    TELEXPRESS                            TYMSHARE
    VM PERSONAL COMPUTING                 WINDMILL SOFTWARE, INC.

    DO YOU WISH TO SEE THE CURRENT MENU AGAIN (Y/N):y
```

Figure 3.5: Uninet Information System Main Menu and Sign-on and Trouble Reporting Information

```
        U N I N E T   I N F O R M A T I O N    S Y S T E M

        INFORMATION LAST UPDATED ON 05-JUL-84

*************************************************************************

DO YOU WANT THE OUTPUT FORMATTED FOR A CRT (Y/N) ?n

ENTER OPTION OR ZERO -0- TO LIST AVAILABLE OPTIONS ?0

AVAILABLE INFORMATION OPTIONS

    1 - LIST NETWORK ACCESS PHONE NUMBERS BY CITY
    2 - LIST NETWORK ACCESS PHONE NUMBERS BY STATE
    3 - LIST NETWORK ACCESS PHONE NUMBERS BY AREA CODE
    4 - LIST SERVICE CHANGE INFORMATION
    5 - LIST SIGN-ON AND TROUBLE REPORTING INFORMATION
    6 - LIST INTERNATIONAL INFORMATION
    7 - LIST UNINET MESSAGES

   99 - END INFORMATION MANAGER

ENTER OPTION OR ZERO -0- TO LIST AVAILABLE OPTIONS ?5

* * * OPTION  5 LIST SIGN-ON AND TROUBLE REPORTING INFO

POSITION TO TOP OF PAGE AND HIT CARRIAGE RETURN

 SIGN-ON

1. TURN ON TERMINAL AND COUPLER OR DATA SET

2. DIAL YOUR LOCAL UNINET ACCESS TELEPHONE NUMBER OR 1-800 NUMBER
   THE TELEPHONE SHOULD RING, ANSWER AND PROVIDE A HIGH PITCHED
   DATA TONE.

3. PLACE THE TELEPHONE INTO THE COUPLER OR PUSH THE DATA BUTTON
   ON YOUR DATA SET. THE FOLLOWING MESSAGE WILL APPEAR AT YOUR
   TERMINAL. THIS IS A REQUEST FOR A TERMINAL IDENTIFIER.

        L?

   THIS MESSAGE MAY APPEAR GARBLED (POSSIBLY AS X"S) IF YOUR
   TERMINALS SPEED HAS NOT YET BEEN DETERMINED BY UNINET

4. RESPOND TO THIS MESSAGE BY TYPING A CARRIAGE RETURN,
   THEN TYPING A PERIOD AND CARRIAGE RETURN.
   THE FOLLOWING MESSAGE WILL BE RETURNED:

        UNINET PAD XXXXXX PORT YY
        SERVICE:

"XXXXXX" IS THE NAME OF THE UNINET PACKET ASSEMBLER/DISSASSEMBLER
(PAD) AND "YY" IS THE PORT NUMBER
IF YOU GET GARBLED CHARACTERS, HIT BREAK AND RE-ENTER
CARRIAGE RETURN, PERIOD, CARRIAGE RETURN.
```

(continued on next page)

Figure 3.5: Uninet Information System Main Menu and Sign-on and Trouble Reporting Information (cont.)

```
5. ENTER YOUR HOST IDENTIFIER AND A CARRIAGE RETURN
   AFTER THE SERVICE PROMPT.

       SERVICE: XXX

   YOU WILL RECIEVE A CONNECT MESSAGE FROM UNINET IF THE
   CONNECTION IS MADE.

       *U001 000 CONECTED TO XXXXXXXX


SIGN-OFF

1. WHEN YOU HAVE DISCONNECTED FROM YOUR HOST, HANG UP THE TELEPHONE
   AND TURN OFF TERMINAL AND COUPLER OR DATA SET.

SOLVING NETWORK ACCESS PROBLEMS

   MOST PROBLEMS THAT YOU ENCOUNTER RELATE TO NETWORK ACCESS
   AND CAN BE RESOLVED BY YOU. SOME OF THESE PROBLEMS ARE LISTED
   BELOW WITH THEIR CORRECTIVE ACTION. IF YOU ARE UNABLE TO RESOLVE
   THE PROBLEM, PLEASE REPORT IT TO YOUR HOST OPERATIONS CENTER.

   RING-NO-ANSWER          HANG UP AND TRY AGAIN

   TONE-NO-RESPONSE        CHECK YOUR TERMINAL AND COUPLER
                           SWITCH SETTINGS, CABLE CONNECTIONS
                           AND POWER-ON SETTINGS. TRY AGAIN

   FAST BUSY SIGNAL        LOCAL TELEPHONE LINES ARE TEMPORARILY
                           OVERLOADED. WAIT A FEW MINUTES AND
                           TRY AGAIN.

   SLOW BUSY SIGNAL        TELEPHONE NUMBER IS TEMPORARILY BUSY.
                           WAIT A FEW MINUTES AND TRY AGAIN.

   TERMINAL DROPS          HANG UP AND RE-DIAL.

   RANDOM CHARACTERS       TRY DISCONNECTING AND RE-DIAL.

   TONE-NO-TONE            THIS OCCURS WHEN TONE IS LOST WHILE
                           PLACING RECEIVER IN COUPLER AND
                           CAUSES YOUR TERMINAL TO BE UNRESPONSIVE.
                           DISCONNECT RECEIVER FROM COUPLER
                           HANG UP, AND RE-DIAL.
```

AT&T Direct Distance Dialing

AT&T's direct distance dialing (DDD) can be used to reach any online service from anywhere in the U.S. and Canada, but the cost can be prohibitive—up to $35 per hour—especially for lengthy online sessions.

Lower-Priced Long-Distance Services

Lower-cost long-distance services that compete with AT&T—like MCI and GTE's Sprint—may be used to gain access to online services, but they too, are more expensive than data communications networks.

The above access methods are usually used only when you do not have immediate access to one of the low-cost data communications networks. A very small number of online services are not available on the public data communications networks because they are relevant only to a single city or area code; a local or long-distance call is required to gain access. But these specialized services are not the subject of this book.

If technical difficulties prevent you from gaining access to a particular online service through a data communications network, most online services provide a direct-access phone number that you can call by using AT&T's direct distance dialing or long-distance services like MCI and GTE Sprint to gain access to online databases. The online service vendors and the data networks have customer service phone numbers that you can call for help with technical problems.

Dedicated Digital Leased Land Lines

If your company is a high-volume user of online services, you can arrange for a dedicated digital leased land line to each of those services's host computers. Leased lines dedicated to digital data communications can transmit data at speeds up to 9600 baud or 960 cps. (The highest transmission rate for PSNs, which use voice-grade telephone lines, is 1200 baud or 120 cps.) Arrangements for dedicated data lines are made with the local telephone company.

OTHER COMMUNICATIONS TECHNOLOGIES

The telecommunications industry is continuing to research and develop new technologies as alternatives to the sometimes decades-old copper-wire land-based telephone networks.

Satellite Communications

Communications satellites are playing an increasing role in both the telephone systems and non-telephone communications. Some wire services, such as United Press International (UPI), utilize a network of satellites to beam news data around the world. An individual online user may some day use his own satellite antenna to receive (and send) online information. Some data communications networks are now utilizing satellites rather than telephone networks for data transmission. The PSNs discussed above may eventually shift to satellites from telephone.

Cable Television

Another online technology being researched is cable television (CATV). Portions of the television bands not used for picture transmission (blanking intervals—the black lines you see when the picture rolls) can be used for data transmission. One-way CATV data transmission (cabletext) is used by hotel directory services over room television sets. Partial two-way transmission is used in a technology called teletext, whereby a user can specify which screens of data he wants directed to his TV from menus that scroll past his screen. Truly interactive CATV technology has not yet been perfected. Videotex (also called videotext or viewdata) is the vehicle being investigated for interactive CATV, but most of the services now being tested still use the telephone for transmission in one or both directions.

Fiber Optics

Fiber optics is another technology being researched by the telecommunications industry. It has the potential for far greater carrying capacity at much lower cost in much less space than the millions of miles of copper wire and cable now used by telephone companies. When perfected, fiber optics could reduce the cost of online services, but any saving would probably be offset by the installation costs. Faster data transmission speeds and greater efficiency will result, however. (Similarly, laser disk technology is being tested as a storage medium for computer data storage, with the potential for online services to store hundreds of times more data in far less space than that required by magnetic disk technology. This has tremendous implications for personal computer data storage potential as well.)

With all of the research and development occurring in data and voice communications, online services will benefit in greater efficiency and possibly lower costs.

SUMMARY

Although other communications technologies are being developed, the telephone system is now the primary medium for connecting terminal users to online services. Packet-switching data communications networks provide an efficient, inexpensive method of accessing commercial online information services over the phone. Unlike voice telephone systems, PSNs are designed specifically for digital data communications. The vast majority of online services are available over PSNs, and access to public PSNs is available from most U.S. cities.

Now that you are familiar with PSNs, you are ready to sign up for the information services you need to assist you in making intelligent business decisions. In the chapters that follow, we'll look at specific information services' offerings and how they can benefit you.

4

Overview of Major Online Services

By mid-1984, there were more than 250 online information services commercially available. Collectively, they offered access to more than 2000 individual databases. In this chapter, we will look at some of the larger, more popular and easier-to-use services of potential value to you, the business person. The criteria for inclusion are:

- information content of business interest
- ease of use
- compatibility with personal business computers

Compatibility is particularly important because of the tremendous growth in the number of personal computers being used in both large and small businesses for a multitude of tasks. The various IBM Personal Computer models, including some of the "work-alike" compatibles, are good examples of small computers that are evolving into multipurpose office workstations; they can be used for letter and report writing, financial analysis, business planning, filing and retrieval of documents, computer-to-computer data communications, and tapping external information services and sources.

It is through personal computers and public packet-switching data communications networks that the vast majority of business people will become familiar with online information services. Although a few online services require special dedicated terminals, the services covered in this chapter are all available to anyone with a typical small business computer equipped with a modem and data communications software or a standard data terminal. (One or two also require terminal emulation software.)

FOUR KINDS OF ONLINE SERVICES

Online services can be categorized into four types:

- popular information utilities
- full-text retrieval services

- library research services

- numeric data services

The distinction generally depends on their origins and user orientation (that is, whether they were designed for the average user of a personal computer or the trained professional information or data processing manager) or on the type of information being sought (whether it is basically textual or numeric in nature). However, these four basic types of online services are beginning to overlap somewhat in the databases and services they offer and in the customer groups they intend to serve.

As noted in Chapter 1, almost all of the online service providers are aware of the fast-growing market of personal computer users and are developing services aimed at this market. The popular information utilities and full-text services were specifically designed for these customers; the library research and numeric data services are releasing new personal computer services, which are considerably easier to use. Specific instances will be mentioned throughout this book, and Chapter 10 includes descriptions of some of the special software packages offered by these services.

Some of the most popular and easy-to-use online information services, by category, are:

- popular information utilities

    Dow Jones News/Retrieval Service

    CompuServe Information Service

    The Source

- full-text retrieval services

    Mead Data Central

    NewsNet

- library research services

    Dialog Information Services

    Knowledge Index (Dialog)

Bibliographic Retrieval Services (BRS)

BRS/After Dark (BRS)

SDC Orbit Search Service (SDC Information Services)

- numeric data services

ADP Network Services

I.P. Sharp Associates

Infomagic (I.P. Sharp)

The following pages provide an overview of these services. The kinds of business-related databases each service offers are outlined, and relative cost ranges for subscribing to and using each are discussed. Table 4.1 presents summary information about the services.

Specific information about many of the databases each service offers—and what those databases can do for you—is detailed in Chapters 5-9. Many other databases are available. Check one of the database directories listed in Appendix B for those that are of interest to you.

Descriptions and prices here—and throughout this book—are as of mid-1984. Remember that the online field is changing all the time; contact vendors for the latest information before you make a choice.

POPULAR INFORMATION UTILITIES

The popular information utilities have developed along with the rapid growth in the use of small computers since 1977. As noted in Chapter 1, personal computer hobbyists wanted facilities for communicating with each other to transmit messages and programs.

Established timesharing services began offering such services as electronic mail, bulletin boards for exchange of hobby information and online computer programming. In response to consumer demand they added news and business information. CompuServe Information Service and The Source are the two most widely used of the services that grew out of computer timesharing operations.

Table 4.1: Major Online Service Vendors Offering Databases of Business and Related Information

Service Name Parent Company	Type of Service	Ease of Use*	Data Networks	Micro Software
Dow Jones News/Retrieval Service Dow Jones and Co., Inc.	Popular utility	2	Telenet Tymnet Uninet	■

CompuServe Information Service
  CompuServe, Inc.
  H&R Block, Inc.
	Popular
	utility
		1	Telenet
			Tymnet
			Own net
				■

The Source
  Source Telecomputing Corp.
  Readers Digest Association, Inc.
	Popular
	utility
		3	Telenet
			Uninet
			Own net
				■

Mead Data Central Mead Corp.	Full text	1	Telenet Leased	■

NewsNet
  NewsNet, Inc.
  Independent Publications, Inc.
	Full text	3	Telenet
			Tymnet
			Uninet	

Dialog Information Services
  Dialog Information Services, Inc.
  Lockheed Corp.
	Library
	research
		5	Telenet
			Tymnet
			Uninet
				■

Knowledge Index
  Dialog Information Services, Inc.
  Lockheed Corp.
	Library
	research
		4	Telenet
			Tymnet
			Uninet	

Bibliographic Retrieval Services (BRS)
  Bibliographic Retrieval Services, Inc.
  Indianhead Technology Group, Inc.
	Library
	research
		4	Telenet
			Tymnet
			Uninet	

BRS/After Dark
  Bibliographic Retarieval Services, Inc.
  Indianhead Technology Group, Inc.
	Library and
	utility
		2	Telenet
			Tymnet
			Uninet	

SDC Orbit Search Service
  SDC Information Services
  System Development Corp.
  Burroughs Corp.
	Library
	research
		4	Telenet
			Tymnet
				■

ADP Network Services Automatic Data Processing, Inc.	Numeric	5	Autonet Tymnet	■
I.P. Sharp Associates I.P. Sharp Associates Ltd.	Numeric	5	Telenet Tymnet	■
Infomagic I.P. Sharp Associates Ltd.	Numeric	2	Telenet Tymnet	

■ - required   □ - optional
*Ease of use on a scale of 1 (very easy for novice) to 5 (difficult for novice)

Table 4.1: Major Online Service Vendors Offering Databases of Business and Related Information (cont.)

Electronic Mail	Online Computing	Start-up Fee	Annual Subscription	Monthly Minimum Charge	Lower Night Rates	Auto Credit Card Charge
■		■	□		■	
■	■	■	□		■	
■	■	■			■	■
			■			
■		■		■		
			□			
		■		■	■	■
■		■	□			
■		■		■	■	■
■			□			
	■		■			
	■					
		■				

Dow Jones News/Retrieval Service (DJNRS) grew out of the demand for online stock price quotation services, and today includes news, electronic mail and many other online features of interest to the average personal computer user.

DOW JONES NEWS/RETRIEVAL SERVICE

The Dow Jones News/Retrieval Service is the most widely used popular information utility. Founded in 1882, Dow Jones and Company is publisher of *The Wall Street Journal* and *Barron's* financial weekly. Dow Jones entered the online services business in 1974 as a joint venture with Bunker Ramo Corp., offering stock quotes to stock brokerage firms and professional investors. The early service was very expensive, and subscribers were linked to Dow Jones' computer by dedicated leased phone lines.

The present Dow Jones News/Retrieval Service began in 1977 when the company added stories from *The Wall Street Journal* and *Barron's* and sold the service over the Telenet and Tymnet data networks at lower prices attractive to business users. Dow Jones bought out Bunker Ramo in 1979 and began offering more new databases and services. In 1980, DJ announced that Apple computers could access the services, followed, in 1981, by Radio Shack TRS-80, IBM Personal Computers and Commodore Pet Microcomputers.

The inclusion of general interest and reference information, such as Grolier's *Academic American Encyclopedia*, Cineman movie reviews, and sports and weather news, is making Dow Jones a mass market general information utility, even though its emphasis is on business and financial services. News/Retrieval is available on the Telenet, Tymnet and Uninet data networks.

Business Information Available

Dow Jones News/Retrieval Service offers six main categories of information, four of which are business-oriented. These are listed in the Dow Jones master menu shown in Figure 4.1, along with the welcome message. The business and financial databases available in these categories are summarized in Table 4.2.

Dow Jones Business and Economic News

As Figure 4.2 indicates, there are three databases available as part of Dow

Figure 4.1: Dow Jones News/Retrieval Service Welcome Message and Master Menu

```
        DOW JONES NEWS/RETRIEVAL
          COPYRIGHT (C) 1984
        DOW JONES & COMPANY, INC.
          ALL RIGHTS RESERVED.

MONDALE PICKS GERALDINE
FERRARO AS RUNNING MATE,
SEE //NEWS. DATA-BASE LIST
IN //MENU.
ENTER QUERY
        //menu
          Master Menu
        Copyright (C) 1984
     Dow Jones & Company, Inc.

PRESS    FOR
  A    Dow Jones Business And
          Economic News Services
  B    Dow Jones Quotes
  C    Dow Jones Text-Search
          Services
  D    Financial And Investment
          Services
  E    General News And
          Information Services
  F    Mail Service and
          Free Customer Newsletter
```

Jones Business and Economic News. The Dow Jones News (DJNEWS) database contains full-text stories from *The Wall Street Journal, Barron's* and the Dow Jones News Service (Broadtape) wire. Stories are as current as 90 seconds old and go as far back as three months. The Weekly Economic Update (UPDATE) database gives statistics and analyses of the week's economic events and forecasts for the coming month. The Wall Street Journal Highlights Online (WSJ) contains headlines and summaries of major stories in the current and four previous issues from 6 a.m. every business day. (See Chapter 5 for more information.)

Dow Jones Quotes

The Dow Jones Quotes section (see Figure 4.3) provides a stock price

Table 4.2: Selected Business and Financial Databases on Dow Jones News/Retrieval Service

Database Title	Subject/Content
Dow Jones Business and Economic News	
Dow Jones News	WSJ, *Barron's*, Broadtape
Weekly Economic Update	Economic indicator summary
Wall Street Journal Highlights Online	Major stories and items
Dow Jones Quotes	
Current Quotes	AMEX, NYSE, OTC exchanges
Historical Quotes	Weekly, monthly, quarterly histories
Historical Dow Jones Averages	Industrials, transportation, utilities
Dow Jones Text-Search Services	
Wall Street Journal	Full text, all stories
Dow Jones News	Full text, all stories
Financial and Investment Services	
Disclosure II	SEC filings on 9500 public companies
Corporate Earnings Estimator	Forecasts for 3000 U.S. firms
Forbes Directory	Corporate rankings
Japan Economic Daily	Kyodo economic news wire
Media General Database	Income, price, volume data
Merrill Lynch Weekly Research Highlights	Financial analysis
MMS Weekly Economic Survey	Money Market Services
Official Airline Guide Electronic Edition	Current air schedules and fares

quotation service from the New York, American and over-the-counter (OTC) exchanges. The Current Quotes (CQ) database provides updated prices and trading information, delayed 15 minutes, throughout the trading day. The Historical Dow Jones Averages (DJA) and the Historical Quotes (HQ) databases permit you to track the history of issues you are particularly interested in. Chapter 7 contains further discussion of Dow Jones Quotes.

With special software for your personal computer, available from Dow Jones (see Chapter 10), you can automatically report and analyze your personal or corporate portfolio of securities, either existing or planned, to determine their performance on a day-to-day basis, and historically to examine their past track records.

Dow Jones Text-Search Services

The Dow Jones Text-Search Services database consists of two subfiles (see

Figure 4.2: Dow Jones Business and Economic News Services Menu

```
            Dow Jones Business
        And Economic News Services

    For help, type code and HELP.
       (Example: //DJNEWS HELP)

      TYPE        FOR
    //DJNEWS   90-Day News From The
               Broadtape, Selections
               From Barron's And The
               Wall Street Journal

    //UPDATE   Weekly Economic Up-
               date: A Roundup Of The
               Past Economic Week

    //WSJ      Wall Street Journal
               Highlights Online:
               Summaries Of The Past
               Five Editions Of The
               Wall Street Journal
```

Figure 4.3: Dow Jones Quotes Menu

```
            Dow Jones Quotes

    For help, type code and HELP.
        (Example: //CQ HELP)

      TYPE         FOR
    //CQ        Current Price Quotes
                On Stocks And Other
                Financial Instruments,
                Delayed 15 Minutes

    //DJA       Historical Dow Jones
                Averages: Daily Sum-
                maries Of The 4 Dow
                Jones Market Averages

    //HQ        Historical Stock Mar-
                ket Price Quotations
```

Figure 4.4). One contains the full text of all stories from *The Wall Street Journal* from January 1984 through the current day. The other offers the full text of stories from Dow Jones News (selected articles from *The Wall Street Journal* and *Barron's* plus the Broadtape) since June 1979. With Text-Search, you search for articles using any substantive keywords found in the text. You may specify word relation using several logical operators, as discussed in Chapter 1. The Text-Search Services database is discussed further in Chapter 5.

Financial and Investment Services

The Financial and Investment Services menu (see Figure 4.5) contains several databases on finances of public corporations and on securities analysis. The Disclosure II database consists of reports filed with the Securities and Exchange Commission by more than 9400 public companies. Corporate Earnings Estimator contains projected earnings for 3000 major public corporations, based on reports from 60 leading brokerage firms. The Forbes Directory ranks the largest U.S. corporations by sales, profits, assets and market value. Media General contains more than 50 selected items about companies trading on the three major U.S. exchanges. The Money Market Services database forecasts leading economic indicators based on interviews with economists and financial analysts at leading financial institutions. Several of these are described in more detail in Chapter 7. Also

Figure 4.4: Dow Jones Text-Search Services Menu

```
Dow Jones Text-Search Services

   For help, type //TEXT HELP

   TYPE      FOR
 //TEXT    Text-Search Services

            1. Wall Street Journal
               Full-Text Version
               From January 1984

            2. Dow Jones News
               From June 1979
               *   *   *
 For an overview, type //DJHELP
```

Figure 4.5: Dow Jones Financial and Investment Services Menu

```
                Financial and
            Investment Services

    For help, type code and HELP.
        (Example: //DSCLO HELP)

       TYPE           FOR
    //DSCLO     Disclosure II:  Finan-
                cial And Management
                Information On 9,400
                Public Companies

    //EARN      Corporate Earnings
                Estimator: Consensus
                Earnings Forecasts For
                3,000 U.S. Companies

    //FORBES    Forbes Directory:
                Rankings of Top
                Corporations And
                Major U.S. Industries

    //KYODO     Japan Economic Daily:
                Same-Day Coverage of
                Business and Economic
                News From Japan
```

included are the Merrill Lynch Weekly Highlights of Investment Research, the Japan Economic Daily (see Chapter 5) and the Official Airline Guide Electronic Edition (see Chapter 9).

Subscription and Cost

Dow Jones has several subscription plans available for varying levels of usage. There is a modest sign up fee of $50 for a standard service subscription and two discount plans for high volume users: Blue Chip and Executive. The Blue Chip membership is $50 to sign up and $75 per year, with a 33.3% discount for non-prime-time rates. The Executive plan is $50 per month and offers a 33.3% discount during both prime and non-prime time. Standard database access fees average $54 per hour during the business day and $6 per hour evenings, weekends and holidays. Actual charges vary with the database being accessed. Dow Jones subscriptions may be purchased in most personal computer retail stores.

COMPUSERVE INFORMATION SERVICE

CompuServe, Inc., a Columbus, OH, timesharing company founded in 1970, began providing remote online computing and programs to personal computer hobbyists during evenings and weekends in 1979. The service, called MicroNet, is still available, along with news, online magazines, stock quotes and other information, added in 1980. CompuServe, which is now available 24 hours a day, is currently the second most popular online service among personal computer users. In addition to information, CompuServe provides several communications features including electronic mail, a subscriber directory, a CB radio simulator or online conferencing feature, and special interest bulletin boards, which put you in touch with others sharing the same interests. Since 1980, CompuServe has been a wholly owned subsidiary of H&R Block, Inc.

CompuServe is easy to use. You can select any of the available databases from a menu or you can go directly to a specific database from anywhere in the system. A user manual is available from CompuServe. There are information and features for the entire family, which makes the service popular in homes with personal computers. There is also a considerable amount of business information available. CompuServe is available via Telenet and Tymnet as well as on its own data communications network.

Business Information Available

Table 4.3 summarizes the primary business database services available on CompuServe. Figure 4.6 illustrates the CompuServe online welcome message and main menu of available services. CompuServe's Business and Financial Services menu of databases is illustrated in Figure 4.7. Of these, the News and Financial Analysis and Investments and Quotations databases are of greatest interest to the general business user. Also included are brokerage services, electronic banking, discussion forums and several personal financial programs. General news, both national and international, is provided from the Home Services menu (item 1 in Figure 4.6).

News and Financial Analysis

In CompuServe's News and Financial Analysis section (also shown in Figure 4.7) the Business Information Wire provides the full text of the Canadian Press wire service, covering U.S. and Canadian business news. The Business Wire, a separate database, also covers current news articles, press releases and other business news. News-A-Tron Commodities gives you news and price data on commodities traded on the major U.S. commodity exchanges.

Table 4.3: Selected Business and Financial Databases on CompuServe Information Service

Database Title	Subject/Content
News and Financial Analysis	
Business Information Wire	U.S. and Canada business news
The Business Wire	Press releases and news
News-A-Tron Commodities	Commodities news and prices
Stevens Business Reports	Analysis and commentary
The Computer Wire	Computer news and analysis
Business & Law Review	Legal articles and reports
MMS Financial Analysis	Money Market Services
Evans Economics, Inc.	Economic forecasts and analysis
Investments and Quotations	
Microquote	Data on 43,000 stocks
Quick Quote	Current stock price data
Standard & Poor's Analysis	Performance of 3000 companies
Value Line Data Base II	Analysis of 1700 public firms
News-A-Tron Commodities	News and price indexes
Rapaport Diamond System	Diamond investing
Shareholders Freebies	News of perks for shareholders
Other Databases of Business Interest	
AP Videotex	Business, national world news
InfoWorld	Weekly computer magazine
Information on Demand	Document find and deliver service
Personal Computing	Monthly computer magazine
St. Louis Post-Dispatch	Full-text newspaper
Washington Post	Full-text newspaper
Executive Information Service*	
Institutional Brokers' Estimate System	Earnings projections
Site-Potential	Marketing demographics
Stats II	Statistical data handling

*Also includes all databases listed above.

These are described further in Chapter 5.

Stevens Business Reports are written for small businesses by Mark A. Stevens, a nationally syndicated columnist. The Computer Wire is a news service covering the computer and data processing industry. The Business and Law Review database reviews current news and events covering business legal issues. The MMS (Money Market Services) Financial Analysis database offers forecasts of leading economic indicators provided by analysts of major financial institutions. Evans Economics, Inc., is an economic news, forecast and analysis service of Michael K. Evans, a nationally known econometrician.

Figure 4.6: CompuServe Information Service Welcome Message and Main Menu

```
COMPUSERVE  INFORMATION  SERVICE

20:44 CDT   THURSDAY   12-JUL-84

[[[[[[[[[[[[[[[**]]]]]]]]]]]]]]]    COMPUSERVE         PAGE CIS-1
[             N E W             ]
[               &               ]    COMPUSERVE  INFORMATION  SERVICE
[       N O T E W O R T H Y     ]
[   IN THE ELECTRONIC MALL (TM) ]    1 HOME SERVICES
[         ----------            ]    2 BUSINESS & FINANCIAL
[ METROPOLITAN ADDS INFORMATION]     3 PERSONAL COMPUTING
[ PAN AM UPDATES CATALOG       ]     4 SERVICES FOR PROFESSIONALS
[ FINANCIAL MARKET CHANGES DATA]     5 THE ELECTRONIC MALL (TM)
[ 1984 OLYMPIC GAMES CONTEST   ]     6 USER INFORMATION
[         ----------            ]    7 INDEX
[   TYPE GO NNW AT ANY PROMPT   ]
[[[[[[[[[[[[[[[**]]]]]]]]]]]]]]]    ENTER YOUR SELECTION NUMBER,
                                     OR H FOR MORE INFORMATION.
KEY S OR <ENTER> TO CONTINUE!        !
```

Figure 4.7: CompuServe Business and Financial Services Menu and News and Financial Analysis (News/Reports) Menu

```
COMPUSERVE          PAGE FIN-1
                                      COMPUSERVE          PAGE FIN-10
BUSINESS AND FINANCIAL SERVICES
                                                NEWS/REPORTS
1 NEWS & FINANCIAL ANALYSIS           1 BUSINESS INFORMATION WIRE
2 INVESTMENTS & QUOTATIONS            2 THE BUSINESS WIRE
3 COMMUNICATIONS                      3 NEWS-A-TRON COMMODITIES
4 BROKERAGE & BANKING                 4 STEVENS BUSINESS REPORTS
5 REFERENCE LIBRARY                   5 THE COMPUTER WIRE
6 DISCUSSION FORUMS                   6 BUSINESS & LAW REVIEW
7 TRAVEL SERVICES                     7 MMS FINANCIAL ANALYSIS
8 PERSONAL FINANCE                    8 EVANS ECONOMICS, INC.


LAST MENU PAGE. KEY DIGIT           LAST MENU PAGE.  KEY DIGIT.
OR M FOR PREVIOUS MENU.             !
!1
```

Investments and Quotes

The main Investments & Quotations menu is shown in Figure 4.8. MicroQuote contains more than 50 items of daily, weekly and monthly data on more than 43,000 stocks, bonds, options and other securities traded on 10 major stock exchanges and over the counter. Quick Quote provides quotes on individual securities, delayed 15 minutes, from the New York, American and OTC stock exchanges. News-A-Tron Commodities is also available on this menu.

Standard & Poor's Analysis contains descriptive profiles and financial data on more than 3000 public corporations (see Chapter 6). Value Line Data Base II contains over 400,000 annual and quarterly time series on more than 200 variables of more than 1700 companies traded on the New York, American

Figure 4.8: CompuServe Investment and Quotations Menu

```
COMPUSERVE          PAGE FIN-20   COMPUSERVE              PAGE FIN-56

     INVESTMENTS & QUOTATIONS                   QUOTATIONS

                                   $1  CURRENT-DAY STOCK PRICES
   1 MICROQUOTE                    $2  PRICING HISTORY, ONE SECURITY
 $ 2 QUICK QUOTE                   $3  PRICE HISTORY, MULT. ISSUES
 $ 3 STANDARD AND POOR'S ANALYSES  $4  DIVIDEND HISTORY
   4 VALUE LINE DATA BASE II       $5  TICKER, CUSIP LOOKUP
   5 NEWS-A-TRON COMMODITIES       $6  NEWS-A-TRON (COMMODITIES)
   6 RAPAPORT   DIAMOND SYSTEM
   7 SHAREHOLDER'S FREEBIES        LAST MENU PAGE. KEY DIGIT
 $ INDICATES CHARGES IN ADDITION   OR M FOR PREVIOUS MENU.
 TO CONNECT TIME MAY BE INCURRED.  COMPUSERVE           PAGE FIN-55

                                        FUNDAMENTAL FINANCIAL
 LAST MENU PAGE. KEY DIGIT                    INFORMATION
 OR M FOR PREVIOUS MENU.
 !m                                  1 VALUE LINE INFORMATION
                                    $2 VALUE LINE ANNUAL REPORTS
                                    $3 VALUE LINE DATA RETRIEVAL
                                    $4 STANDARD & POOR'S ANALYSIS
                                     5 SHAREHOLDER FREEBIES

                                   LAST MENU PAGE. KEY DIGIT
                                   OR M FOR PREVIOUS MENU.
```

and OTC exchanges (see Chapter 7). The Rapaport Diamond System is a trading service for investors in diamonds. Shareholders Freebies covers news about perks and benefits for investors in public stock.

Other CompuServe Databases

Additional databases of business interest on CompuServe from the Home Service menu include AP Videotex, a news wire from the Associated Press, especially formatted for the popular information utilities (see Chapter 5); InfoWorld and Personal Computing, electronic versions of the magazines of the same names, which cover the personal computer industry; Information on Demand (IOD), a service providing document search and delivery; and The St. Louis Post-Dispatch and The Washington Post, electronic versions of those newspapers (see Chapter 5).

Executive Information Service

CompuServe's Executive Information Service (EIS) is a special edition of the information service for business people. It contains all of the business and financial databases in the regular service plus some additional databases, as shown in Table 4.3: Institutional Brokers' Estimate Systems (IBES), a stock earnings forecasting service; Site-Potential, a database of marketing demographics; and Site II, a database for statistical handling of demographic data.

There is also special software available for the IBM Personal Computer that lets IBM users sign on automatically and use all of CompuServe's business and financial services immediately and easily, even if they've never been online before (see Chapter 10). EIS also connects the IBM PC to the Official Airline Guide Electronic Edition (see Chapter 9).

Subscription and Cost

CompuServe subscriptions are available at most personal computer retail stores. There is a modest sign-up fee of $19.95, but you should plan to purchase user manuals, which will bring the cost to about $50. Hourly database access charges average $12.50 during the business day and $6 in non-prime time for 300 baud transmission; for 1200 baud transmission, the rates are $15.00 and $12.50 respectively. A few databases and services cost extra—these are indicated by a dollar sign ($) to the left of the service name in the CompuServe menus, as shown in Figure 4.8.

THE SOURCE

The Source calls itself "America's Information Utility" and is similar to CompuServe in the types of databases and services offered. The Source is operated by Source Telecomputing Corp., which began service in 1979 as The Telecomputing Corp. of America. In 1980, it was bought by the Reader's Digest Association, Inc.

The Source can be used either in a menu-driven mode, for new and infrequent users, or in a command-driven mode, which allows more experienced users to bypass the menus. Like Dow Jones and CompuServe, The Source offers several business and financial databases and packages as well as general interest information, electronic mail, games and other entertainment features. There are also business and financial analysis computer programs available online. The Source can be used over Telenet, Tymnet and SourceNet, its own network.

Business Information Available

Table 4.4 summarizes the business and financial databases available from The Source. Figure 4.9 shows the welcome message, main menu and Business Update menu.

Table 4.4: Selected Business and Financial Databases and Services on The Source

Database Title	Subject/Content
Business Update	
Financial Headlines	Weekly business news (UPI)
Business Horizons	The week in review (UPI)
U.S. News Washington Letter	*U.S. News & World Report*
The Board Room	Corporate advice and news
Stockcheck	UPI stock quotes
Market Indicators	News of market conditions
Commodities Index	News on the economy
Currency	Exchange rate reports
Bizdex (Business and Financial Services Index)	
Stockcheck	UPI stock quotes
Media General Data Base	Analysis of 3000 public companies
Management Contents, Ltd.	Abstracts of 27 publications
Information on Demand	Document search and delivery
Embassy Institute Tax Service	Tax advice and information
Foldex Stock Portfolio Management	Personal portfolio analysis

Figure 4.9: The Source Welcome Message, Main Menu and Business Update (Bizdate) Menu

```
Welcome, you are connected to THE SOURCE
Last login Friday 04 Nov 83 14:53:40

(C) COPYRIGHT SOURCE TELECOMPUTING CORPORATION 1983

WELCOME TO THE SOURCE
1   USING THE SOURCE
2   TODAY
3   BUSINESS UPDATE
4   THE SOURCE MAIN MENU
5   WHAT'S NEWS
COMMAND LEVEL
Enter item number or HELP   3

            BUSINESS UPDATE
            ===============
            Weekend Edition
         November 5 & 6, 1983

1.  STOCKCHECK
2.  MARKET INDICATORS: Interest Rate Fears Drive Stocks Lower
3.  COMMODITIES INDEX: Gold Settles Lower
4.  CURRENCY: Dollar Soars to Record Highs
5.  FINANCIAL HEADLINES: The Business Week in Review
6.  BUSINESS HORIZONS: Roundup of This Week's Stories
7.  U.S. NEWS WASHINGTON LETTER
8.  THE BOARD ROOM: The Never Never Land of the Debt Question
9.  BIZDEX:  A Guide to THE SOURCE Business Services

Enter item number or HELP   9
```

Business Update

The Business Update (Bizdate), "a daily business tabloid," provides the day's and week's major business and financial news, including Financial Headlines and Business Horizons from the United Press International (UPI) news wires. The U.S. News Washington Letter from *U.S. News and World Report* is updated weekly. The Board Room offers business and financial analysis and opinion from various sources. See Chapter 5 for more details.

The Stockcheck database, also from UPI, lets you look at the latest New

York, American and OTC stock price quotes, delayed 15 minutes. Market Indicators compiles current information from UPI on the stock, securities and commodities markets. For more information on these databases, see Chapter 7. Commodities market indicators and the latest gold and currency rates are available in Commodities Index and Currency, respectively.

Bizdex

Bizdex is an online index to business and financial services available on The Source. As Figure 4.10 indicates, Bizdex refers the user to Stockcheck, U.S. News Washington Letter and Bizdate itself, as well as to several other services. Media General's Stock Analysis contains over 50 items of data for companies listed on the three major exchanges. The Management Contents Ltd. database provides abstracts of current and recent articles from 27 leading business journals; this is a small subset of the full Management Contents database available on BRS, Dialog and SDC Orbit library research services (see Chapter 8).

The Source also has a tax advisory service online (Embassy Institute Tax Services), several computational programs, a financial modeling program, a stock portfolio management program (Foldex), a document retrieval and search service (IOD), and a database management program for your business records. All of these services also may be obtained through The Source's main menu.

Subscription and Cost

Like Dow Jones and CompuServe, subscriptions to The Source are available at most personal computer retail stores. The subscription cost is $100. The hourly connect rate is $20.75 during prime time and $7.75 during non-prime time.

FULL-TEXT RETRIEVAL SERVICES

Like the popular information utilities, full-text services are fairly recent additions to the online industry. In the early years of online retrieval, magnetic storage devices were not efficient enough to store large amounts of text. Now, however, the technology of dense magnetic disk storage enables storing the entire text of newspapers, magazines, newsletters, professional and technical journals, laws and legal cases, and encyclopedias. Since many of these are general interest publications, and others are designed for professional end users, full-text systems are designed to be easy to use. Of particular interest to business users are Mead Data Central and NewsNet.

Figure 4:10: The Source Business and Financial Services Index (Bizdex)

```
BIZDEX:  An index to Business and Financial Services on THE SOURCE

A Daily Business Tabloid................................BIZDATE
    Provides market indicators, commodities index, currency,
    financial headlines and much more on a daily basis.

Stockcheck..........................................STOCKCHECK
    Provides the latest stock market quotations from United Press
    International.  STOCKCHECK also is available from Option 1 of the
    BIZDATE menu.

Media General's Stock Analysis..........................STOCKVUE
    Provides current and historical data for over 3,100 common
    stocks traded on the NYSE, AMEX, and OTC.

Management Contents, Ltd................................CONTENTS
    Provides abstracts from 27 leading business periodicals.

Document Retrieval and Search Services...................IOD
    For General Information and Current Rates.............HELP IOD

Exchange of Corporate Goods and Services................BARTER

U.S. News Washington Letter (updated weekly).............USNEWS

Embassy Institute Tax Services..........................TAX

Index to Computational Programs........................HELP COMPUDEX
    Includes programs to compute loan or bond interest rates,
    cashflow values, depreciation schedules, equity capital
    costs, amortization schedules, mortgage analysis, sales
    commissions, and more.

Financial Modelling for Business Planning...............HELP MODEL1
    (Free Manual Required, see HELP SYSDOC)

Infox Business Data Base Management.....................HELP INFOX
    Useful for braod range of accounting procedures.  (Manual
    Required, see HELP SYSDOC)

Stock Portfolio Management..............................HELP FOLDEX
```

MEAD DATA CENTRAL

Mead Data Central (MDC) is a division of Mead Corp., the paper and forest products company of Dayton, OH. MDC began electronic publishing services in 1973 when it launched Lexis, an online full-text legal research service (see Chapter 9). In 1980, it introduced Nexis, a full-text news research service (see Chapter 5). In 1983, Nexis became the online vendor for The New York Times Information Service's (NYTIS) InfoBank and New York Times Online databases. NYTIS is now a major database supplier to MDC. MDC has become one of the most successful online service vendors; most large U.S. law firms and many smaller ones use Lexis. Nexis is widely used by libraries and by business and professional people.

MDC pioneered full-text interactive retrieval online with keyword-in-context (KWIC) phrase searching. The MDC system searches the entire text of every requested article, story or legal case for the correct phrase in the context specified. MDC's services are extremely easy to use with its custom UBIQ terminals, which have special keys for the various search and display functions. MDC has offered special software which emulates the UBIQ terminal functions for IBM and Wang Personal Computers and the Apple II. Other personal computers will be added in late 1984. MDC services are available via Telenet or dedicated leased lines directly from Dayton.

Business Information Available

The complete range of MDC full-text database services is extensive. The service line now includes:

- Lexis legal research service

- Nexis news research service

- Lexpat patent research service

- the complete Encyclopaedia Britannica

- NAARS (National Automated Accounting Research Service)

- Associated Press Political Service

- MDC system access to Dialog Information Service

Table 4.5 lists the major MDC services of interest to business and professional people.

Subscription and Costs

MDC has two subscription plans. The higher-cost leased line subscription plan offers volume discounts for heavy users; a subscription to Nexis is $50 per month. The lower-cost dial access plan for less frequent users is available on the Telenet data network at an average cost of $28 per hour for Nexis. For

Table 4.5: Selected Databases from Mead Data Central

Database Title or Type	Subject/Content
Lexis Legal Research Libraries	
U.S. code, regulations and cases	Federal laws and U.S. courts
Tax law and cases	IRS and federal taxes
Securities law and cases	SEC and federal rulings
Trade regulations and cases	FTC regulations and rulings
Patent, trademark and copyright	Infringement cases and rulings
Communications law and cases	FCC regulations and rulings
Labor law and cases	Labor regulations and rulings
Bankruptcy cases	Bankruptcy decisions
Energy regulations and determinations	DOE regulations and rulings
Public contracts cases and determinations	Contract decisions
Federal Register	Full text of Federal Register
State law libraries	Code and cases, 50 states and DC
United Kingdom law libraries	Code and cases of U.K.
French law libraries	Code and cases of France
Auto-Cite	Case citations
Shepard's Citations	Case citations
Matthew Bender	Full text of publications
American Bar Association	Constitution, bylaws, ethics
Lexpat patent research	Full text of U.S. patents 1975
Nexis News Research Libraries	
Newspapers	Full text, 15+ newspapers
Magazines	Full text, 30+ magazines
Wire Services	Full text, 10+ news wires
Newsletters	Full text, 40+ newsletters
Miscellaneous Services and Databases	
National Automated Accounting Research System	AICPA annual reports, literature
Associated Press political service	Candidates, issues, results
Encyclopaedia Britannica	Macropaedia and micropaedia
Forensic Services Directory	Listings of experts and consultants

more information, you can contact MDC at its headquarters (see Appendix C). MDC also has regional sales offices in several major cities; check your phone directory.

NEWSNET

NewsNet was established in 1982 by NewsNet, Inc., a subsidiary of Independent Publications, Inc., of Philadelphia. NewsNet offers the full text of electronic editions of more than 175 topical and special interest business, financial and technical newsletters. Many of the newsletters are available online before the print editions are mailed to subscribers. A few are not available in print at all: they are only published electronically via NewsNet. NewsNet also offers the Public Relations (PR) and UPI news wires.

All newsletters may be searched using keywords or phrases. With a feature called NewsFlash, you can establish your own automatic updating or current awareness profile based on your particular interests. Each time you log on, you are alerted to new articles matching your profile. You may then scan the headlines and read any articles of interest. NewsNet is an excellent way to keep up on the latest trends and developments of your competitors and other industries of interest.

NewsNet is fairly easy to use. There are online menus and self-help tutorials which are of considerable aid in navigating through the system. Figure 4.11 shows the NewsNet online welcome, with its copyright message and typical bulletins announcing new services. NewsNet is available over Telenet, Tymnet and Uninet.

Business Information Available

Table 4.6 lists selected NewsNet databases in some of the the larger business and technical categories. Additional databases are listed in the discussion of NewsNet in Chapter 5. The categories with the most newsletters are the high technology areas of computers and electronics, publishing and broadcasting (which includes electronic publishing, online database services and videotex), and telecommunications. The finance, investments and taxes categories also each include several newsletter databases. NewsNet is growing continuously, with several new newsletters or other services being added every month.

Subscription and Cost

There is no fee to sign up as a NewsNet subscriber, but there is a monthly

Figure 4.11: NewsNet Welcome Message and News Bulletins

```
NewsNet System 18.3B(75)
On At 20:56 11/01/83
Last On At 14:13 11/01/83
                * * * * * * * * * * *
                * NEWSNET *   FOR THE BUSINESS INFORMATION EDGE
                * * * * * * * * * * *


Copyright NewsNet, Inc. 1983.  No part of any NEWSNET
transmission may be reproduced, stored in a retrieval
system, or transmitted in any form or by any means without
prior written permission.  Contents of publications are
copyrighted by the publisher and may not be reproduced
without prior written permission.  All rights reserved.

--> At any time, touch <RETURN> for assistance, or type HELP for
even more details.

*** THE BUSINESS COMPUTER (EC22) now available on NewsNet!! ***

*** DEFENSE R&D UPDATE (AE03) now available on NewsNet!! ***

*** EDITORS ONLY (PB13) now available on NewsNet!! ***

Enter command or <RETURN>
-->
```

minimum charge of $15. The text of the newsletters can be read for an hourly access charge of between $24 and $120; the rate is established by the newsletter publisher. Because publishers of both print and electronic editions often want to protect their print subscriptions, they offer subscribers a preferred hourly rate, usually 50% less than the non-subscriber rate. Subscriptions are available directly from NewsNet, Inc. (see Appendix C).

LIBRARY RESEARCH SERVICES

The library research services, also called bibliographic search services, were pioneers of the commercial online information industry. Originally intended for use by information specialists, as noted in Chapter 1, they were designed to handle huge numbers of bibliographic records identifying and abstracting scientific and technical publications. These services now cover more than 100

Table 4.6: Selected Business and Financial Newsletter Databases on NewsNet

Database Title	Subject or Publisher
Business and Management	
Altman & Weil Report to Legal Management	Business legal issues
The Corporate Shareholder	Corporate investing
The Entrepreneurial Manager	New business management
Executive Productivity	Management efficiency
The Exporter	Trade Data Reports, Inc.
International Intertrade Index	Imports and exports
Media Science Reports	Advertising
Office Automation Update	News and products
PR Newswire	Corporate press releases
Finance and Accounting	
Banking Regulator	Reports, Inc.
Credit Union Regulator	Reports, Inc.
Federal Reserve Week	Business Publishers, Inc.
Financial Management Advisor	Financial advice
Investments	
News-A-Tron Daily Industrial Index Analyzer	Economic indicators
Fedwatch	Money Market Services
Ford Investment Review	Ford Investor Services
Howard Ruff's Financial Survival Report	Investment advice
Insight	Money Market Services
Low-Priced Stock Alert	Idea Publishing Corp.
Market Consensus Alert	Idea Publishing Corp.
Penny Stock Preview	Idea Publishing Corp.
Real Estate Investing Letter	Harcourt Brace Jovanovich Newsletter Bureau, Inc.
The Stanger Report	Investing news
Stock Advisor's Alert	Idea Publishing Corp.
Tax Shelter Insider	Newsletter Management Corp.
Trude Latimer's Stock Trader's Hotline	Investment tips
Wall Street Monitor: Weekly Market Digest	Market analysis
Taxes	
CCH State Tax Review	Commerce Clearing House, Inc.
CCH Tax Day: Digest of Federal Taxes	Commerce Clearing House, Inc.
Charitable Giving	Tax angles
Corporate Acquisitons & Dispositions	Mark A. Stephens, Ltd.
Employee Retirement Plans	Mark A. Stephens, Ltd.
IRS Practices & Procedures	Mark A. Stephens, Ltd.
Tax Notes Today	Tax Analysts
Tax Notes Bulletin Service	Tax Analysts

million publications—virtually 90% of the world's published scientific and technical literature—from research journal articles to patents. They are now adding directory, numeric and full-text databases as well.

The major services also offer smaller, easier to use subsets of their services for personal computer users; these cover the major business databases. The primary commercial library services—Dialog, BRS and SDC Orbit—and their personal computer utility offshoots are described below.

DIALOG INFORMATION SERVICES

Dialog Information Services, Inc. is the world's largest bibliographic database vendor in terms of the number of databases offered, total information content and the number of customers—over 60,000 in 1984. Dialog contains roughly 100 million records, each identifying a publication or other document, such as a magazine, newspaper or journal article, a patent, a technical report, a book, a thesis, a dissertation, etc. Dialog began commercial service in 1972 as a division of Lockheed Missiles & Space Company, Inc. and now, as Dialog Information Services, Inc., is a subsidiary of Lockheed.

Dialog is designed for librarians and information managers whose job it is to retrieve information. It is neither obvious nor easy to use unless you have had prior experience or training, or are willing to sit down with a user manual and teach yourself. The search protocol is command-driven and requires construction of keyword phrases using logical operators to indicate word relationships. The system's prompts and error messages are incomprehensible to the uninitiated. There are no menus, and the prompt from Dialog for your entry is simply a question mark ("?"). (See Figure 1.4 in Chapter 1.) The Dialog sign-on message, with news bulletins, and a list of some available databases are shown in Figure 4.12.

Because of both the value and the amount of information in the Dialog system, much of which may be helpful to business and professional end users, Dialog has created Knowledge Index, a somewhat simpler version, available after business hours (see below). In addition, other companies have developed menu-driven microcomputer software to take the mystery out of Dialog (see Chapter 10). Dialog has announced that it is working on the next generation of its search system, which will be much more appealing to the more casual user.

Dialog is well known among professional librarians in corporations,

Figure 4.12: Dialog Sign-on Message, News Bulletins and Partial List of Databases

```
XXXXXXXX LOGON File1 Tue 10jul84 17:42:07 Port098

DIALOG News (Enter ?NEWS for details):
  Available July 1:
    MOODY'S CORPORATE PROFILES (File
      555)
    STANDARD & POOR'S CORPORATE
      DESCRIPTIONS (File 133)
  Free time in July:
    FOOD SCIENCE AND TECHNOLOGY
      ABSTRACTS (File 51)--$37.50
      combined connect time and
      TYPEs/DISPLAYs.
  Announcements:
    Price change on TRIS (File 63) now
    in effect.
    Price change on METADEX (File 32)
    now in effect.
? explain filesd

D&B DUN'S MARKET IDEN 10+            516
D&B MILLION DOLLAR DIRECTORY         517
D&B PRINCIPAL INT'L BUSINESSES       518
Dairy Science Abstracts               50
DIALINDEX                            411
DIALINDEX (ONTAPS)                   290
DIALOG PUBLICATIONS                  200
DIF                                  229
Directory Industry Data Sources      189
DISCLOSURE II                        100
DISCLOSURE SPECTRUM/OWNERSHIP         540
DISSERTATION ABSTRACTS ONLINE         35
DM2 (Defense Mkt Meas Sys)            59
DOE ENERGY                           103
DRUG INFORMATION FULLTEXT            229
Drug Literature Index         72,73,172
Drug Research Reports                 42
DRUGDOC                       72,73,172
Dun's Market Identifiers 10+         516
?
```

government agencies and academic institutions. If you work for a large organization, Dialog is probably available in your library or information center. Some business people are beginning to use Dialog themselves—the more basic search techniques are not too difficult to learn. You can also always go to a library or an information broker for Dialog service. Dialog is available on the Telenet, Tymnet and Uninet networks.

Business Information Available

There are about 40 databases on Dialog that are of immediate interest to business users. They can be grouped into five categories:

- business periodical indexes and abstracts

- business news

- business and economic statistics

- business companies (directories and encyclopedias)

- patents and trademarks

Many of the Dialog databases in these categories are summarized in Table 4.7 and are discussed in greater detail in Chapters 5-8. Most of those marked as available on Knowledge Index are described briefly below.

You may order printouts to be mailed to you of any search results, and photocopies of most documents identified can be obtained from suppliers participating in the Dialorder document delivery service. Current awareness profiles may be established on many of the databases.

Subscription and Cost

There is no sign-up fee or required monthly minimum for a basic open access Dialog account. Database hourly access rates vary from $15 per hour for special practice databases to $165 per hour (one patents database is $300); the average price is about $70 to $75 per hour. Special volume discount, guaranteed monthly minimum and pre-paid annual subscription accounts are available. Contact Dialog Information Services (see Appendix C) for details.

Table 4.7: Selected Business, Financial and Economic Databases on Dialog

Database Title	Subject/Content	Also on Knowledge Index
Business Periodical Indexes and Abstracts		
ABI/Inform	Business management	X
Adtrack	Magazine ad index	
Arthur D. Little Online	Index to reports	
Economic Literature Index	International economics	
Harvard Business Review Online	Full-text articles	
Industry Data Sources	Industry analysis	
Insurance Abstracts	Insurance literature	
Management Contents	Business management	X
Predicasts F&S Indexes	Industry literature	
Predicasts PROMT	Technology markets	
Business News		
Magazine ASAP	Full-text magazines	
Magazine Index	Popular magazines	X
National Newspaper Index	*New York Times, Washington Post*	X
Newsearch	Daily magazine/newspaper	X
Standard & Poor's News	Corporate news	X
Trade & Industry ASAP	Full-text trade journals	
Trade & Industry Index	200 trade journals	X
UPI News	U.S., international news	
Washington Post	Index to articles	
Business and Economic Statistics		
BI/Data Forecasts	Macroeconomics, 35 countries	
BI/Data	Time series, 135 countries	
BLS Consumer Price Index	Bureau of Labor Statistics data	
BLS Labor Force Statistics	Bureau of Labor Statistics data	
BLS Producer Price Index	Bureau of Labor Statistcs data	
Predicasts Economic Forecasts	U.S. and international	
Predicasts Annual Time Series	U.S. and international	
Business Companies		
Commerce Business Daily	Federal contract awards	
D&B - Dun's Market Identifiers 10+	Companies with 10 or more employees	
D&B - Million Dollar Directory	Companies with sales of $500,000 or more	
D&B - Principal International Businesses	Non-U.S. companies	
Disclosure II	9500 public companies	
EIS Industrial Plants	Manufacturing company directory	

(continued on next page)

Table 4.7: Selected Business, Financial and Economic Databases on Dialog (cont.)

Database Title	Subject/Content	Also on Knowledge Index
EIS Nonmanufacturing Establishments	Service company directory	
Electronic Yellow Pages	U.S. business directory	
EnergyNet	Energy company directory	
Predicasts PTS Annual Report Abstracts	Public companies	
Patents and Trademarks		
Claims	U.S. patents	
PatLaw	U.S. patent law	
TradeMarkScan	Registered and pending trademarks	

KNOWLEDGE INDEX

In 1983, Dialog introduced Knowledge Index, a simplified, compact version of its bibliographic information service. This new service, aimed at the user of personal computers, offers more than 40 of the major Dialog databases. Knowledge Index is available only in the evenings and on weekends—times when use of the regular Dialog service is very low.

Knowledge Index uses the same basic format as the large library service with many of its cryptic prompts and messages, but the command language is simplified. In addition, there are self-help tutorials available online for the inexperienced user, and Dialog provides new subscribers with a user manual for Knowledge Index.

Business Information Available

Knowledge Index databases are grouped into 12 broad categories. The welcome message and the first five of these database groups are shown as they appear online, in Figure 4.13. Some of those of business interest are described very briefly below.

The business category includes ABI/Inform, which contains citations and abstracts from more than 600 periodicals since 1971, and The Trade and Industry Index, which offers abstracts and citations from more than 3000

Figure 4.13: Knowledge Index Welcome Message and Partial List of Database Categories

```
LOGON AT 19:38:29 EST TUESDAY 11/01/83
WELCOME TO KNOWLEDGE INDEX

For instructions on how to use
Knowledge Index, enter HELP KI or ?
Otherwise enter your commands.
September billing info now available.
**Type BULLETIN for KI news.

?help sections
HELP SECTIONS.  There are 12 different
sections available in KNOWLEDGE INDEX.
Each section contains one or more data-
bases.  For an explanation of the data-
base(s) in each section, enter HELP fol-
lowed by the first four letters in the
section name.  The database name is the
same as the section name but followed by
a number.  At this time all of the sec-
tions except five have only one data-
base.
                          -
Section name          Database name
AGRI - AGRIculture
   Database:  AGRICOLA       (AGRI1)


BOOK - BOOKs
   Database:  BOOKS IN PRINT      (BOOK1)
   (Copyright by R.R. Bowker Co.)
BUSI - BUSIness
   Database:  ABI/INFORM        (BUSI1)
   (Copyright by Data Courier, Inc.)
   Database:  TRADE AND INDUSTRY
        INDEX                    (BUSI2)
   (Copyright by Information Access
   Corp.)
COMP - COMPuters and Electronics
   Database:  INSPEC            (COMP1)
   (Copyright by Institution of
   Electrical Engineers)
   Database:  INTERNATIONAL
        SOFTWARE DATABASE        (COMP2)
   (Copyright by Imprint Software)
   Database:  MICROCOMPUTER INDEX (COMP3)
   (Copyright by Microcomputer
   Information Services)
CORP - CORPorate News
   Database:  STANDARD & POOR'S
        NEWS                     (CORP1)
   (Copyright by Standard & Poor's)
```

business and trade journals and more than 1200 additional selected publications, dating from 1981. The corporate news section includes Standard & Poor's News, a database of full-text financial stories on over 10,000 corporations from June 1979 to date. The magazines and newspapers sections cover three related databases—Magazine Index, National Newspaper Index and Newsearch, which covers updates to the previous two. More on these databases can be found in Chapter 5. (See Chapter 8 for a discussion of ABI/Inform.) The medicine section abstracts the major literature of the legal and medical professions.

Subscription and Cost

Database access costs on Knowledge Index are much lower than on the parent Dialog service. The sign-up fee is $35 and includes two hours of connect time and an instruction manual. The hourly connect fee is $24. Additional information and subscriptions are available from Dialog Information Service. All charges and fees are billed to a credit card.

BIBLIOGRAPHIC RETRIEVAL SERVICES

Bibliographic Retrieval Services (BRS) is a library research service with about 80 databases covering all subject disciplines. The main emphasis of BRS is on medical and educational databases, serving academic and government institutions, but an increasing number of business and economic databases is being offered. To reach new and expanding end-user markets, BRS is creating new online services and products, such as BRS/After Dark (see below).

The BRS search interface is somewhat cryptic to the new user—it is a command-driven system designed for the use of information professionals. BRS offers training courses and user manuals, and these are recommended if you want to use the system efficiently. You can learn the basics in a one day training program for beginners. Figure 4.14 shows the BRS sign-on message, a bulletin and other information. The BRS service is available via the Telenet, Tymnet and Uninet networks.

Business Information Available

There are several databases on BRS of interest to business people. These are listed in Table 4.8. If you are a medical professional, BRS has a significant number of databases and a new service, BRS/Medical Colleague, that offers the full text of medical journals and texts (see Chapter 9). You can order printouts of search results for next-day mailing, and current awareness profiles can be established for mailing of any new records retrieved from future updates.

Subscription and Cost

Several BRS subscription plans are available. Hourly database access fees vary from about $20 to $120 per hour, depending on the database and subscription plan. The open access account requires a $50 annual subscription fee, and the average hourly database access charge is $65 to $70. Prepaid group subscription plans provide discounts based on the amount of prepayment or the amount of guaranteed monthly use. Contact BRS customer service (see Appendix C) for more information.

BRS/AFTER DARK

Designed for personal computer users, BRS/After Dark is a much simplified, easier-to-use version of the regular BRS service. It is available on evenings and weekends. Offering a subset of the major BRS databases (as

Figure 4.14: Sign-on Message, News Bulletin System Menu and Partial List of Databases on BRS

```
BROADCAST MESSAGE CHANGED 07/06/84 AT 13:18:49.
ENTER 'Y' OR 'N' FOR BROADCAST MESSAGE._:    y


UPDATE TRAINING SESSIONS ARE SCHEDULED FOR INDIANAPOLIS, BOISE,
  PORTLAND AND SEATTLE. SEE NEWS DOC #8  OR CALL OUR TRAINING OFFICE
  (800) 441-9996 FOR DETAILS. IN PA CALL COLLECT 215-527-4116.
  THE BRS USERS' MEETING WILL BE AT THE MCCORMACK INN IN CHICAGO ON
  SEPT 24-25TH.  DETAILS HAVE BEEN MAILED TO YOU IN THE JUNE BULLETIN.


ENTER DATA BASE NAME_:     news


  *SIGN-ON    02.45.41                    07/08/84:

#######################################
SYSTEM NEWS                       2          3-31-83
DATABASES ONLINE                  3          WEEKLY
DATABASES OFFLINE                 4          3-25-83
X FILES                           5          WEEKLY
DATABASE CHARGES                  6          6-12-84
UPCOMING PRICE CHANGES            7          6-5-84
     .
     .
     .
PLEASE ENTER THE DOCUMENT NUMBER.  DO NOT ENTER DOC=N

ENTER DOCUMENT NUMBER RANGE
_:    9


THE FOLLOWING IS A LIST OF THE DATABASE NAMES AND THEIR
SEARCH LABELS FOR ALL PUBLICLY-AVAILABLE BRS DATABASES:
DATABASE NAME                     SEARCH LABEL
#
ABI INFORM                               INFO
ABLEDATA                                 ABLE
ABSTRAX 400                              A400
ACADEMIC AMERICAN ENCYCLOPEDIA DATABASE  AAED
     .
     .
     .
```

Table 4.8: Selected Business and Financial Databases on BRS

Database Title	Subject/Content	Also on BRS/After Dark
Business and Financial		
ABI/Inform	Business management	x
Fintel	Financial Times London	
Harvard Business Review Online	Full-text articles	x
Index to Frost & Sullivan Reports	Market research	
Industry Data Sources	Industry information	
Management Contents	Business management	x
Predicasts Annual Reports Abstracts	Public companies	
Predicasts F&S Indexes	Industry articles	
Predicasts Economic Forecasts	U.S. and international	
Predicasts Annual Time Series	U.S. and international	
Predicasts PROMT	Technology markets	
Patents, Specifications and Standards		
Industry & International Standards	Index to standards	
Military & Federal Specifications	Index to specs	
PatData	U.S. patents	x
Voluntary Standards Information Network	Standards cooperation	

indicated in Table 4.8), After Dark is evolving into a popular information utility like CompuServe or The Source. Among the available services are the database search service, an online newsletter and MCI electronic mail. Figure 4.15 shows the welcome message, main menu and a partial list of databases.

Business Information Available

Among the five categories of databases on After Dark, as shown in Figure 4.15, is "business and financial." This category includes: ABI/Inform; Harvard Business Review Online (abstracts of all articles since 1971 and full text of all articles since 1976); Management Contents (indexes and abstracts from over 560 international business and management publications); and PatData (abstracts all of more than 500,000 patents issued by the U.S. Patent Office since 1975). As with the regular BRS service, you may order offline printouts of records from any of these databases to be mailed to you.

Subscription and Cost

BRS/After Dark is considerably less expensive than its parent library

Figure 4.15: BRS/After Dark Welcome Message, Main Menu, Database Category Menu and Partial List of Databases

```
WELCOME TO BRS AFTER DARK

PLEASE TYPE IN SCREEN LINE LENGTH (20, 40 OR 80)
PLEASE TYPE IN THE NUMBER OF LINES ON YOUR SCREEN (20,21,22,ETC.)
      PLEASE SEE IMPORTANT INFORMATION IN MENU ITEM 6.
      MANY NEW ENHANCEMENTS HAVE BEEN ADDED TO THE SEARCH
      SERVICE!  ALSO, NEWSLETTER, MENU ITEM 2, NOW
      OPERATIONAL!

TONIGHT'S MENU IS:

NUMBER          ITEM
   1            LOOKING FOR INFORMATION?...SEARCH SERVICE
   2            WANT TO HEAR THE LATEST?...NEWSLETTER SERVICE
   3            NEED A PROGRAM?...SOFTWARE SERVICE
   4            KEEP IN TOUCH!...ELECTRONIC MAIL SERVICE
   5            LET'S MAKE A DEAL!...SWAP SHOP
   6            WHAT'S NEW?...NEW SYSTEM FEATURES
   7            WANT TO CHANGE YOUR SECURITY PASSWORD?...
                  SECURITY

TYPE IN MENU ITEM NUMBER AND HIT ENTER KEY FOR DESIRED SELECTION
        1

YOU ARE NOW CONNECTED TO THE BRS AFTER DARK SEARCH SERVICE.
THE FOLLOWING CATEGORIES OF DATABASES ARE AVAILABLE FOR
SEARCHING.
CATEGORY     DESCRIPTION

    1         SCIENCE AND MEDICINE DATABASES
    2         BUSINESS AND FINANCIAL DATABASES
    3         REFERENCE DATABASES
    4         EDUCATION DATABASES
    5         SOCIAL SCIENCES AND HUMANITIES DATABASES

TYPE IN CATEGORY NUMBER THEN HIT ENTER KEY FOR
CATEGORY OF DATABASES DESIRED.    2

BUSINESS AND FINANCIAL DATABASES
********************************
DATABASE NAME                         LABEL

ABI/INFORM                            INFO
HARVARD BUSINESS REVIEW               HBRO
MANAGEMENT CONTENTS                   MGMT
PATDATA                               PATS
```

research service. There is a one time sign-up fee of $50. Hourly database connect charges range from $6 to about $30, depending on database royalties. Usage fees are charged automatically to your credit card on a monthly basis. Contact BRS for more information.

Wiley Executive Information Service

In conjunction with BRS, the publisher John Wiley & Sons, Inc. offers an Executive Information Service, using the BRS/After Dark system and four BRS databases: ABI/Inform, Harvard Business Review Online, Management Contents and the Academic American Encyclopedia. There is a $100 per month fee which allows unlimited access to these four files.

SDC ORBIT SEARCH SERVICE

A major vendor of patent abstracts databases, SDC Orbit Search Service is a commercial service of System Development Corp. (SDC), Santa Monica, CA, a Burroughs Corp. company. Orbit is a library research service that specializes in petrochemical, pharmaceutical and patent research and development. Its primary customers are R&D departments of major corporations in the petroleum, chemical and pharmaceutical industries. SDC developed the prototype Orbit system under contract to the National Library of Medicine in 1968 and began commercial operation in 1973.

Orbit is an extremely sophisticated search system which is a little easier for the uninitiated to use than is Dialog. There are two levels of system prompts and messages—short and long—for experienced and beginning users, respectively. Figure 4.16 shows the Orbit welcome message and a list of available databases. The prompt messages in the figure are in the long format. A new-user training session and user manuals are recommended for anyone who wants to use this service. SDC has announced SearchMaster, a microcomputer software interface to simplify using Orbit and developing technical search strategies.

Business Information Available

The business-related databases available on the Orbit system are summarized in Table 4.9. Accountants Index from the American Institute of Certified Public Accountants (AICPA) provides citations to the journal literature on accounting and related fields. ABI/Inform is also available. Both are discussed in Chapter 8. Banker indexes *The American Banker*. Orbit offers access to a huge collection of patent abstracts in the World Patent Index

Figure 4.16: SDC Orbit Welcome Message, System Bulletins and Databases

```
HELLO FROM SDC/ORBIT IV.   (07/08/84   11:42 P.M.   PACIFIC TIME)
ENTER SECURITY CODE:
XXXXXXXXXX

PROG:
****
ELECTRONIC MAIL SERVICE NOW AVAILABLE!   ENTER EX MAIL FOR DETAILS!
****
INSPEC IS NOW PROXIMITY SEARCHABLE!   SEE EXPLAIN INSPEC FOR DETAILS.
****
NEW TRAINING SCHEDULES!   ENTER EX TRAINING AUSTRALIA, EX TRAINING CANADA,
EX TRAINING EUROPE OR EX TRAINING U.S.
****
YOU ARE NOW CONNECTED TO THE ORBIT DATABASE.
FOR A TUTORIAL, ENTER A QUESTION MARK.   OTHERWISE, ENTER A COMMAND.

USER:
files

PROG:
YOU ARE NOW CONNECTED TO THE ORBIT DATABASE.
THE FOLLOWING DATABASES ARE AVAILABLE TO YOU:
ACCOUNTANTS    ASI           BANKER         CAS-ED
CASSI          CAS6771       CAS7276        CAS77
CA82           CDEX-ED       CHEMDEX        CHEMDEX2
CHEMDEX3       CIN           CIS            COLD
COMPENDEX      CRECORD       DBI            EBIB
EIMET          ENERGYLINE    ENVIROLINE     EPIA
ERIC           FEDREG        FOREST         FSTA
GEOREF         GRANTS        INFORM         INSPEC
LABORDOC       LC/LINE       LISA           MANAGEMENT
MDF/I          METADEX       MONITOR        NDEX
NTIS           NUC/CODES     ORBCHEM        ORBIT
ORBPAT         P/E NEWS      PAPER          PAPERCHEM
PIE            POWER         PSYCHINFO      RINGDOC UDB
SAE            SDF           SPORT          TROPAG
TSCA PLUS      TULSA         USCLASS        USGCA
USPA           USP70         USP77          VETDOC UDB
WATERLIT       WPI-ED

SS 1 /C?---SEARCH STATEMENT 1 OR COMMAND?
USER:
```

Table 4.9: Selected Business and Technical Databases on SDC Orbit

Database Title	Subject/Content
Business and Management	
ABI/Inform	Business management
Accountants Index (AICPA)	Accounting literature
Banker	*The American Banker*
The Christian Science Monitor	Index to contents
Management Contents	Business management
Newspaper Index	Index to 9 dailies
Petrochemical Technology and Patents	
Apilit	American Petroleum Institute literature
Apipat	American Petroleum Institute patents
CA Search	Chemical literature
Chemical Economics Handbook	SRI International
PE/News (Petroleum & Energy News)	Platt's Oilgram
Tulsa (Petroleum Abstracts)	Petroleum production
US Patent Classification	Patent Office classes
US Patents Database	U.S. patents
World Patent Index	Patents of 14 countries

database, covering patents from 14 major industrialized countries from 1964 to date, and the U.S. Patents database containing abstracts and full text of front page information of U.S. patents issued since 1970. Several other petroleum, chemical and pharmaceutical databases make Orbit worthwhile if you are in a petrochemical business that does extensive research and development. See Chapter 8 for more details on the patent databases, Apilit, Apipat and CA Search.

Subscription and Cost

Orbit is available through several subscription plans and costs a minimum of $100 per month. Database access costs vary from $35 to $165 per hour, depending on the database and the subscription plan chosen; the average hourly rate is $80 to $85. Contact SDC Information Services (see Appendix C) for more details.

NUMERIC DATA SERVICES

Numeric data services have traditionally been the domain of data-processing professionals, financial analysts and statisticians. Typically offered by computer timesharing companies, numeric databases consist of economic time series and forecasts, financial balance sheets, stock performance ratios or other number series, presented in tabular format. Data can be manipulated using various statistical and financial analysis programs.

These services are products of the era before personal computers appeared on the scene. Like the library research database vendors, numeric data services are command-driven and are not easy to use without manuals and training. However, also like the library services, these companies are designing interfaces that will enable them to market their services to personal computer users in business and the professions.

Described below are two numeric database vendors: ADP Network Services and I.P. Sharp Associates, which offers two retrieval services.

ADP NETWORK SERVICES

ADP Network Services is a division of Automatic Data Processing, Inc., founded in 1949 as a computer timesharing services company. The company has four main divisions: Commercial Services, Financial Services, Special Services and Network Services. ADP Network Services operates the Autonet packet-switching data communications network described in Chapter 3.

ADP offers online services with more than 30 numeric databases of financial, investment and economic data. Other ADP services can help businesses with strategic planning, project management, economic forecasting and computer applications development. The ADP databases are available over the Autonet, Telenet and Tymnet data networks.

Business Information Available

The numeric databases available from ADP are grouped into six categories:

- U.S. economic data

- international economic data

- corporate financial data

- banking data

- investment data

- miscellaneous

The databases are summarized in Table 4.10 and described briefly below.

U.S. Economic Data

U.S. economic databases include economic time series, indicators and forecasts, such as the Conference Board, Consumer Price Indexes, Producer Price Indexes, Long Term Projections, Short Term Projections, Flow of Funds from the Federal Reserve Board and the U.S. Economic Data Bank.

International Economic Data

International economic time series of indicators and projections are also available: European Economic Indicators, Main Economic Indicators (25 Organization for Economic Cooperation and Development—OECD—countries), International Financial Statistics (more than 160 world economies) and Quarterly National Accounts (indicators for 25 OECD nations from 1960 to date).

Corporate Financial Data

The primary corporate financial databases are Standard & Poor's Compustat II (summary financial data for more than 6000 public industrial, telecommunications and utility corporations), Value Line Data Base II (essential market and financial and 11 years of historical data for 1600 major industrial, utility, transportation, finance and retail companies), and Exstat (covering 2500 British, European and Japanese companies). More about Compustat II and Value Line Data Base II is presented in Chapter 7.

Banking Data

The four banking databases are BANCALL (Federal Reserve Board Call Reports on over 14,000 FDIC commercial banks since 1978), Bancompare (10 years of annual reports, 10-K and 10-Q, and call report data on 280 major banks and holding companies), Compustat Banking (annual data since 1961 of the largest U.S. bank holding companies) and Savings and Loan (data on 4000 FSLIC companies from 1974 to date).

Investment Data

ADP offers two databases of investment data: Fastock from Muller Data Corp. (12 years of daily price, dividend and trading volume history for stocks, bonds and mutual funds) and Foreign Exchange (Bache Halsey commentary and daily exchange rates for up to six years).

Table 4.10: Selected Economic and Financial Databases on ADP

Database Title	Subject/Content
U.S. Economic Data	
Business Conditions Digest	500+ monthly indicators 1947+
Conference Board	1000+ business time series 1951+
Consumer Price Indexes	Cost of living, consumption
Long-Term Projections	10 year macroeconomic forecasts
Producer Price Indexes	Cost of goods and services
SCAN200	200 popular indicators 1947+
Short-Term Projections	2-year macroeconomic forecasts
Flow of Funds	Sources, uses of funds 1952+
U.S. Economic Database	Major economic sectors 1947+
International Economic Data	
European Economic Indicators	Major country indicators
Main Economic Indicators	25 OECD countries 1960+
International Financial Statistics	160 world economies
Quarterly National Accounts	25 OECD countries 1960+
Corporate Financial Data	
Compustat II Geographic	3000 corporations by region
Compustat II Industrial	Industries traded in U.S.
Compustat II Line of Business	6000 companies by business
Compustat II Telecommunications	U.S. telecommunications firms and subsidiaries
Compustat II Utility	250+ class A utilities
Disclosure II	9500 public company SEC filings
Exstat	2500 U.K., European, Japanese firms
Mergers & Acquisitions Database	Tenders, mergers, buyouts 1979+
Value Line Data Base II	Analyses of 1700 companies
Banking Data	
BANCALL	Financials for 14,000 FDIC banks
Bancompare	280 major banks 10-Ks, 10-Qs
Compustat II Banking	Bank holding companies 1970+
Savings and Loan	400 FSLIC S&L firms, 1974+
Investment Data	
Fastock	Price, volume, dividend histories
Foreign Exchange	6 years daily exchange rates
Miscellaneous Data	
Bank of England	400 financial variables
Bridge Data	Real-time stocks, options
Central Statistical Office	200 economic variables from Bank of England
Prognos	Forecasts of developing and developed countries

Miscellaneous Data

There are four miscellaneous databases: Bank of England (over 400 financial variables, updated quarterly), Bridge Data (real-time U.S. stock and options prices), Central Statistical Office (2000 U.K. economic variables) and Prognos (5- and 10-year forecasts of key economic indicators for developed and developing countries).

Subscription and Costs

The ADP database service annual subscription fee is is $1000. Contact ADP directly, at its headquarters (see Appendix C) or in several major cities—check your phone directory.

I.P. SHARP ASSOCIATES

I.P. Sharp Associates, Ltd. is a privately held Canadian computer timesharing and online database services company. It has major offices in the United States as well as 19 other countries. Founded in 1964 as a software development firm, I.P. Sharp is today the world's largest online vendor of numeric database services. The company's services fall into four main groups: timesharing, proprietary software development, special systems and public databases. I.P. Sharp services are available over the Telenet and Tymnet networks, as well as Sharp's own network and the DataPac networks in Canada.

Business Information Available

I.P. Sharp offers access to more than 95 databases containing more than 40 million economic and financial time series. The databases are grouped into the following categories:

- aviation

- economics

- energy

- finance

- actuarial and miscellaneous

Table 4.11 presents a selected list of the available databases; some of these are highlighted below.

Table 4.11: Selected Economic and Financial Numeric Databases on I.P. Sharp

Database Title	Subject/Content	Also on Infomagic
Aviation		
Aircraft Accidents	Accident data on plans, 20,000 lbs.+	
Commuter Online Origin-Destination	Point-to-point commercial traffic	
International Air Travel Statistics	Passengers U.S.-foreign ports	
Official Airline Guide	Flight schedules	x
Economics		
BI/Data Forecasts	Macroeconomics 35 countries	x
BI/Data	Time series 135 countries	x
Citibase	U.S. economic indicators	x
Citiforecast	250 macroeconomic time series	
International Financial Statistics	Economies of 200+ countries	
Organization for Economic Cooperation & Development	OECD countries economic data	
U.S. Consumer Price Index	Consumer goods and spending	
U.S. Producer Price Index	Goods and services statistics	
U.S. Flow of Funds Quarterly	Sources and uses of funds	
Energy		
DeWitt Petrochemical Newsletters	Analysis and price forecasts	
Energy Futures Group	Energy forecasts	x
Lundberg Survey	U.S. petroleum production	x
Petroleum Argus Market & Prices	Daily price reports	
Petroleum Intelligence Weekly	Production and prices news	
U.S. Petroleum Imports	Statistics on shipments U.S.	
Finance		
Agdata Agricultural Commodities	Daily market and exchange rates	
Commodities	Volume and price for U.K. and North America	
Currency Exchange Rates	World currencies 10 markets	
Disclosure II	SEC filings 9400 public companies	x
Federal Reserve Board Weekly	Weekly banking and monetary statistics	
Money Market Rates	Interest and currency rates	
Nastock	North American stock markets	x
Toronto Stock Exchange 300 Index	Top 300 Canadian stocks	x
U.S. Banks	Balance, income 15,000+ banks	
U.S. Stock Options	Daily put and call options	

Aviation Databases

Some of the I.P. Sharp aviation databases are Aircraft Accidents (data on all accidents of jet and turboliner aircraft of 20,000 pounds or over), International Air Travel Statistics (between U.S. and foreign ports, excluding Canada) and Origin-Destination (results of a continuous survey of domestic itineraries of 10% of passengers on U.S. carriers).

Economics Databases

Selected economics databases include Business International Corp.'s BI/Data Forecasts (textual and numeric forecasts of 35 major countries) and BI/Data (over 20,000 economic and demographic time series for 135 countries), Citibase (U.S. economic statistics), Citibank Economic Forecast (250 quarterly macroeconomic time series), International Financial Statistics (over 200 countries), OECD (economic data on OECD countries), U.S. Consumer and Producer Price Indexes, and U.S. Flow of Funds Quarterly (for 50 major sectors). More details about the Business International Corp. databases and Citibase are given in Chapter 7.

Energy Databases

Among the databases in the energy category are the Petroleum Argus Daily Market Report and Petroleum Prices (Europe), DeWitt Petrochemical Newsletter and Price Forecasts (weekly analytical reports), U.S. Petroleum Imports (all shipments into the U.S. of foreign oil and oil products), Lundberg Survey files (Dealer Buying Price, Survey Share of Market and Survey Wholesale Prices—all are U.S.) and the Petroleum Intelligence Weekly (production statistics, crude and spot prices).

Financial Databases

A few of the databases of U.S. financial data are Agdata Agricultural Commodities (price and volume data), Commodities (volume and price data for all major commodities on the London and North American markets), Currency Exchange Rates (major currencies on 10 world markets), Disclosure II, Federal Reserve Board Weekly, Money Market Rates, U.S. Banks and U.S. Stock Options.

Subscription and Cost

Subscriptions are available directly from I.P. Sharp Associates, and costs average between $70 and $100 per hour. Open access accounts without annual or monthly subscription fees are available. Detailed service and cost information may be obtained from I.P. Sharp in Toronto (see Appendix C) and in major U.S. cities.

INFOMAGIC

I.P. Sharp Associates has repackaged some of its numeric databases in a menu-driven, easy-to-use retrieval program for personal computer users, known as Infomagic.

Business Information Available

Infomagic provides access to more than 15 of the larger and more popular databases from the collection on the primary I.P. Sharp service. Some are indicated in Table 4.11. Figure 4.17 illustrates the welcome message and introductory user information, including commands. Figure 4.17 also shows that databases are available in the same four main categories as on the I.P. Sharp primary database service: finance, economics, aviation and energy.

Figure 4:17: Infomagic Welcome Message, System Commands and Database Category List

```
WELCOME TO INFOMAGIC.  ENTER  DESCRIBE  FOR DOCUMENTATION.

TERMINAL OPTIONS SET FROM PREVIOUS INFOMAGIC SESSION.
ENTER  TERM  TO RESET OPTIONS.

ENTER DATABASE:

                        INFOMAGIC

      INFOMAGIC IS A SYSTEM WHICH ALLOWS USERS TO RETRIEVE DATA
INTERACTIVERLY FROM I.P. SHARP'S PUBLIC DATABASES.  SHOULD YOU REQUIRE
FURTHER INFORMATION AT ANY PROMPT, TYPE: HELP.

AS WELL, THE FOLLOWING COMMANDS ARE AVAILABLE AT ANY PROMPT:

'EXIT', 'QUIT', 'OFF', '>OFF' - CAUSES USER TO LEAVE INFOMAGIC SYSTEM

'STOP', 'BACK' - RETURN TO PREVIOUS PROMPT (SAME AS EXIT AT 1ST PROMPT)

'TOP'  - RETURN TO THE FIRST PROMPT

'TERM'  - SET TERMINAL OPTIONS SUCH AS PAGE WIDTH AND PAGE DEPTH

'DESCRIBE' - PRINTS THIS MESSAGE AT THE FIRST PROMPT OR A
             DESCRIPTION OF A DATABASE ONCE IT HAS BEEN CHOSEN.

ENTER DATABASE: help

ENTER DATABASE CODE OR  HELP  FOR A LIST OF DATABASE CATEGORIES
ENTER DATABASE: help

THE FOLLOWING DATABASE CATEGORIES ARE AVAILABLE

1. FINANCE
2. ECONOMICS
3. AVIATION
4. ENERGY

ENTER A NUMBER CORRESPONDING TO THE CATEGORY DESIRED: 1
```

Subscription and Cost

Infomagic has a flat hourly connect rate of $60 for 300 baud transmission and $120 for 1200 baud transmission. There is no sign-up fee.

WHICH SERVICES TO USE

With all of these services available, which do you need? It depends on your business, your job and your personal situation. No one will need all of these services and databases. Even if you did, they all have such different command languages and search protocols that you would have difficulty learning to use all of them effectively. In the following chapters, we will take a closer look at the types of services and information available in order to help you decide which online services will best meet your specific information needs.

5

General Business and Industry News

Today there are more online services and databases oriented toward business information than any other single category. Yet this is a fairly recent occurrence; throughout the 1970s, the dominant type of online information was scientific and technical. The business information now available is of four primary types:

- full-text news stories and articles

- indexes to and abstracts of business and technical research

- directory information about companies

- financial data, including stock quotes, balance sheets and forecasts

In this chapter we'll concentrate on the full-text business and industry news services and some of the index and abstract services. Specific company, financial and economic information will be covered in Chapters 6 and 7.

USES OF BUSINESS NEWS SERVICES

The business and industry online services are an excellent and convenient way to track what is happening in any industry, trade or group of companies you regularly follow for business or personal investing purposes. You can maintain up-to-the-minute knowledge of stock prices, corporate earnings and economic indicators. You can keep abreast of the latest news about companies, products, acquisition opportunities, industry trends and governmental activities. You can gain access to valuable analyses, forecasts, summaries and reviews of developments in various industries and the economy as a whole.

BUSINESS NEWS SERVICES

The following online information services offering electronic news will be discussed in this chapter:

- Dow Jones News/Retrieval Service

- CompuServe Information Service

- The Source

- Dialog Information Services

- NewsNet

- Nexis

The first four services provide access to both full-text and bibliographic abstracts of major news sources as part of their overall service. NewsNet and Nexis are devoted entirely to full-text news information.

You can connect with all of these services through any common micro-computer, modem and communications software, with the exception of Nexis. Until recently, Nexis, a service of Mead Data Central, required a special dedicated terminal and Mead's own data communication lines, leased as part of a subscription to the service. Nexis is now also available to users of several brands of microcomputers, including IBMs and Apples, but the user must still buy special software from Mead as a part of the subscription package.

DOW JONES NEWS/RETRIEVAL SERVICE

As we mentioned in Chapter 4, Dow Jones News/Retrieval Service (DJNRS) is the most popular and widely used of any of the major news online services. DJNRS had more than 140,000 individual subscribers by mid-1984 and is growing at the rate of about 5000 new users each month. Most of the news on DJNRS comes from Dow Jones' *The Wall Street Journal* and *Barron's* weekly. The Dow Jones News Service (The Broadtape) constitutes most of the remainder. Each of these sources contributes to one or more business and economic databases on DJNRS:

- Dow Jones News (DJNEWS)

- Weekly Economic Update (UPDATE)

- Wall Street Journal Highlights Online (WSJ)

- Text-Search Services (TSS)

- Japan Economic Daily (KYODO)

Each database serves different purposes, as explained in the following descriptions. All are full text, except Wall Street Journal Highlights Online, which provides summaries. In addition to these business and economic news databases, DJNRS offers three general news databases: News/Retrieval World Report (NEWS), News/Retrieval Sports Report (SPORTS) and News/Retrieval Weather Report (WTHR). The DJNRS news databases are summarized in Table 5.1.

Many users of DJNRS search the business and economic news databases along with the Dow Jones stock quotes databases, which will be discussed in Chapter 7. You can also purchase special microcomputer software from Dow Jones that enables you to establish current awareness, or interest profiles. This software automatically searches and retrieves information on specific companies of interest to you each time you sign on, eliminating the need to type in various symbols. Special Dow Jones software will be covered in more detail in Chapter 10.

Dow Jones News

The Dow Jones News (DJNEWS) database includes selected stories from *The Wall Street Journal, Barron's* and the Dow Jones News Service (The

Table 5.1: Selected News Databases on Dow Jones News/Retrieval Service

Database Title	Frequency of Updating	Period Covered
Business and Economic News Services		
Dow Jones News (DJNEWS)	Continuous, with 90-second delay	Latest 3 months
Weekly Economic Update (UPDATE)	Weekly	Latest week
Wall Street Journal Highlights Online (WSJ)	Daily	Latest 5 days
Text-Search Services		
Text-Search Services (TSS)	Daily	Since 6/79
Financial and Investment Services		
Japan Economic Daily (KYODO)	Daily	Latest 5 days
General News		
News/Retrieval World Report	Daily	Latest week
News/Retrieval Sports Report	Daily	Latest week
News/Retrieval Weather Report	Twice daily	Latest week

Broadtape). DJNEWS is as current as the last 90 seconds and goes back as far as 90 days. The DJNEWS database is updated continually throughout the day. Thus you can maintain up-to-the-minute knowledge about companies, industries, government regulations and economic events.

News in DJNEWS may be searched in the categories of company, industry or government agency. News about any of more than 6000 U.S. and more than 700 Canadian companies, all publicly owned, can be retrieved by entering the company's stock symbol. A complete list of corporate stock symbols is included in *The Dow Jones News/Retrieval Fact Finder*, a handy book that new subscribers receive. For U.S. companies, the stock symbol must be prefaced by a dot or period; for Canadian companies, it must be preceded by .T. (for Toronto exchange).

When you enter the appropriate preface and stock symbol, a list of all headlines in the database pertaining to that company will be displayed. To retrieve only the most recent headlines, follow the preface and stock symbol with 01 (zero-one). Browse through the headlines screen by screen. When you see a headline of interest, enter the number preceding the headline to get the full text of the story.

The same general procedure is used to retrieve stories in the industry and government categories. The *Fact Finder* lists the symbols used for various industries and government agencies. They must be preceded by I/ or G/.

In addition, you can do a free-text search of the same news stories by using the Text-Search Services (TSS) database (see below). Or, as noted above, special software may be used to provide automatic retrieval of news based on your own interest profile. An example of information from DJNEWS is shown in Figure 5.1.

Weekly Economic Update

The editors of Dow Jones compile a weekly summary, analysis and forecast of current economic news in the Weekly Economic Update (UPDATE) database. UPDATE consists of five sections:

- Executive Summary
- Economic Week
- Statistical Highlights

Figure 5.1: A Full-text Story from Dow Jones News (DJNRS)

```
N   AIRQC        01/03 BC  -1/2
/AIRQC LABOR                /BCY AIR/
   07/12 AIR FLORIDA NEARS ACCORD
  (WJ) WITH THREE EMPLOYEE GROUPS
    MIAMI -- AIR FLORIDA, WHICH STOPPED
FLYING JULY 3 AND FILED FOR
BANKRUPTCY-LAW PROTECTION FROM
CREDITORS, SAID IT IS "NEARING
AGREEMENTS" WITH EMPLOYEE GROUPS ON
TERMS UNDER WHICH SOME EMPLOYEES WILL
RETURN TO WORK WHEN THE CARRIER TRIES
TO RESUME FLYING.
    AIR FLORIDA, WHICH HAS RECALLED
ABOUT 100 OF ITS 1,200 EMPLOYEES FOR
LIMITED OPERATIONS, EXPECTS TO RESUME
ITS MIAMI-LONDON ROUTE AND SOME
DOMESTIC AND CENTRAL AMERICAN ROUTES,
BUT A DATE HASN'T BEEN SET.
    FLIGHT ATTENDANTS HAVE AGREED TO
TAKE A 25% PAY CUT, BUT THE AGREEMENT
HASN'T YET BEEN SIGNED BY THEIR
INDEPENDENT ASSOCIATION'S OFFICERS, THE
COMPANY SAID. PILOTS AND MACHINISTS
ALSO ARE NEARING ACCORDS ON TERMS UNDER
WHICH THEY WOULD RETURN TO WORK. AND
RAMP WORKERS SAY THEY HAVE AN
UNDERSTANDING THAT THE CARRIER WON'T
ABROGATE ITS LABOR CONTRACT.
    "THEY'VE SAID THEY'LL GO BY
SENIORITY AND NOT ABROGATE THE
CONTRACT" WITH THE RAMP WORKERS, SAID
WILBUR SPURLOCK, PRESIDENT AND GENERAL
CHAIRMAN OF DISTRICT 146 OF THE
INTERNATIONAL ASSOCIATION OF MACHINISTS
AND AEROSPACE WORKERS.
```

- Analysis

- The Month Ahead

When you enter UPDATE, you are shown a welcome screen that describes the database and how to move through it to retrieve the information you need. A menu of the five categories listed above is also shown, enabling you to select the category you want by entering the category number.

The Executive Summary is a capsule review of the past week's economic news. Economic Week is a day-by-day review of the past week's economic developments and major economic indicators. Statistical Highlights provides tables and charts of data from the Economic Week indicators. Analysis provides commentaries by leading economic analysts on the short- and long-term outlook for the economy. Finally, The Month Ahead is a four-week calendar of dates for release of key economic indicators. The menu and a portion of Economic Week from UPDATE are illustrated in Figure 5.2.

Wall Street Journal Highlights Online

Each business day the headlines and summaries of major stories in that day's issue of *The Wall Street Journal* can be selected and read in the Wall Street Journal Highlights Online (WSJ) database. The database is current from 6:00 a.m. Eastern Time.

In addition to the issue of the day, the four most recent isues are available. WSJ is an excellent way to preview the current *Journal* and to review any issue you may have missed during the past four business days. You are always given the choice when entering WSJ of scanning the current day's *Journal* or looking at the previous four editions. For any headline or summary of interest, you can find the complete story in the DJNEWS database. WSJ contains edited selections from the "Business and Finance," "World Wide," "Heard on the Street" and "Abreast of the Market" columns in addition to major news stories. Figure 5.3 shows the introductory message and menus plus sample headlines from WSJ.

Text-Search Services

All stories that have appeared in the DJNEWS database since June 1979 are maintained in the Text-Search Services (TSS) database. In addition, TSS includes the full text of all stories from *The Wall Street Journal* either published or scheduled to be published since January 1, 1984. TSS is updated daily.

You may search for stories in TSS using any substantive words from headlines and text, such as names of companies, persons or products, geographic names, events, numbers, dates, etc. Keyword search phrases are

Figure 5.2: Menu and Part of the Economic Week from the Weekly Economic Update (DJNRS)

```
THE WEEKLY ECONOMIC UPDATE
      COPYRIGHT (C) 1984
   DOW JONES & COMPANY INC.
        JULY 9, 1984

   MADE AVAILABLE FRIDAY NIGHT
AND UPDATED MONDAY TO HIGHLIGHT
   THE PAST ECONOMIC WEEK.

PRESS      FOR
  1        EXECUTIVE SUMMARY
  2        ECONOMIC WEEK
  3        STATISTICAL HIGHLIGHTS
  4        ANALYSIS
  5        THE MONTH AHEAD
       2

UPDATE 7/9/84 P102 ENDS AT 111

      Economic Week
      July 2 to July 8
```

```
            Monday, July 2

    Factory orders rose 1.9% in
May, the Commerce Department
reported.
    The gain brought new orders
to a seasonally adjusted
$193.24 billion from $189.72
billion in April.
    In the previous month,
factory orders dropped 3.4%.
    The increase was paced by a
10.6% rise in orders for non-
defense capital goods, which
are considered an indicator of
investment spending.
    The department also said
spending on new construction
rose 1.8% during May. In April,
spending fell a revised 1.5%.
    The value of new construc-
tion spending in May ran at a
seasonally adjusted annual rate
of $310.4 billion, up from a
revised $305 billion rate.
```

constructed using various logical connectors or operators, such as "and," "or," "near" and so on.

The primary advantage of TSS over DJNEWS is that a much broader and more flexible set of search keys is available to you. TSS is, thus, a little more difficult to use than DJNEWS, but it does contain more than 180,000 exclusive news stories and is ideal for detailed research on a company, industry or other topic. A special user guide for TSS is available from Dow Jones at no charge.

It is recommended that you first search DJNEWS for your topic. If that does not yield the news stories that you need, search TSS using keywords and phrases. A typical full-text news story from the TSS database appears in Figure 5.4.

Figure 5.3: Introductory Message and Menus and Headlines from the Wall Street Journal Highlights Online (DJNRS)

```
     THE  WALL  STREET  JOURNAL          PRESS    FOR
         HIGHLIGHTS  ONLINE
          COPYRIGHT  (C)  1984         1      FRONT  PAGE
     DOW  JONES  &  COMPANY,  INC.     2      EDITORIALS
                                       3      FRONT  PAGE  --  SECTION  2
     THIS  DATA  BASE  ENABLES  YOU    4      MARKET  NEWS
   TO  VIEW  ONLINE  HEADLINES  AND    5      BACK  PAGE
   SUMMARIES  OF  MAJOR  STORIES  IN            1
   THE  WALL  STREET  JOURNAL.  FOR
   DETAILS  ON  THESE  AND  OTHER      WSJ  07/12/84   -1-    FRONT  PAGE
      STORIES,  PLEASE  SEE            PRESS    FOR
        THURSDAY'S  JOURNAL            1    LONG  BEFORE  THE  'RUN'
                                            AT  CONTINENTAL  ILLINOIS,
                                            BANK  HINTED  OF  ITS  ILLS
   PRESS    FOR                         2    BESIDES  BEING  AN  ARTIST,
     A    THURSDAY'S  EDITION               CHRISTO  IS  MAIN  ASSET
     B    PREVIOUS  EDITIONS                CLAIMED  BY  CVJ  CORP.
          a                            3    WHAT'S  NEWS  --  BUSINESS  &
                                            FINANCE
   WSJ  07/12/84                       4    WHAT'S  NEWS  --  WORLD-WIDE
                                       5    BUSINESS  BULLETIN
     THE  WALL  STREET  JOURNAL        6    GERMAN  SPAS  WISH
   THE  EDITION  FOR  THURSDAY,             THE  OLD  BAD  DAYS
        JULY  12,  1984                     WERE  BACK  AGAIN
```

Japan Economic Daily

The Kyodo English Language News Service wire is provided by Dow Jones as the Japan Economic Daily (KYODO) database. It is a daily database of Japanese and international economic news from the Japanese perspective. Since so much international business is conducted between Japan and the United States, this database is an excellent source of news and economic indicators for many U.S. business people.

COMPUSERVE INFORMATION SERVICE

CompuServe, currently the second most popular online information service for personal computer users, offers a wide variety of databases and services of interest to business people. As noted in Chapter 4, CompuServe's Executive Information Service (EIS) includes all of the business-related

Figure 5.4: A Full-text Story from Text-Search Services (DJNRS)

```
        DOCUMENT=        1 OF       11    PAGE =     1 OF     15
AN      840712-0010.
HL         What's News --
           World-Wide
DD      07/12/84
SO      WALL STREET JOURNAL (J)
TX         MONDALE WILL ANNOUNCE his running mate at midday, aides
        said.
           The Democratic presidential candidate's choice accepted
        the offer in a phone conversation last night. They are to
        appear together today in St. Paul, Minn., for the
        announcement. Earlier, Mondale's aides showed strong
        continuing interest in New York Rep. Geraldine Ferraro and
        San Francisco Mayor Dianne Feinstein. Ferraro said she was
        asked for health and financial data. Another potential
        choice: San Antonio, Texas, Mayor Henry Cisneros. Mondale
        hasn't spoken with Hart in two weeks.
           Jackson has been ruled out, a Mondale aide said. Sources
        close to Lloyd Bentsen said Mondale wasn't any longer
        considering the Texas senator.
```

services and databases from its regular consumer information service, plus some additional databases specifically for executives and managers. Special software can be purchased for IBM Personal Computers to simplify signing on and retrieving information from the EIS databases.

Among the news databases available are the following:

- The Business Information Wire

- The Business Wire

- News-A-Tron Commodities

- AP Videotex

- The St. Louis Post-Dispatch

- The Washington Post

These databases are summarized in Table 5.2 and are described briefly below. Since CompuServe is continually adding new databases and dropping ones that are not used frequently, you should check the latest offering before subscribing, to be sure that the databases you need are available.

The Business Information Wire

The Business Information Wire (BIW) comes from the Canadian Press Wire Service. It contains the full text of Canadian and U.S. business news stories plus selected international news items. BIW covers 17 categories of news, including finance, communications, labor and agriculture. A typical story from BIW is illustrated in Figure 5.5.

The Business Wire

The Business Wire (not to be confused with the BIW, above) is a separate news wire covering business, financial and economic news. It is updated several times daily and is compiled from press releases and news items covering hundreds of companies.

News-A-Tron Commodities

The News-A-Tron Commodities database is produced by Herman Communications, Inc. and provides current prices from the major commodities exchanges, as well as news on the commodities and stock markets. Prices and news of grains, livestock, metals, financial commodities and instruments, stock market indicators, commodity options and foreign currencies are included. News-A-Tron is updated daily. The news and analysis menu and stock market highlights from News-A-Tron are shown in Figure 5.6.

Table 5.2: Selected News Databases on CompuServe Information Service

Database Title	Frequency of Updating	Period Covered
Business Information Wire (BIW)	Continuous	Latest 24 hours
The Business Wire	Continuous	Latest 24 hours
News-A-Tron Commodities	Daily	Latest 24 hours
AP Videotex	Continuous	Latest 24 hours
St. Louis Post-Dispatch (SLPD)	Daily	Latest 24 hours
Washington Post (WP)	Daily	Latest 24 hours

Figure 5.5: Initial Menu and Part of a Story from the Business Information Wire (CompuServe)

```
THE CANADIAN PRESS     PAGE BIW-1        OR AUTOMATIC SEAT BELTS IN NEW
                                         CARS BEGINNING WITH SOME 1987
BUSINESS    INFORMATION    WIRE          MODELS, BUT WILL LET AUTOMAKERS
*********************************         OFF THE HOOK IF ENOUGH STATES
1   NEWS CATEGORY LIST                   PASS MANDATORY SEAT BELT LAWS,
2   WHAT IS (CP)?                        REAGAN ADMINISTRATION SOURCES
3   WHAT IS THE BIW?                     SAID TODAY.
4   USER INFORMATION                        TRANSPORTATION SECRETARY
                                         ELIZABETH DOLE WAS SAID BY AIDES
        COPYRIGHT (C) 1984               TO HAVE STRUGGLED TO DEVELOP A
            (CP)                         PLAN THAT WOULD BE ACCEPTED BY
        THE CANADIAN PRESS               ALL SIDES IN THE 15-YEAR
                                         CONTROVERSY. BUT ADVOCATES AND
LAST MENU PAGE. KEY DIGIT                CRITICS OF AIR BAGS AGREE THE
OR M FOR PREVIOUS MENU.                  GOVERNMENT'S RULE WILL BE
                                         CHALLENGED IN COURT.
                                            EVEN BEFORE TODAY'S FORMAL
THE CANADIAN PRESS   PAGE BIW-238        ANNOUNCEMENT OF THE ORDER,

CP 11:53 EDT 11-07-84                                    .
   WASHINGTON (AP) - THE U.S.                            .
GOVERNMENT IS ORDERING AIR BAGS                          .
```

AP Videotex

The AP Videotex database is formatted for CompuServe and other information utilities by the Associated Press from its various news wires. AP Videotex is updated continuously throughout the day. News and information items are arranged in menus for easy retrieval. The full text of major national, world, Washington, political and financial news stories is available, as well as local Ohio news (CompuServe is headquartered in Columbus) and sports.

Electronic Newspapers

Two electronic newspapers are available on CompuServe: *The Washington Post* (WP) and the *St. Louis Post-Dispatch* (SLPD). The WP is an abbreviated "newsletter" version of the full newspaper, and you must subscribe to it separately, through CompuServe, for an additional fee. The WP newsletter enables you to spot check news highlights on a daily basis and

Figure 5.6: News and Analysis Menu and Stock Market News from News-A-Tron (CompuServe)

```
COMPUSERVE        PAGE OSC-1

----------------------------
NEWS-A-TRON INDICES ANALYSIS
----------------------------

1 INDUSTRIAL INDEX ANALYSIS

2 S&P ANALYSIS

3 KC VALUE LINE ANALYSIS

4 STOCK MARKET NEWS

LAST MENU PAGE. KEY DIGIT
OR M FOR PREVIOUS MENU.
!4
```

```
COMPUSERVE           PAGE OSC-40

NEWS-A-TRON STOCK MARKET NEWS
 12:00 NOON EDT  07/12/84

  THE DOW JONES INDUSTRIAL
AVERAGE IS TRADING AT 1106.88
DOWN 1.66. NEW YORK STOCK
EXCHANGE VOLUME IS 35 MILLION
SHARES WITH UP VOLUME AT 14
MILLION AND DOWN VOLUME AT 14
MILLION. THE HIGH FOR TODAY IS
1115.28 AND THE LOW 1115.28. THE
DOW JONES TRANSPORTATION INDEX
IS TRADING AT 467.48 UP .61 WITH
THE UTILITIES AVERAGE AT 125.52
UP .48.

  NYSE COMPOSITE 87.04 +.08
  NYSE INDUSTRIALS 102.29
  NYSE TRANSPORTATIONS 77.92
  NYSE UTILITIES 44.06
  NYSE FINANCIALS 79.14
```

to review the WP's editorial perspective on various issues. It covers local (Washington, DC) news, selected feature articles, and national and world news. There is no additional charge for the SLPD, which provides a midwestern regional perspective on the news.

CompuServe, in cooperation with the American Newspaper Publishers Association (ANPA), experimented with 12 electronic newspapers a few years ago, but found that most people would not give up their printed newspapers in favor of reading entire stories on a video display screen. It is doubtful that online services will ever displace newsprint, but electronic news wires and newspapers are a nice complement to print because they can be updated continually.

THE SOURCE

The Source is third in popularity after Dow Jones News/Retrieval and CompuServe as a business and general-purpose online information service for personal computer users. As with CompuServe, databases are continually being added to and deleted from The Source's offerings.

As noted in Chapter 4, Bizdex (Business Services Index) provides an index to all business-related services available on The Source. A primary feature is the Business Update (Bizdate) database, which provides daily summaries of business and economic news, financial and commodities markets and economic indicators each business day, and weekly summaries on weekends. Much of the information in Bizdate comes from United Press International (UPI). The Source also offers the complete UPI international, national, state and business wires as a database.

We will discuss Bizdate offerings below and follow with a look at other Bizdex services and the UPI database.

Business Update

The Business Update (Bizdate) menu includes the following files:

- Stockcheck

- Market Indicators

- Commodities Index

- Currency

- Financial Headlines

- Business Horizons

- U.S. News Washington Letter

- The Board Room

The Bizdate files are summarized in Table 5.3; all are briefly described below with the exception of Stockcheck, which is covered in Chapter 7.

Market Indicators

The Market Indicators file lists a number of spot references, including the hourly condition of the stock markets, plus gold and metal prices, and

Table 5.3: Selected News Databases on The Source

Database Title	Frequency of Updating	Period Covered
Business Update (Bizdate)	Daily	Latest week
Stockcheck	Continous	Latest week
Market Indicators	Hourly	Latest week
Commodities Index	Continuous	Latest week
Currency	Twice daily	Latest week
Financial Headlines	Continuous	Latest week
Business Horizons	Continuous	Latest week
U.S. News Washington Letter	Weekly	Latest 4 weeks
The Board Room	Weekly	Latest week
United Press International News Wires	Continuous	Latest 24 hours

mutual fund prices from United Press International (UPI). (See Chapter 7 for additional information.)

Commodities Index

The Commodities Index file includes price quotes for various commodities groups as well as general commodities and economic news. This information is supplied by Commodity News Service and is updated throughout the day. A sample list of headlines from this file is shown in Figure 5.7.

Currency

The Currency file reports on the status of the dollar and more than 25 foreign currencies on the New York and foreign exchanges. Data are provided by Multi National Computer Models, Inc., and the file is updated twice daily.

Financial Headlines

The Financial Headlines file includes headlines and summaries of economic stories, both domestic and international, from the UPI business wire. The file is updated continuously.

Business Horizons

The Business Horizons file contains selected business stories from UPI. As with other UPI databases, this one is updated throughout the business day.

Figure 5.7: General News Headlines from the Commodities Index of the Business Update (The Source)

```
-->CNS GENERAL

1   0815 GMT LDN FOREIGN EXCHANGE OPEN--1/25--UCN
2   0905 GMT LDN/DOLLAR CROSS RATES--1/25--UCN
3   1205 GMT LDN/DOLLAR CROSS RATES--1/25--UCN
4   STERLING EFFECTIVE EXCHANGE RATE INDEX--1/25--UCN
5   LDN GOLD MIDDAY: LOWER ON  U.S. MONEY NEWS--1/25--UCN
6   DAILY COMMODITY CALENDAR
7   LDN FOREIGN EXCHANGE MIDDAY: DOLLAR FIRMS--1/25--UCN
8   SOVIET OFFICIAL SPENDS 10 DAYS IN PEKING, TALKS TO OFFICIALS
9   NY MONEY MARKET RATES--1/25--UCN
(ENTER S TO MAKE A SELECTION)

-END- S

ENTER ITEM NUMBER(S) OR HELP: 9
NY MONEY MARKET RATES--1/25--UCN
COMM PAPER (BANK)
3 DAYS 13.50
14 DAYS 13.50
30 DAYS 13.75
```

U.S. News Washington Letter

The U.S. News Washington Letter file, from *U.S. News & World Report,* is updated every Monday morning and consists of news summaries of federal government activities relating to business. It covers both political and economic news. The four most recent issues are always available online. A typical display from this database is shown in Figure 5.8.

The Board Room

The Board Room file provides opinion and commentary on current business and economic issues from a variety of businesses, institutions and individual analysts. The data are updated weekly.

Bizdex

In addition to Bizdate, the Bizdex menu includes a number of other business

Figure 5.8: Headlines from the U.S. News Washington Letter of the Business Update (The Source)

```
-->USNEWS

U.S. NEWS WASHINGTON  LETTER

        FOR THE WEEK OF
        3 OCTOBER 1983

1   FOOD FRICTION
2   ECONOMIC INSIGHT
3   TURMOIL, LAME DUCKS, BEER
4   SHORT TAKES
5   COLLECTING, PAYING, SELLING
6   FOREIGN RETIREMENT
7   ALIEN WORKERS
8   PAST ISSUES

ENTER ITEM NUMBER OR HELP  3

TURMOIL, LAME DUCKS, BEER
-------------------------

LEBANON'S NOT THE ONLY HOT SPOT WASHINGTON'S
MONITORING
```

databases and services, as we saw in the previous chapter (Figure 4.10). Much of the information in Bizdex is updated rapidly and continually, and you can spot check market conditions at any time by entering the following keywords:

- DOW (Dow Jones indexes)

- NYSE (New York Stock Exchange indexes)

- GOLD (gold prices and status of trading)

- METALS (metals market activity)

- SP (Standard & Poor's indexes)

- CURRENCY (exchange rates)

You can also obtain the latest prices for specific stocks, money markets and commodities with Stockcheck (see Chapter 7). In addition, The Source offers a portfolio-management service that automatically tracks a group of stocks specified by you to match your investments. This service, part of Stockvue, is also covered in Chapter 7.

United Press International News Wires

In addition to providing several items for the Business Update, as mentioned above, the complete UPI international, national, state and business news wires are available as a database on The Source. Whereas Business Update provides summaries and highlights of business and economic news, the UPI database contains all of the news stories transmitted by UPI each day. Furthermore, stories in UPI may be searched and retrieved using keywords and keyword phrases, while Business Update information is available only by selecting the appropriate menu number. UPI is still easy to use; you are prompted at every step, as illustrated by Figure 5.9. UPI stories are updated continually and retained for 24 hours.

Figure 5.9: Initial Tutorial for Selecting News Stories from the UPI Database (The Source)

```
-->UPI

....UPI DATA NEWS IS ON-LINE!
TYPE "HELP" OR "QUIT" AT ANYTIME....

NATIONAL (N), REGIONAL (R), OR STATE (S) NEWS, FEATURES (F), OR
"STOP"?    N

PICK GENERAL (G), BUSINESS (B), SPORTS (S), OR
MISCELLANEOUS (M).   G

KEYWORDS (PRESS RETURN FOR ALL STORIES).   defense

ENTER STARTING DATE, OR PRESS RETURN FOR TODAY.

PICK A STARTING STORY NUMBER FROM 1 (THE EARLIEST) TO 31
(THE LATEST).   31

READ FORWARD IN TIME (RF), READ BACKWARD (RB) , SCAN
FORWARD (SF) OR SCAN BACKWARD (SB)?   sb
```

DIALOG INFORMATION SERVICES

The largest of today's online information services in terms of sheer volume of information is Dialog Information Services, Inc. As discussed in previous chapters, Dialog emphasizes bibliographic databases. Most of its news databases consist of abstracts and indexes to newspapers, magazines and other publications, although some full-text databases are also available. Among the news databases offered by Dialog are the following:

- National Newspaper Index

- Magazine Index

- Magazine ASAP

- Trade & Industry Index

- Trade & Industry ASAP

- Newsearch

- Standard & Poor's News

- UPI News

- World Affairs Report

The first six databases are produced by Information Access Co. (IAC). All of the above databases are summarized in Table 5.4.

The majority of Dialog's news databases are updated only weekly or monthly, so they are better suited to retrospective research than to current awareness. There are, however, three exceptions: Newsearch, Standard & Poor's News and UPI News are updated daily. The information in these databases is eventually added to corresponding retrospective files. As noted in Chapter 4, several of these databases are available on Knowledge Index.

We will first describe the IAC databases and follow with Standard & Poor's News, UPI News and World Affairs Report.

Information Access Co. Databases

IAC indexes a wide variety of news publications. It produces printed

Table 5.4: Selected News Databases on Dialog Information Services

Database Title	Database Type	Frequency of Updating	Period Covered (Starting Month/Year)
National Newspaper Index	Index	Monthly	1/79
Magazine Index	Index	Monthly	1/73
Magazine ASAP	Full text	Monthly	1/83
Trade & Industry Index	Abstract	Monthly	1/81
Trade & Industry ASAP	Full text	Monthly	1/83
Newsearch	Index	Daily	Latest 45 days
Standard & Poor's News	Abstract	Daily	6/79
UPI News	Full text	Daily	4/83
World Affairs Report	Abstract	Monthly	1/70

indexes, computer output microfilm (COM) indexes and seven online indexes: National Newspaper Index, Magazine Index, Magazine ASAP, Trade & Industry Index, Trade & Industry ASAP, and Newsearch, which are discussed here, and the Legal Resource Index, which is discussed in Chapter 8. Magazine ASAP and Trade & Industry ASAP provide full text as well as indexing.

National Newspaper Index

The National Newspaper Index fully indexes three major newspapers: *The New York Times* (city edition), *The Christian Science Monitor* (western edition) and *The Wall Street Journal*. Abstracts are not included in this database. Figure 5.10 shows two bibliographic records from the National Newspaper Index.

Magazine Index

The Magazine Index database indexes and provides source references to more than 435 popular magazines, including all those indexed by *The Reader's Guide to Periodical Literature*. As with the National Newspaper Index, abstracts are not included in this database.

Magazine ASAP

Magazine ASAP is a new database offering full text as well as indexing of articles appearing in more than 50 of the magazines covered by Magazine Index, including *Advertising Age* and *Computers & Electronics*.

Figure 5.10: Two Bibliographic References from the National Newspaper Index (Dialog)

```
File111:National Newspaper Index - 79-84/Jun
(Copr. IAC)

1/5/1
0845643    DATABASE: NNI File 111
  Weaned  on 'Billie Jean';  tinyboppers:  Michael's moonwalking munchkins.
(Michael Jackson)
  Kastor, Elizabeth
  Washington Post    v107   pC1   May 26   1984
  col 6    039 col in.
  illustration; photograph
  EDITION: Sat
  NAMED PEOPLE: Jackson, Michael-influence
  DESCRIPTORS: singers-influence; rock musicians-influence

1/5/2
0845332    DATABASE: NNI File 111
  Jacksons  on  the  way;   Michael's  mom  says  tour  includes Washington.
(entertainer Michael Jackson)
  Harrington, Richard
  Washington Post    v107   pE1   May 22   1984
  col 2    011 col in.
  illustration; portrait
  EDITION: Tue
  CAPTIONS: The Jackson brothers.
  NAMED PEOPLE: Jackson, Michael-performances; Jackson, Katherine-planning
  DESCRIPTORS: rock musicians-performances
```

Trade & Industry Index

The Trade & Industry Index provides indexing and abstracts for articles appearing in more than 330 business, industry and trade publications as well as 1200 additional publications. Information from the Public Relations (PR) news wire is also included in this database. Trade & Industry Index offers business- and industry-related records from the other IAC databases, including the Legal Resource Index.

Trade & Industry ASAP

Trade & Industry ASAP provides indexing and the full text of articles from more than 85 of the publications covered by the Trade & Industry Index, including all of the major business and trade journals.

Newsearch

The Newsearch database is the only IAC database that is updated daily. It offers information about all of the publications covered by the Magazine Index, the National Newspaper Index and the Legal Resource Index. After 45 days, entries from Newsearch are added to the corresponding retrospective databases. Newsearch provides indexed bibliographic citations only—abstracts are not available. Thus, Newsearch is helpful primarily in tracking current articles of interest in publications that you can readily obtain elsewhere for reading. Sample Newsearch headlines are shown in Figure 5.11. Complete citations for articles of interest can then be retrieved.

Figure 5.11: Headlines from Newsearch (Dialog)

```
File211:NEWSEARCH
(Copyright IAC)

1/6/1
1141211    DATABASE: TI File 148
  NEXIS provides information retrieval services for Democratic National
Convention.

1/6/2
1137142    DATABASE: TI File 148
  Free Congress Foundation and Moral Majority Foundation plan Family Forum
III.

1/6/3
1137102    DATABASE: TI File 148
  Former President Gerald R.  Ford suggests shorter schedules for major
political conventions.

1/6/4
1137076    DATABASE: TI File 148
  Both Democratic and Republican conventions will be served by AT&T
communication services.

1/6/5
1129312    DATABASE: TI File 148
  ITT Corp.  will operate press centers at both Democratic and Republican
conventions in San Francisco and Dallas. (F Y I)
```

Standard & Poor's News

The Standard & Poor's News database is equivalent to the Daily News Section of Standard & Poor's *Standard Corporation Records* publications. The daily file of this database is updated daily; each week entries from the daily file are added to the retrospective file, which goes back to June 1979. The database includes information about more than 10,000 publicly owned companies. Its companion, Standard & Poor's General Information database, is discussed in Chapter 6.

UPI News

Various United Press International news wires are offered by more online information services than any other electronic information source. The version on Dialog includes full text of the final editions of stories transmitted via the UPI international news wire, which provides comprehensive coverage of international, U.S. and Washington, DC, news.

The advantage of using UPI on Dialog is in the powerful full-text searching features that can retrieve words in complex phrases exactly as they occur in the text. The major disadvantage is that stories are two days old by the time they appear online in Dialog's UPI News database, even though the file is updated daily. If you want to keep abreast of news within the hour, use the UPI databases on The Source or NewsNet (see below). Figure 5.12 is a typical UPI News story as it appears on Dialog.

World Affairs Report

The World Affairs Report database, produced by the California Institute of International Studies, provides commentary and analysis of world events by comparing coverage from a wide variety of published news sources, including *Pravda, Tass* and *Izvestia* from the Soviet press. Editorial descriptions examine the Soviet viewpoint in contrast to that of the U.S.

NEWSNET

NewsNet transmits electronic editions of more than 175 specialty business, financial and technical newsletters. There are far too many newsletters to discuss individually, but areas best covered are finances, investments, taxes, computers, electronics, telecommunications, broadcasting and publishing (both electronic and print). Tables 5.5 and 5.6 list some representative newsletter databases and their updating frequency.

With NewsNet you can scan far more newsletters much faster than you could ever do with print subscriptions. Newsletters usually appear online before their print counterparts reach subscribers' desks. Back issues are maintained online as well.

Also included in NewsNet service are the Public Relations (PR) news wire and several UPI news wires: the business and financial wire, the domestic news wire, the political wire, the international news wire and the sports wire.

Figure 5.12: The Full Text of a News Story from UPI News (Dialog)

```
STORY TAG: perot
BY: CARMICHAEL, DAN
DATELINE: DALLAS (UPI)    June 02, 1983
TIME: 21:31pd    CYCLE: pm
PRIORITY: Deferred    WORD COUNT: 0321
```

A four-year dispute between Electronic Data Systems Corp. and Iran, accented by a daring commando-style prison raid, ended with computer magnate H. Ross Perot accepting $2.5 million less than the Tehran government owed him.

EDS operated a data processing center for a number of Iranian government agencies, but the government stopped paying in June 1978.

In a three-sentence announcement, Perot said he and his company had settled all its claims against Iran for $16.5 million. He was owed $19 million.

"They stopped paying, and we moved our employees out of Iran," EDS spokesman Jerry Dalton said Wednesday after announcing the settlement.

"They captured two of our remaining employees just before the revolution. We eventually broke them out."

In a February 1979 rescue mission arranged by Perot, a 14-member commando squad of EDS employees with combat experience in Vietnam infiltrated an Iranian prison and staged the largest jailbreak in history, spiriting the two employees out of the country and freeing 11,000 other prisoners.

Shortly thereafter Iran became embroiled in the revolution highlighted by the taking of the 52 American hostages. They were released under a negotiated agreement that required all American claims against Iran to be sent to an international tribunal.

EDS, however, was the only American corporation to complete successfully its litigation against Iran before that accord was reached.

In 1981, Perot sued the American government, challenging the hostage release agreement. In response, a court ordered federal marshals to take custody of $20 million of Iranian money frozen in a New York City bank.

Table 5.5: Selected Full-text High Tech Newsletters on NewsNet

Database Title	Frequency of Updating	Period Covered (Starting month/year)
Computers and Electronics		
The Business Computer	Weekly	10/83
Computer Insider	Bi-weekly	12/83
Computer Market Observer	Weekly	9/82
E-COM News	Bi-weekly	11/83
IBM Outlook	Monthly	6/84
Mini/Micro Bulletin	Weekly	9/82
Personal Computers Today	Monthly	12/82
Seybold Report on Professional Computing	Monthly	9/83
Electronic Publising and Broadcasting		
IIA Friday Memo (Information Industry)	Weekly	1/82
NewsNet's Online Bulletin	As news occurs	8/82
Online Database Report	Monthly	3/82
Public Broadcasting Report	Bi-weekly	5/82
Seybold Report on Publishing Systems	Bi-weekly	1/82
Television Digest	Weekly	3/82
Worldwide Videotex Update	Monthly	12/82
Research and Development		
Federal Research Report	Weekly	1/82
Hi Tech Patents: Data Communications	Bi-weekly	3/83
Hi Tech Patents: Fiber Optics Technology	Bi-weekly	3/83
Hi Tech Patents: Laser Technology	Bi-weekly	3/83
Research Monitor News	Weekly	1/82
Telecommunications		
CableNews	Weekly	1/82
Cellular Radio News	Monthly	11/82
Communications Daily	Daily	1/82
Data Channels	Bi-weekly	1/82
Fiber/Laser News	Bi-weekly	1/82
Interconnection	Bi-weekly	1/84
LAN (Local Area Networks)	Monthly	5/82
Mobile Phone News	Bi-weekly	1/84
Satellite News Bulletin Service	As news occurs	4/82
Telephone News	Weekly	1/82
VideoNews	Bi-weekly	1/82
ViewText	Monthly	5/82

Table 5.6: Selected Full-text Business and Industry Newsletters on NewsNet

Database Title	Frequency of Updating	Period Covered (Starting month/year)
Aerospace		
Defense Industry Report	Bi-weekly	8/83
Defense R&D Update	Monthly	10/83
Corporate Communications and Management		
The Corporate Shareholder	Bi-weekly	1/82
Sid Cato's Newsletter on Annual Reports	Monthly	9/83
Entrepreneurial Manager's Newsletter	Monthly	11/81
Executive Productivity	Monthly	6/82
Office Automation Update	Monthly	6/82
Energy		
Daily Petro Futures	Twice daily	6/83
International Petroleum Finance	Bi-weekly	1/84
Solar Energy Intelligence Report	Weekly	1/82
Finance and Accounting		
American Banker	Daily	1/84
Banking Regulator	Weekly	1/82
EFT Report (Electronic Funds Transfer)	Bi-weekly	1/84
Federal Reserve Week	Weekly	7/83
Fintex All-Day U.S. Money Market Monitor	3 times daily	Latest 5 weeks
Government and Regulatory		
Compliance Alert: Federal Register Digest	Weekly	1/84
Grants and Contracts Alert	Daily	6/82
Grants and Contracts Weekly	Weekly	5/82
Investments		
Energies, Trends, Cycles	Monthly	9/83
Howard Ruff's Financial Survival Report	Weekly	10/83
Low-Priced Stock Digest	Monthly	9/83
The Stranger Report	Monthly	10/83
Tax Shelter Insider	Monthly	6/82
Wall Street Monitor: Weekly Market Digest	Weekly	11/83
The Wellington Alert Bulletin Service	Twice weekly	12/83
Public Relations		
Contacts Daily Report	Daily	6/84
PR Newswire	Hourly	7/83
Trade Media News	Bi-weekly	6/84
Taxation		
CCH State Tax Review	Weekly	1/83
CCH Tax Day: A Digest of Federal Taxes	Daily	8/83
Corporate Acquisitions & Dispositions	Monthly	1/82

A highly useful feature of NewsNet is NewsFlash, which enables you to establish a keyword current awareness profile of companies, products or other topics you particularly want to follow. Unlike Dow Jones and CompuServe, NewsNet's interest-profile searching capability does not require special software. Each time you sign on, NewsFlash automatically searches the databases for new information corresponding to your profile and tells you in a message what items were found. NewsFlash is an extremely powerful feature that lets you scan headlines and selectively read the stories retrieved at each update. The various UPI news wires available on NewsNet, updated continuously throughout each business day, can be searched only via the NewsFlash feature. Other databases can also be searched using keywords and simple keyword phrases.

An example of a message resulting from a NewsFlash update is shown in Figure 5.13.

NEXIS

Nexis, a service of Mead Data Central, provides more full-text news stories than any other online information service. However, as noted previously, you must have a Mead terminal or special terminal-emulation software in order to gain access to Nexis.

Nexis offers general and business news and selected additional information from many major newspapers, magazines, newsletters and wire services. Included in Nexis service are the late city edition of *The New York Times* and The New York Times Information Bank, originally designed to give reporters access to current and retrospective articles from a wide variety of

Figure 5.13: Message Indicating New Articles Found to Match a NewsFlash Curent Awareness Profile (NewsNet)

```
NEWSFLASH NOTIFICATION

*****************************************************************
     2 Total NewsFlash Hits. Use STOP to stop and delete all.
     New hits = 2        Saved Items = 0

     TX12    12/6/83 == IRS + WITHHOLDING == Headline-->1
             IRS RELEASES TABLES FOR WITHHOLDING DISTRIBUTIONS
             FROM QUALIFIED PLANS
     TX12    12/6/83 == IRS + REGULATION* == Headline-->2
```

publications. Some of the news sources covered in full text by Nexis are listed in Table 5.7.

Table 5.7: Selected Full-text Databases on Mead Data Central's Nexis

Database Title	Frequency of Updating	Period Covered (Starting month/year)
Newspapers	Daily, 48-72	
American Banker	hour delay	1/79
Christian Science Monitor		1/80
Japan Economic Journal		6/80
News York Times		6/80
Oil and Gas Journal		1/78
Washington Post		1/77
Magazines	Weekly or	
ABA Banking Journal	monthly	1/80
Aviation Week & Space Technology		1/75
Business Week		1/75
Chemical Week		1/75
Coal Age		1/81
Congressional Quarterly Weekly Report		1/75
Dun's Business Monthly		1/75
The Economist		1/75
Electronics		1/81
Engineering News-Record		1/81
Newsweek		1/75
Offshore		1/81
U.S. News & World Report		1/75
Newsletters	Variable,	
Advertising Compliance Service	according to	9/81
Defense & Foreign Affairs Daily	publication	1/81
Latin America Economic Report		1/73
Latin America Political Report		1/67
Mining Journal		1/81
Raylux Financial Service Newsletter		9/81
Synfuels Week		8/80
Wire Services	Hourly or daily	
Associated Press world, national, business wires		1/77
Jiji Press Economic News Service (Japan)		1/80
Reuters European News Report		9/80
States News Service		12/81
UPI world, national, business, sports wires		9/80
Xinhua (China News Agency)		1/77

OTHER NEWS SERVICES

There are other news-oriented online services, but those described above are the most popular. *The Philadelphia Daily News* and *The Philadelphia Inquirer* are available online from Philadelphia Newspapers, Inc. on its Vu/Text service. The two electronic newspapers are updated daily. The *Daily News* is online from January 1980, while the *Inquirer* is available from January 1981.

In Canada the Info Globe online news service, owned and operated by *The Toronto Globe and Mail*, provides electronic access to the full text of all news and editorials from that paper, updated daily at 8 a.m. to coincide with the current printed edition. A complete back file of stories is maintained online from November 14, 1977, and the *Globe and Mail's Report on Business* is available from January 1, 1978.

SUMMARY

Online news services are an easy, convenient way to keep track of companies, industries and products you are interested in. Online news databases, particularly those that are updated daily or even more frequently, allow you to maintain up-to-the-minute knowledge of business, industry, trade and economic news. Competitors, mergers and acquisitions activity, market indicators and industry trends can be monitored via online newspapers, news wires, newsletters and trade magazines. Many online services allow you to establish current awareness interest profiles and automatically alert you to relevant news stories as they appear online.

In addition to general business news, detailed information about companies—their assets, locations, executives, board members, products and services, and financial condition—is available online. Chapters 6 and 7 will discuss the databases and online information services that provide these kinds of information.

6

Information on Specific Businesses and Companies

One of the most sought-after types of online information is basic data about corporations, small companies and other businesses. Until very recently, information of this sort was difficult to obtain online. By 1984 numerous directory databases had become available to fill this need, and more are appearing all the time.

The kinds of data most frequently provided by directory databases include company names, addresses and phone numbers, number of employees and other indicators of size, and information about major lines of business, ownership, parent and subsidiary companies, and executives, directors and other principals. Some directory databases also include financial data, such as sales, profits, earnings and stock performance. In this chapter we will focus on the fundamental corporate data provided by directory databases. Financial data will be covered in Chapter 7.

USES OF COMPANY INFORMATION

Directory information about companies can be used for many and varied purposes, including acquisitions and merger analysis, planning new ventures and diversification, identifying existing and potential competitive activity, monitoring growth industries and new products, finding international trade opportunities, making corporate and personal investment decisions and locating suppliers, consultants, clients and customers.

BUSINESS DIRECTORY DATABASES

Online directories of information about corporations and other businesses exist on several online services. Dow Jones News/Retrieval Service and Dialog Information Services have the most directory databases to offer. Some directory databases, particularly those that include financial information, are also available from numeric database vendors.

The databases covered in this chapter include the following files and database families:

- Disclosure

- Investext

- PTS Annual Reports Abstracts

- Dun & Bradstreet

- Economic Information Systems

- Electronic Yellow Pages

- Forbes Directory

- International Listing Services

- Standard & Poor's Corp.

- U.S. Department of Commerce

These sources and some of the terms by which they can be searched are summarized in Table 6.1. Most directory databases can be searched by company name and address. Ticker symbols and Dun's company numbers (assigned by Dun & Bradstreet and used to identify companies not only on the Dun & Bradstreet databases but on some other databases as well) are also common searchable items. Standard Industrial Classification (SIC) codes may also be used in some cases to search for companies involved in particular kinds of businesses. Other identifying numbers and codes that can be used to retrieve information about companies will be noted below.

The rest of this chapter will discuss the content and applications of the databases listed above and show you sample online records from them.

DISCLOSURE DATABASES

The Disclosure databases, from Disclosure, Inc., are some of the most widely used for fundamental corporate data. They include basic and financial data for thousands of public companies, derived mainly from filings required by and made to the U.S. Securities and Exchange Commission (SEC). The various SEC reports on public companies have always been in the public domain, but Disclosure, Inc. was the first company to publish them electronically and make them available online. The two databases produced

Table 6.1: Selected Online Directory Databases of Corporations, Businesses and Industries

Producer / Database Title	Vendors	Name and Address	Dun's Number	Ticker Symbol	SIC Codes	Financial Data*
Disclosure, Inc.						
Disclosure II	Dow Jones, I.P. Sharp, Dialog	X	X	X	X	X
Disclosure/Spectrum Ownership		X	X	X	X	X
Business Research Corp.						
Investext	Dialog	X		X	X	X
Predicasts, Inc.						
PTS Annual Reports Abstracts	Dialog, BRS	X	X	X	X	X
Dun & Bradstreet, Inc.						
Dun's Market Identifiers 10+	Dialog	X	X	X	X	
Million Dollar Directory		X	X	X	X	
Principal International Businesses		X	X		X	
Economic Information Systems, Inc.	Dialog					
EIS Industrial Plants		X			X	
EIS Nonmanufacturing Establishments		X			X	
Market Data Retrieval, Inc.	Dialog					
Electronic Yellow Pages		X			X	
Forbes, Inc.						
Forbes Directory	Dow Jones	X		X		X
Standard and Poor's Corp.						
Standard & Poor's General Information File	CompuServe	X		X		
International Listings Service	Dialog				X	X
U.S. Department of Commerce	Dialog					
Commerce Business Daily (CBD)		X				
Trade Opportunities		X				
Foreign Traders Index		X			X	

*Financial data covered in Chapter 7.

by Disclosure, Inc., are Disclosure II and Disclosure/Spectrum Ownership; the latter is produced jointly with Computer Directions Advisors, Inc. Both Disclosure databases are available through Dow Jones News/Retrieval, Dialog and I.P. Sharp (on both primary and Infomagic services).

Disclosure II

The Disclosure II database has proven to be one of the most popular databases to appear online in recent years. Disclosure II provides information on more than 9400 public corporations and includes companies listed on the New York, American and over-the-counter (OTC) stock exchanges. Information contained in the database is extracted from annual business/financial (10-K and 20-F) reports, quarterly income (10-Q) statements, proxy reports, registration statements and other reports filed with the SEC.

A complete corporate record in Disclosure II can be quite long. Each company record may contain the following items:

- basic company resume (shown in Figure 6.1)

- subsidiaries (shown in Figure 6.2)

- officers and directors (shown in Figure 6.3)

- text of management discussion (shown in Figure 6.4)

- balance sheet (shown in Figure 7.1, Chapter 7)

- income statement (shown in Figure 7.1)

- earnings, operating and stock ratios (shown in Figure 7.2)

- business segment data (shown in Figure 7.2)

- list of reports filed with the SEC and filing dates

Other kinds of information may also be included, but not every record will have all of the possible items. The items illustrated here and in Chapter 7 are most representative of what is contained in Disclosure II. This database is updated weekly.

Figure 6.1: A Basic Company Resume from Disclosure II (Dialog)

```
SOUTHERN PACIFIC CO
DISCLOSURE CO NO: S528300000
CROSS REFERENCE: NA
ONE MARKET PLAZA
STEUART STREET TOWER
SAN FRANCISCO  CA  94105
TELEPHONE: 415-541-2000
INCORPORATION: DE
EXCHANGE: OTH
TICKER SYMBOL: SX
FORTUNE NO: NA
CUSIP NO: 0008435711
D-U-N-S NO: 04-525-5767
SIC CODE(S): 4011; 4213; 4613
PRIMARY SIC CODE: 4011
CURRENT OUTSTANDING SHARES: 1,000   (SOURCE: 10-Q        03/31/84)
SHARES HELD BY OFF & DIR: NA
NUMBER OF SHAREHOLDERS: 1
NUMBER OF EMPLOYEES: 34,500
FISCAL YEAR END: 12/31

AUDITOR CHANGE: NA
AUDITOR: PRICE WATERHOUSE
AUDITOR'S REPORT: QUALIFIED; SUBJECT TO, PROBABLE DISPOSAL OF RAILROAD AND
TRUCKING ASSETS AND OPERATIONS BY INTERSTATE COMMERCE COMMISSION

DESCRIPTION OF BUSINESS
----------------------
ENGAGED IN PROVIDING TRANSPORTATION SERVICES BY RAIL AND TRUCK; PIPELINE
OPERATIONS; REAL ESTATE AND NATURAL RESOURCE ACTIVITIES; COMMUNICATIONS
SERVICES; AND INSURANCE AND FINANCIAL SERVICES.

OWNERSHIP
---------
SANTA FE SOUTHERN PACIFIC CORP., 100%
```

Disclosure/Spectrum Ownership

New in 1984, the Disclosure/Spectrum Ownership database expands upon the information in Disclosure II by providing detailed and summary ownership data for about 5000 of the 9400 companies in the latter database. The ownership data comes from Computer Directions Advisors, Inc.,

Figure 6.2: Subsidiary Information from Disclosure II (Infomagic)

```
SUBSIDIARIES
------------
GTE  PRODUCTS  OF  CONNECTICUT  COPRORATION;*  GTE  COMMUNICATIONS
PRODUCTS  CORPORATION;**  GTE  AUTOMATIC  ELECTRIC  INCORPORATED;***
GTE BUSINESS COMMUNICATIONS SYSTEMS INCORPORATED;*** GTE  LENKURT
INCORPORATED;* GTE PRODUCTS CORPORATION;* GTE FINANCE N.V.;** GTE
EXPORT  FACTORING COMPANY B.V.;* GTE LABORATORIES  INCORPORATED;*
GTE   INTERNATIONAL   INCORPORATED;**   GTE   TELECOMMUNICAZIONI
S.P.A.;**  GTE  SYLVANIA  DANADA  LIMITED;**  GTE  ATEA  N.V.;  GTE
TELENET  INCORPORATED;*  GTE  TELENET  HOLDING  CORPORATION;*  GTE
TELENET   INFORMATION   SERVICES   INCORPORATED;   ANGLO-CANADIAN
TELEPHONE  COMPNY;  BRITISH  COLUMBIA  TELEPHONE  COMPANY;**  AEL
MICROTEL  LIMITED;**  CANADIAN  TELEPHONE S AND  SUPPLIES  LTD.;*
DOMINION  DIRECTORY COMPANY LIMITED;* QUEBEC  TELEPHONE;  GENERAL
TELEPHONE  COMPANY OF CALIFORNIA;* GENERAL TELEPHONE  COMPANY  OF
FLORIDA; GENERAL TELEPHONE COMPANY OF ILLINOIS; GENERAL TELEPHONE
COMPANY OF INDIANA,  INC.; GENERAL TELEPHONE COMPANY OF KENTUCKY;
GENERAL TELEPHONE COMPANY OF MICHIGAN;  GENERAL TELEPHONE COMPANY
OF MIDWEST; GENERAL TELEPHONE COMPANY OF NORTHWEST, INC.; GENERAL
TELEPHONE  COMPANY  OF  OHIO;  GENERAL  TELEPHONE  COMPANY   OF
PENNSYLVANIA;  GENERAL  TELEPHONE COMPANY OF  SOUTHEAST;  GENERAL
TELEPHONE  COMPANY  OF SOUTHWEST;  GENERAL TELEPHONE COMPANY  OF
WISCONSIN;  GTE  DIRECTORIES  CORPORATION;  HAWAIIAN  TELEPHONE
COMPANY;  GTE CREDIT CORPORATION; GTE DATA SERVICES INCORPORATED;
GTE INVESTMENT MANAGEMENT CORPORATION; GTE MOBILNET INCORPORATED;
GTE  REALTY CORPORATION;  GTE SATELLITE CORPORATION;  GTE SERVICE
CORPORATION; GTE SHAREHOLDER SERVICES INCORPORATED
```

publishers of the well-known *Spectrum* series of corporate ownership reports. Disclosure/Spectrum Ownership includes the following information for each company:

- company resume and stock summary

- details of institutional holdings (Spectrum 3)

- details of 5% ownership (Spectrum 5)

- details of insider ownership (Spectrum 6)

- ownership summary

Figure 6.3: A Listing of Officers and Directors from Disclosure II (Infomagic)

```
OFFICERS
--------
NAME/ AGE/ TITLE/ REMUNERATION
MCLEAN, R. J./ 62/ EXECUTIVE VICE PRESIDENT, SUBSIDIARY OFFICER/ $250,000
HOYT, L. E./  57/  SENIOR VICE PRESIDENT / NA
DENTON, W. R./  52/  VICE PRESIDENT / NA
PHELPS, L. M./  39/  VICE PRESIDENT / NA
PILZ, D. F./  57/  VICE PRESIDENT / NA
SAGE, J. A./  48/  VICE PRESIDENT / NA
TAGGART, R. W./  45/  VICE PRESIDENT / NA
WATERMAN, H. A./  64/  VICE PRESIDENT, LEGAL COUNSEL / NA
WOOD, L. T./  52/  VICE PRESIDENT, CONTROLLER / NA
MCPHEE, B. G./  48/  ASSISTANT VICE PRESIDENT, TREASURER / NA
HILL, A. E./  61/  SECRETARY / NA
BIAGGINI, B. F./  66/  CHAIRMAN OF THE BOARD, CHIEF EXECUTIVE OFFICER (PRX
04-04-83)  / $475,000
FURTH, ALAN C./  60/  PRESIDENT (PRX 04-04-83)  / $343,750
MCNEAR, DENMAN K./  57/  SUBSIDIARY OFFICER (PRX 04-04-83)  / $328,750
SICILIANO, ROCCO C./  61/  SUBSIDIARY OFFICER (PRX 04-04-83)  / $377,724

DIRECTORS
---------
NAME/ AGE/ TITLE/ REMUNERATION
PROXY: 04/04/83
BECHTEL, STEPHEN D., JR./ 57/  NOMINEE / NA
BIAGGINI,  B.  F./   66/   CHAIRMAN OF THE BOARD,  CHIEF EXECUTIVE OFFICER,
NOMINEE / $475,000
DAVIES, PAUL L., JR./  52/  NOMINEE / NA
FURTH, ALAN C./  60/  PRESIDENT, NOMINEE / $343,750
HAYNES, HAROLD J./  57/  NOMINEE / NA
HAZARD, ELLISON L./  71/  NOMINEE / NA
LITTLEFIELD, EDMUND W./  68/  NOMINEE / NA
MCNEAR, DENMAN K./  57/  SUBSIDIARY OFFICER, NOMINEE / $328,750
MILLER, ARJAY/  67/  NOMINEE / NA
MILLER, RICHARD K./  57/  NOMINEE / NA
MORPHY, MICHAEL A./  50/  NOMINEE / NA
MUDD, HENRY T./  69/  NOMINEE / NA
MUNROE, GEORGE B./  61/  NOMINEE / NA
PARKER, JACK S./  64/  NOMINEE / NA
SICILIANO, ROCCO C./  61/  SUBSIDIARY OFFICER, NOMINEE / $377,724
WRISTON, KATHRYN D./  44/  NOMINEE / NA
```

Figure 6.4: Management Discussion Portion of a Record from Disclosure II (Dialog)

MANAGEMENT DISCUSSION:
1980 COMPARED WITH 1979. SALES IN 1980 INCREASED 4% FROM 1979 TO $3 BILLION, WHILE INCOME DECREASED 22% FROM 1979 TO $136 MILLION (BEFORE AN EXTRAORDINARY GAIN OF $12.5 MILLION). ALTHOUGH SALES AND INCOME IN PAPER MANUFACTURING INCREASED FROM 1979, OUR PERFORMANCE WAS TEMPERED BY THE HIGHER COST OF RESIDUAL WOOD CHIPS AT OUR PACIFIC NORTHWEST PAPER MILLS. WOOD CHIP COSTS, WHICH ROSE TO LEVELS MORE THAN DOUBLE THOSE OF THE PREVIOUS YEAR, DECLINED DURING THE FOURTH QUARTER DUE TO HIGH INVENTORY LEVELS AND REDUCED OVERSEAS DEMAND. PAPER MANUFACTURING INCOME WAS ALSO NEGATIVELY IMPACTED BY A STRIKE WHICH RESULTED IN APPROXIMATELY 21,000 TONS OF LOST PRODUCTION IN 1980. PRICES FOR MOST PAPER PRODUCTS INCREASED IN 1980, BUT COSTS INCREASED MORE. SALES AND INCOME FROM OUR PACKAGING AND OFFICE PRODUCTS BUSINESS INCREASED 12% AND 16%, RESPECTIVELY, FROM 1979. PERFORMANCE OF THE PACKAGING BUSINESSES WAS HELPED BY INCREASED SELLING PRICES FOR MOST PRODUCTS, AND THE INCREASE IN OFFICE PRODUCTS INCOME WAS DUE PRIMARILY TO INCREASED SALES. THE DEPRESSION IN THE HOMEBUILDING INDUSTRY SEVERELY IMPACTED OUR WOOD PRODUCTS AND BUILDING MATERIALS BUSINESSES. AS A RESULT OF HIGH INTEREST RATES AND A DECREASE IN THE AVAILABILITY OF MORTGAGE FUNDS, HOUSING STARTS PLUNGED TO 1.29 MILLION IN 1980, WELL BELOW THE 1.74 MILLION LEVEL OF 1979. POOR MARKET CONDITIONS FOR WOOD PRODUCTS CAUSED THE SHARP DECREASE IN OUR WOOD PRODUCTS BUSINESS. BOTH SELLING PRICES AND VOLUMES WERE DOWN, REFLECTING THE MUCH LOWER DEMAND CAUSED BY FINANCING RESTRAINTS. BECASUE OF THAT LOW DEMAND, MOST MILLS OPERATED AT REDUCED LEVELS AND OR WERE CLOSED FOR VARYING PERIODS OF TIME IN 1980. THE COMPANY'S BUILDING MATERIALS DISTRIBUTION AND HOUSING BUSINESSES REPORTED A LOSS FOR THE YEAR. THE BUILDING MATERIALS DISTRIBUTION DIVISION SUFFERED A MODEST LOSS FOR THE YEAR DUE TO THE POOR HOUSING MARKET AND COSTS ASSOCIATED WITH THE ASSIMILATION OF ITS 1979 EXPANSION. SALES DECREASED 11% FROM 1979. CONSIDERING THE ADDITIONS TO OUR DISTRIBUTION FACILITIES IN LATE 1979, THIS REPRESENTED A SIGNIFICANT DECLINE IN RELATIVE VOLUME. THE HOUSING DIVISION OPERATED AT A SUBSTANTIAL LOSS IN 1980. DURING THE YEAR, THE COMPANY CLOSED A HOUSING PLANT AND SOLD ITS CABINET DISIVISON. OTHER INCOME, NET (SEE NOTE 1 OF THE NOTES TO FINANCIAL STATEMENTS) WAS DOWN PRIMARILY BECAUSE OF THE DECLINE IN THE PERFORMANCE OF BOISE SOUTHERN, A JOINT VENTURE. BOISE SOUTHERN'S 1980 EARNINGS DECLINE WAS DUE TO THE DEPRESSED WOOD PRODUCTS MARKET RESULTING FROM THE HOUSING DEPRESSION; INABILITY TO PASS ON THE HIGHER COSTS OF MANUAFCTURING LINERBOARD; MAJOR MECHANICAL PROBLEMS WHICH RESULTED IN SIGNIFICANTLY REDUCED PRODUCTION AT THE DE RIDDER, LOUISIANA, PAPER MILL; AND ADDITIONAL INTEREST EXPENSE RESULTING FROM THE RECENT EXPANSION. INTEREST EXPENSE FOR 1980 WAS $49 MILLION, WHICH IS NET OF $25 MILLION OF CAPITALIZED INTEREST REALTED TO CAPITAL PROJECTS. THE AMOUNT OF INTEREST CAPITALIZED IN 1981 WILL BE LESS DUE TO THE PLANNED REDUCTION IN QUALIFYING CAPITAL PROJECTS. THE EFFECTIVE TAX RATE IN 1980 WAS 16%, COMPARED WITH 21.5% IN 1979. THIS REDUCTION WAS CAUSED PRIMARILY BY INCREASED INVESTMENT TAX CREDITS FROM THE COMPANY'S CAPITAL PROGRAM AND A HIGHER PROPORTION OF TIMBER CAPITAL GAINS INCOME. DUE TO A PLANNED REDUCTION IN CAPITAL EXPENDITURES FOR 1981, THERE WILL BE A SIGNIFICANT REDUCTION IN INVESTMENT TAX CREDITS. CONSEQUENTLY, THE 1981 EFFECTIVE TAX RATE IS EXPECTED TO INCREASE.

Figure 6.5 is an example of a full company record from Disclosure/Spectrum Ownership as it appears on Dialog. This database is updated quarterly.

You may wish to search Disclosure/Spectrum Ownership in conjunction with Disclosure II to obtain complete summary information about a company. This can be done by using the Disclosure company number, which appears in the company resume and is used to identify the company on both Disclosure databases.

Figure 6.5: A Full Company Record from Disclosure/Spectrum Ownership (Dialog)

```
0005204
LOUISIANA LAND & EXPLORATION CO
DISCLOSURE CO NO: L855000000
CROSS REFERENCE: NA
EXCHANGE: NYS
TICKER SYMBOL: LLX
CUSIP NO: 0005462684
SIC CODES: 1311; 2911; 1081; 6552; 1021
PRIMARY SIC CODE: 1311
NUMBER OF SHAREHOLDERS: 14,874
CLASS OF STOCK: COM
OUTSTANDING SHARES: 31,391,000
CLOSING PRICE: 29.50
MARKET VALUE($MILLIONS): 926
   AS OF: 03/31/84
```

INSTITUTIONAL HOLDINGS (SPECTRUM 3)

INSTITUTIONAL HOLDER	RANK	LATEST QTR CHG IN SHS	SHARES HELD	FILING DATE
ADAMS EXPRESS CO	37	0	100,000	03/31/84
AETNA LIFE & CASUALTY CO	99	-4,200	1,600	03/31/84
AMERICAN NATL B&T/CHICAG	31	-5,200	116,276	03/31/84
AMERICAN TEL & TEL INDEX	50	0	37,400	03/31/84
AMERITRUST COMPANY	15	-56,800	234,780	03/31/84
ANALYTIC INVESTMENT MGMT	58	-22,600	26,900	03/31/84
BABSON DAVID L & CO	98	0	1,800	03/31/84
BANKAMERICA CORP	81	0	9,995	03/31/84
BANK OF CALIFORNIA N A	36	2,580	101,744	12/31/83

(continued on next page)

Figure 6.5: A Full Company Record from Disclosure/Spectrum Ownership (Dialog) (cont.)

TEXAS COMMERCE BANCSHRS	51	-1,900	36,809	03/31/84
TORCHMARK CORPORATION	37	-15,000	100,000	03/31/84
TRAINER WORTHAM & CO	95	0	2,678	03/31/84
TRAVELERS CORP	80	-4,790	10,060	03/31/84
UNION TRUST BANCORP/MD	82	0	9,100	03/31/84
UNITED STATES TRUST/N Y	43	25,460	86,650	03/31/84
VALLEY NATL BK/ARIZONA	56	-400	28,100	03/31/84
WARBURG PINCUS COUNSELLR	7	172,600	356,600	03/31/84
WELLS FARGO BANK N.A.	20	4,805	202,805	03/31/84
WILMINGTON TRUST COMPANY	75	0	12,920	03/31/84
TOTAL OF 103 OWNERS		2,972,861	12,017,259	
MARKET VALUE($MILLIONS)			355	03/31/84

```
              OWNERSHIP BY 5% OWNERS (SPECTRUM 5)
```

NAME OF OWNER	LOCATION	SHARES HELD	DATE	FORM
PIONEER CORP	TEXAS	2,760,900	01/31/84	13D
TOTAL OF 1 OWNERS		2,760,900		

```
              OWNERSHIP BY INSIDERS (SPECTRUM 6)
```

NAME OF INSIDER	RELATION SHIP	RANK	LATEST TRADE	SHARES HELD	FILING DATE
BROWN R MANNING JR	D	14	200	1,200	01/81
EUMONT JACK V	O	11	0	1,955	02/81
FAULK NILES R	O	9	-1,000	2,385	02/81
GRAHAM FORD M	D	7	-2,000	7,821	07/80
LANGHETEE EDMOND J JR	CB	5	0	12,300	02/81
MCCARTHY EDWARD D	O	12	0	1,430	02/81
MITCHELL DONALD P	O	10	0	2,010	02/81
PARRISH EUGENE M	O	13	0	1,250	02/81
PHILLIPS JOHN G	CB	6	0	7,875	06/80
SECOND CRESCENT INVESTMEN	B	1	0	4,688,600	04/82
TIMKEN W R JR	D	4	-3,776	106,625	01/84
TIMKEN W ROBERT	D	3	-4,000	132,750	01/81
TOOT JOSEPH F JR	D	2	-2,500	165,345	01/84
WILLIAMSON ERNEST L	OD	8	-1,000	6,050	02/81
WILSON LOUIS HUGH	D	15	500	1,000	02/82
TOTAL OF 15 OWNERS			-13,576	5,138,596	

```
                OWNERSHIP SUMMARY
```

	NO. OF OWNERS	SHARES HELD	MARKET VALUE ($MILLIONS)	FILING DATE
INSTITUTIONS (SPEC 3)	103	12,017,259	355	03/31/84
5% OWNERS (SPEC 5)	1	2,760,900	NA	NA
CORPORATE INSIDERS (SPEC 6)	15	5,138,596	NA	NA

INVESTEXT

Also new in 1984, the Investext database, produced by Business Research Corp., covers the full text of research reports on companies and industries generated by the financial analysts of major investment banking firms in the U.S., Canada, Europe and Japan. Among the firms contributing reports to Investext are Smith Barney; Harris Upham & Co.; Kidder, Peabody & Co.; and Scrimgeour, Kemp-Gee (U.K.). Information can be retrieved using the names of these contributing sources, keywords in text, SIC codes or company names or stock symbols.

These reports cover about 2500 companies and include detailed data such as the following:

- market share forecasts

- sales forecasts

- profiles of market leaders

- stock price forecasts

- profit and loss statements

- product costs and margin analysis

- debt structure

- divisional forecasts

- analyses of sales and operating income by segment

- earnings forecasts and analysis

Figure 6.6 illustrates the table of contents of a report. Investext is available on Dialog and is updated weekly.

Applications of Investext include market research, competitive analysis, financial forecasting and business planning. Investext provides data not always found in other files, making it a nice complement to other databases; it covers a smaller number of companies than Disclosure, however.

PTS ANNUAL REPORTS ABSTRACTS

Predicasts, Inc., an established business and market research firm, produces

Figure 6.6: A Table of Contents Record from Investext (Dialog)

```
239841
Union Pacific Corporation - Research
DONALDSON, LUFKIN & JENRETTE, INC.
Joel Price and Luella White

DATE: 840423
REPORT NUMBER: 403567,  PAGE 0 OF 3
This is a(n) COMPANY report.

SECTION/TABLE HEADINGS:
   Stock Price Data 1983-85                               PG 1
   Summary and Recommendation                             PG 1
   First-Quarter Results                                  PG 1
   First-Quarter Results                                  PG 2
   Table 1 - First Quarter Operating Results 1983-84      PG 2
   First-Quarter Results                                  PG 2
   Table 2 - Transportation Sector 1983-84                PG 3
   Champlin Petroleum                                     PG 3
   Table 3 - Champlin First Qu. Operating Income 1983-84  PG 3
   Champlin Petroleum                                     PG 3
   Table 4 - UNP First Qu. Net Income 1983-84             PG 3

COMPANY: UNION PACIFIC CORP.
TICKER SYMBOL: UNP
INDUSTRY CROSS REFERENCE: RAILRD; NATRES
SIC CODES: 6711; 1081; 1311; 1382; 2911; 4011; 6552

SUBJECT DESCRIPTORS:
   STOCK PRICE DATA                                       PG 1
   EARNINGS PER SHARE ESTIMATES                           PG 1
   INVESTMENT RECOMMENDATION                              PG 1
   STOCK VALUATION                                        PG 1
   QUARTERLY RESULTS                                      PG 1
   QUARTERLY RESULTS                                      PG 2
   SALES/EARNINGS ANALYSIS                                PG 2
   SALES/EARNINGS ESTIMATES                               PG 2
   BUSINESS SEGMENT REPORTING                             PG 3
   EARNINGS PER SHARE ESTIMATES                           PG 3
   QUARTERLY RESULTS                                      PG 3
   OPERATING RESULTS/ANALYSIS                             PG 3
   SALES/EARNINGS ESTIMATES                               PG 3
PRODUCT DESCRIPTORS:
   RAILROADS                                              PG 1
   RAILROADS                                              PG 2
   COAL                                                   PG 2
   COAL                                                   PG 3
   NATURAL GAS LIQUIDS                                    PG 3
   NATURAL GAS                                            PG 3
   CRUDE PETROLEUM                                        PG 3
```

a family of databases, both bibliographic and numeric. Of these, one—PTS Annual Reports Abstracts—provides substantive information about companies. (Other Predicasts databases are discussed in Chapters 7 and 8.)

PTS Annual Reports Abstracts covers more than 3000 U.S. and selected international public companies. About 350 new companies are added each month. Corporate annual reports and SEC 10-K reports are the major sources for information in PTS Annual Reports Abstracts.

Primary coverage includes the following data about a company:

- business segment performance

- corporate sales

- operating income

- total assets

- capital expenditures

- corporate goals, plans and strategies

- stock exchange and ticker symbols

Other information, such as advertising and research and development expenditures, is included when available.

Data are presented in three formats that together represent one complete company record. A corporate establishment record is shown in Figure 6.7. A textual abstract is given in Figure 6.8. The third format, a financial abstract, shows numeric information; it is illustrated here, rather than in the next chapter, to let you see all formats at a glance (see Figure 6.9). All three are indexed using Predicasts' expanded SIC codes, event codes and geographic codes—the same codes used in all Predicasts databases.

PTS Annual Reports is particularly useful for finding corporate financial information, market research and industry segment analysis. It may be used with the Disclosure II and Investext databases to ensure the most complete coverage of a company.

The database is available on Dialog and BRS. Text records are updated every three years, and financial abstracts are updated annually.

Figure 6.7: A Corporate Establishment Record from PTS Annual Report Abstracts (Dialog)

```
0160998
InterFirst
PO Box 83209                          ID: 013979
Dallas, TX 75283                      DN: 06-411-7716
United States
214-744-7100


Sales: 709 mil US$                    No. Employees: 9653
Fiscal End: 12/31/83


Stock Exchange: NYS                   Ticker Symbol: IFC
Product Lines:
60200 Commercial Banks
73700 Computer Services
63100 Life Insurance
60201 Commercial Bank Retail Svcs
60202 Commercial Bank Corporate Svcs
```

DUN & BRADSTREET DATABASES

One of the best-known business analysis firms, Dun & Bradstreet, Inc. (D&B), produces several business directory databases. DunsPRINT is the well-known subscription service that provides financial, banking and bill-paying history on more than 4 million public and private companies in the U.S. DunsPRINT is only available directly from Dun & Bradstreet. Subscriptions are expensive, and larger corporations doing a lot of business with other corporations are the primary users of the DunsPRINT service.

D&B has recently added a DunsVOICE service whereby you can get company data by phone simply by pressing the appropriate buttons on your touch-tone telephone when prompted by the computerized voice at the other end. DunsVOICE is also only available directly from Dun & Bradstreet.

However, portions of the more than 4 million reports in DunsPRINT are included in three online databases made available on Dialog by Dun's Marketing Services. These are:

• Dun's Market Identifiers 10+

• Million Dollar Directory

Figure 6.8: A Textual Abstract from PTS Annual Report Abstracts (BRS)

```
AN  108252, 8304.
CI  Electronic Data Systems          ID: 003217
SO  10-K Report, 80.06.30            Year End: June 30, 1982
TI  COMPETITION.
AB      Generally, with respect to both pricing and services rendered,
    there is competition from firms providing business information
    services and from computer manufacturers. These competitors may be
    larger than the Company in terms of capital, resources and personnel
    and/or may be willing to aggressively compete on certain contracts
    which may be key to their own business plans. In addition,
    competition may come from the Company's own customers who decide to
    provide business information services for themselves upon expiration
    of their contracts with the Company. In the event the Company's
    customer who has a contract with the government desires not to
    provide these data processing services internally, the customer is
    required to publicly solicit bids for these services. All of these
    factors can affect the Company's ability to obtain or renew
    contracts.
        Although the Company is in a strong financial position and has
    eighteen years of proven performance, the Company's ability to meet
    competition will depend upon, among other things, its ability to
    maintain price competition, to continue to provide quality service to
    its customers, and to obtain and retain competent personnel.
PN  *Computer-Systems (PC3573001). Computer-Services (PC7370000).
DE  *PC3573001. PC7370000.
EN  *Industry-Structure (EC176).
DE  *EC176..
CN  *United-States (CC1USA).
DE  *CC1USA.
CO  *Electronic-Data-Systems.
SF  Text..
YR  820630.
```

• Principal International Businesses

All three databases follow the same general format and cover both public and private companies. To search the D&B databases in conjunction with each other or with the Disclosure databases or PTS Annual Reports Abstracts, you can use the Dun's company number, which is used to identify companies on all of the above databases.

Let's take a brief look at the D&B databases.

Figure 6.9: A Financial Abstract from PTS Annual Report Abstracts (Dialog)

```
0104973
Ford Motor                                      Annual Report
Corporate ID: 011894             Year Ending December 31, 1983
```

```
                                    bil US$
                         1983    1982    1981    1980    1979
ASSETS BY REGION         23.869  21.962  23.021  24.35   23.52
  United States          13.229  11.410  11.533  12.55   13.35
  Canada                 1.737   1.551   1.669   1.62    1.73
  Europe                 7.736   7.765   8.003   7.69    7.61
  Latin America          2.147   2.506   2.372   2.37    1.75
  Asia-Pacific           2.103   2.506   2.910   2.00    1.72
  Eliminations (-)       3.083   3.775   2.910   1.88    2.64
CAPITAL EXPEND BY REGION 2.333   2.968   2.227   2.77    3.44
  United States          1.096   1.470   1.039   1.42    2.35
  Canada                 0.160   0.073   0.191   0.39    0.18
  Europe                 0.789   0.837   0.653   0.72    0.73
  Latin America          0.205   0.455   0.276   0.17    0.10
  Asia-Pacific           0.083   0.133   0.068   0.06    0.08
RESEARCH & DEVELPMNT EXPEND 1.751 1.764  1.718   1.68    ---
NUMBER OF EMPLOYEES (000)  380.1 379.29 404.81  426.76  494.6
  United States          163.4   155.9   170.8   179.9   239.4
```

```
010   Free World 3710000 Motor Vehicles & Parts 870 assets
1USA United States 3710000 Motor Vehicles & Parts 870 assets
2CAN Canada 3710000 Motor Vehicles & Parts 870 assets
4  E Europe 3710000 Motor Vehicles & Parts 870 assets
3 LA Latin America 3710000 Motor Vehicles & Parts 870 assets
9  A Asia & Oceania 3710000 Motor Vehicles & Parts 870 assets
010   Free World 3710000 Motor Vehicles & Parts 431 total P&E
1USA United States 3710000 Motor Vehicles & Parts 431 total P&E
2CAN Canada 3710000 Motor Vehicles & Parts 431 total P&E
4  E Europe 3710000 Motor Vehicles & Parts 431 total P&E
3 LA Latin America 3710000 Motor Vehicles & Parts 431 total P&E
9  A Asia & Oceania 3710000 Motor Vehicles & Parts 431 total P&E
1USA United States 3710000 Motor Vehicles & Parts 453 expend for R&D
010   Free World 3710000 Motor Vehicles & Parts 531 employment
1USA United States 3710000 Motor Vehicles & Parts 531 employment
```

Dun's Market Identifiers 10+

Dun's Market Identifiers 10+ is a directory of basic location, financial and marketing information on about 1.5 million companies having 10 or more employees. Also included are all parent, headquarters and ultimate owner companies, even if they have fewer than 10 employees. These data come from D&B records updated within the last 18 months. The entire database is updated on a quarterly basis. A sample record appears in Figure 6.10.

Figure 6.10: A Record from Dun's Market Identifiers 10+ (Dialog)

```
0587222
LOCKHEED AIRCRAFT CORP
LOCKHEED SUPPORT SYSTEMS INC
1600 E PIONR BKWY STU 440
ARLINGTON, TX  76011
TELEPHONE: 817-261-0295
TARRANT COUNTY        SMSA: 142   (DALLAS-FT WORTH,TX)


BUSINESS: AIRCRAFT MAINTENANCE

PRIMARY SIC:    4582          AIRPORTS,FLYG FIELDS
```

	CURRENT YEAR	TREND YEAR (DEC 1983)	BASE YEAR (DEC 1980)
SALES ($):	0	0	0
EMPLOYEES HERE:	25	NA	NA
EMPLOYEES TOTAL:	NA		
SALES GROWTH (%):	NA		
EMPLOYMENT GROWTH (%):	NA		

```
SQUARE FOOTAGE: NA
    THIS IS:
    A BRANCH LOCATION
    A PUBLIC COMPANY
DUNS NUMBER:            03-790-0057
HEADQUARTER DUNS:      00-825-5283   LOCKHEED AIRCRAFT CORP
CORPORATE FAMILY DUNS: 00-825-5283   LOCKHEED CORPORATION

CHIEF EXECUTIVE OFFICER:
K E MILLER
```

Million Dollar Directory

D&B's Million Dollar Directory contains summary data on U.S. companies having a net worth of $500,000 or more. The more than 150,000 company records may represent headquarters, subsidiaries or single-location firms. The database is updated annually, and information is current within the preceding 18 months. Figure 6.11 shows a typical entry.

Principal International Businesses

About 60,000 non-U.S. companies from 133 countries are listed in the Principal International Business file. Records for this database are essentially the same as those for the above two databases. Sales figures, when available, are given in both local and U.S. currencies. This database is updated annually.

ECONOMIC INFORMATION SYSTEMS DATABASES

Two directories of companies are produced by Economic Information Systems, Inc. (EIS), a Control Data corporation: EIS Industrial Plants and EIS Nonmanufacturing Establishments. The information comes from business and trade magazines and journals, corporate financial reports, clipping services, state directories, industrial directories, Census Bureau statistics and the companies themselves. Information may be retrieved by company name and address, geographic location, zip code, SIC code, or any combination of these or other items of data. Both EIS databases are available on Dialog and both are updated quarterly.

EIS Industrial Plants

The EIS Industrial Plants database is a directory to more than 200,000 manufacturing plants and industrial and mining firms with 20 or more employees. The companies included have sales of $500,000 or more per year. The database as a whole represents more than 90% of U.S. industrial shipments. Corporate links—i.e., parent or subsidiary—are included for each record where appropriate. An EIS Industrial Plants company record is shown in Figure 6.12.

EIS Nonmanufacturing Establishments

EIS Nonmanufacturing Establishments is the companion to EIS Industrial Plants, and it contains essentially the same information for nonmanu-facturing firms and establishments with 20 or more employees. More than

Figure 6.11: A Record from the Million Dollar Directory (Dialog)

```
0000895
DOW JONES & CO INC
22 Cortlandt St
New York, NY  10007
PHONE: 212-285-5000
NEW YORK COUNTY
```

BUSINESS: Publishes General-Interest Newspapers Books Domestic & Foreign Business Periodicals & Financial News Services

```
PRIMARY SIC:      2711        NWSP PBG PBG PRTG
SECONDARY SIC:    2721        PRCDLS PBG PBG PRTG
SECONDARY SIC:    2731        BOOK PUBLISHING

YEAR STARTED:                 1882

SALES:                        $731,000,000
EMPLOYEES HERE:               NA
EMPLOYEES TOTAL:              5,890

THIS IS:
A MANUFACTURING LOCATION
A HEADQUARTERS LOCATION
A PUBLIC COMPANY

TICKER SYMBOL:  DJ
STOCK EXCHANGE:  NYS

BANK:  Manufacturers Hanover Tr Co
ACCOUNTING FIRM:  Coopers & Lybrand
LAW FIRM:  Patterson Belknap Webb & Tyler

DUNS NUMBER:            00-131-6702
PARENT DUNS:           00-131-6702
CORPORATE FAMILY DUNS: 00-131-6702

CHAIRMAN:                     PHILLIPS, WARREN H. / CH CEO *
PRESIDENT:                    SHAW, RAY / PR CHIEF OPTG OFCR *
CORPORATE SECRETARY:          POTTER, ROBERT S. / SEC *
COUNSEL:                      FAULK, W. G. / VP LGL
MARKETING:                    FLANAGAN, BERNARD T. / MKTG
          .
          .
          .
```

Figure 6.12: A Company Record from EIS Industrial Plants (Dialog)

```
141981
 ELECTRO MOTIVE DIV GM
    9301 55TH ST
    MC COOK, ILLINOIS    60525
    COUNTY :  COOK
    312-387-6000

    37431    RAILROAD EQUIPMENT

    SALES  MIL $ :    0132.3      INDUSTRY % :    03.41
    EMPLOYMENT :    8  (2500-9999)

 GENERAL MOTORS CORP    02674 * PUBLIC
    GENERAL MOTORS BLDG
    DETROIT, MICHIGAN    48202    313-556-5000
```

260,000 companies are included in this directory and, together, represent 85% of each industry's sales. Industries covered include agriculture, construction, transportation, communications, utilities, finance, service, etc.

A sample record from EIS Nonmanufacturing Establishments is illustrated in Figure 6.13.

ELECTRONIC YELLOW PAGES

The largest online directory of businesses, in terms of sheer number of entries, is the Electronic Yellow Pages series of databases produced by Market Data Retrieval, Inc. More than 10 million U.S. businesses, from sole proprietors and professionals to the largest corporations, are covered by this database. It is available on Dialog.

The Electronic Yellow Pages is compiled from all of the 4800 or so U.S. Yellow Pages phone directories and more than 1000 other sources. Typical entries in the database include:

• business name, address, zip code

• area code and telephone number

• city, county and state

Figure 6.13: A Company Record from EIS Nonmanufacturing Establishments (Dialog)

```
302545
  SAFEWAY STORES INC
    4477 S 70TH E AVE
    TULSA, OKLAHOMA    74145
    COUNTY :  TULSA
    918-627-5120

    5411    GROCERY STORES

    SALES  MIL $ :    041.1        INDUSTRY % :    0.04
    EMPLOYMENT :    2  (20-49)

  SAFEWAY STORES INC    05488 * PUBLIC
    4TH & JACKSON ST
    OAKLAND, CALIFORNIA    94660    415-891-3000
```

- SIC code and subject heading

In some cases, information about the following is also included:

- chief officer(s)

- city population

- individual, partnership, corporation, headquarters, branch, subsidiary, etc.

- size (assets, sales, number of employees, office size, etc.)

- advertising class (ordinary Yellow Pages listing, bold-face listing or Yellow Pages display advertisement).

The Electronic Yellow Pages database is divided into the following subfiles, based on SIC code categories:

- Construction Directory (SIC 1521-1799)

- Financial Services Directory (SIC 6020-6141)

- Manufacturers Directory (SIC 1850, 2000-3999)

- Professionals Directory (SIC 6411, 6531, 8011-8091, 8111, 8911, 8931, 8999)

- Retailers Directory (SIC 5200-5999)

- Services Directory (SIC 7000-7999)

- Wholesalers Directory (SIC 5012-5199)

There is also an online index file to the entire database. Companies may be searched and sorted by city, state, zip code, county, SIC code and other parameters. All sections are updated semiannually. Sample entries from this database are shown in Figure 6.14.

THE FORBES DIRECTORY

The publishers of *Forbes* magazine produce annual statistical analyses of public corporations, ranking the top 25 and the top 500 companies in terms of profits, sales, assets and market value. The Forbes Directory database provides these company rankings, along with industry rankings and analyses, online via Dow Jones News/Retrieval. In addition to directory information, this database contains financial and statistical data. It is updated annually and can be searched by company name and address, by ticker symbol or by selecting the appropriate number from the menu. Top 25 report for 1983 is shown in Figure 6.15.

STANDARD & POOR'S GENERAL INFORMATION FILE

Standard & Poor's produces the General Information File, which contains basic descriptive and financial information on more than 3000 major public U.S. corporations. It is updated weekly. The data duplicate some of what is found in Disclosure II, PTS Annual Reports Abstracts and other databases. This database is available on CompuServe and corresponds, in part, to Standard & Poor's Compustat II database, which is covered in Chapter 7.

INTERNATIONAL LISTING SERVICE

One of the newer databases on Dialog's service, International Listing Service from International Listing Service, Inc., fills a need heretofore not met by an online database. This file identifies both public and private entrepreneurial and investment opportunities in manufacturing, mining, transportation, wholesale and retail trade, construction, agriculture, and various other trades, industry segments and services.

Figure 6.14: Business Records from Electronic Yellow Pages Manufacturing and Professional Directories (Dialog)

```
0877523
JOHNSON & LINDLEY INC
1313 FIRST CITY NATL BNK
HOUSTON, TX 77002
TELEPHONE: 713-946-8426
COUNTY: HARRIS

SIC:
2899  .(CHEMICAL PREPARATION MFRS., N.E.C.)
CITY POPULATION: 2 .(2,500-4,999)
NUMBER OF EMPLOYEES: C .(100 - 499)

THIS IS A(N) CORPORATION
               HEADQUARTERS

0937162
ROBERT H FRASER
FRASER & BOGUCKI
3345 WILSHIRE BLVD
LOS ANGELES, CA 90010
TELEPHONE: 213-386-7701
COUNTY: LOS ANGELES

SIC:
8111A .(PATENT ATTORNEYS)
OFFICE SIZE: 5 .(5 OR MORE) PERSON OFFICE
ADVERTISING CLASS: ORDINARY LISTING
CITY POPULATION: 9 .(500,000 AND OVER)

THIS IS A(N) INDIVIDUAL
```

More than 500 records in International Listing Service represent either companies or individuals who wish to purchase or sell businesses, merchandise, equipment or other assets; merge businesses; or obtain or offer equity capital, loans or other financing. The information in this database is obtained from companies, entrepreneurs, investors and other interested parties.

There are four types of records:

• business sought for purchase

Figure 6.15: Top 25 Most Profitable Companies for 1983 from the Forbes Directory (DJNRS)

```
                        PROFITS
                        THE  TOP  25

        RANK                              PROFITS
    1983  1982      COMPANY           ($ MILLIONS)

      1    1      AMERICAN TEL & TEL    5,746.6
      2    2                    IBM     5,485.0
      3    3                  EXXON     4,978.0
      4   13        GENERAL MOTORS      3,730.2
      5    6      GENERAL ELECTRIC      2,024.0
      6   --           FORD MOTOR       1,926.9
      7    5    STANDARD OIL INDIANA    1,868.0
      8    4      STANDARD OIL OHIO     1,731.0
      9    8             SHELL OIL      1,633.0
     10   10    STANDARD OIL CALIF      1,590.0
     11    7    ATLANTIC RICHFIELD      1,547.9
     12    9                  MOBIL     1,503.0
     13   --             BELLSOUTH      1,371.5
     14   18        SEARS,ROEBUCK       1,300.8
     15   11                TEXACO      1,233.0
     16   15          E I DU PONT       1,127.0
     17   --             AMERITECH      1,064.8
     18   --         BELL ATLANTIC      1,026.1
     19   --                 NYNEX        982.7
     20   17                   GTE        964.0
     21   22         PHILIP MORRIS        903.5
     22   --              U S WEST        894.0
     23   --     SOUTHWESTERN BELL        892.7
     24   23       PROCTER & GAMBLE       886.0
     25   14                  GULF        864.0
                        -END-
```

- business for sale (shown in Figure 6.16)

- capital sought

- capital offered

The database is updated monthly.

Figure 6.16: Record of a Business for Sale from International Listing Service (Dialog)

```
01259
   TRANSACTION TYPE: Sell--Business
   ENTRY DATE: 840228
   BUSINESS LOCATION:    USA

   DESCRIPTION OF BUSINESS:   Services-Business  Services-Computer Related
Services, nec
   SIC CODES: 7379
   COMMENTS:
      A privately held software distribution company located in the
Northeast area is interested in being acquired by a company which could
inject cash to support inventory and plant expansion needs for expected
large growth in sales. Sales for 1982 were $1 million. They anticipate 1984
sales to be $30 million, based on current monthly sales volume.
      This company would prefer offers from medium to large size publicly
held companies.
      The company deals with the major microcomputer software houses which
create and market software for Apple, IBM and Commodore hardward.
       Lister reference: Foley -- Boston -- 02084
   TYPE OF ORGANIZATION: Corporation--Privately Held

   GROSS REVENUES......................$8,000,000
   PRICE NEGOTIABLE?....................Yes

   CONTACT: Coopers and Lybrand, Certified Public Accountants
            1800 M Street, N.W., Suite 400
            Washington, D.C.  Washington, D.C.  20036
            USA
   CONTACT PERSON: Bartko, Edward A.,CPA,Audit Partner
   CONTACT PHONE: 202-822-4114
```

Of the databases discussed in this chapter, this is the only one that cannot be searched by company name and address, because the companies listed generally prefer to remain anonymous. However, listings may be searched and retrieved by type of business, financial data (e.g., gross revenue or sales), SIC code, price and geographic location of the contact person or company.

U.S. DEPARTMENT OF COMMERCE DATABASES

The U.S. Department of Commerce produces three online databases that provide information about various kinds of business opportunities. They are:

- Commerce Business Daily

- Trade Opportunities

- Foreign Traders Index

All are available on Dialog.

Commerce Business Daily

Any business that contracts with the U.S. government knows the *Commerce Business Daily* (CBD), published by the U.S. Department of Commerce. This publication is available online, from 1982 to date. The database is updated daily, so announcements are online the same day they appear in the printed edition. The following categories of business announcements are included:

- federal contract awards by military or civilian agencies

- proposed procurements by military and civilian agencies

- surplus U.S. government property sales

- notices of government interests in R&D fields

This database can be searched by the name of the sponsoring agency and by keywords indicating the nature of the contract awarded or the items being procured.

While not strictly a business directory, the CBD database is a good source for monitoring companies that frequently bid for and are awarded government contracts for research and development or supplies and services procurement. The CBD can help you find new sources of federal government business and identify companies against whom you might be competing in bidding for certain government contracts. Procurement and contract award announcements are shown in Figure 6.17.

Trade Opportunities and Foreign Traders Index

Trade Opportunities lists requests by international markets for U.S. goods and services, and the Foreign Traders Index is a directory of non-U.S. firms that either already import goods from the U.S. or express interest in representing U.S. exporters.

Figure 6.17: Procurement and Contract Award Announcements from Commerce Business Daily (Dialog)

0659739
RECEPTACLE, PRESSURE, used on the various acft. NSN 1R 2915-01-161-8377 VH, United Technologies Corp P/N 70307-23905-101, 70 ea. East/west coast destn. Requisition N00383-84-X-P712-NM7. Anticipated date of sol 30 Jul 84. RFQs have been issued to United Technologies Corp, Stratford CT, Parker Hannifin Corp, Irvine CA. See notes 40, 73.
  Sponsor: Naval Aviation Supply Office, 700 Robbins Ave, Philadelphia PA 19111, 215/697-5777
  Subfile: PSU .(U.S. GOVERNMENT PROCUREMENTS, SUPPLIES)
  Section Heading: 29 Engine Accessories
  Legend: STAR
  CBD Date: JULY 19, 1984

0620114
UH-60A BLACK HAWK HELICOPTER. Contract DAAJ09-82-C-A326, Modification P00115, 22 May 1984, quantity 9 ea $562,303, period of performance 1 October 1983 thru 30 September 1984. Awarded to United Technologies Corporation, Sikorsky Aircraft Division (L), North Main Street, Stratford, CT. (150)
  Sponsor: U.S. Army Aviation Systems Command, Directorate for Procurement and Production, 4300 Goodfellow Blvd, St Louis, MO 63120
  Subfile: CSE .(CONTRACT AWARDS, SERVICES)
  Section Heading: L Technical Representative Services
  CBD Date: JUNE 9, 1984

Both databases can be searched by company name, country name and SIC codes. Trade Opportunities is updated weekly and Foreign Traders Index is updated three times a year. A typical record from Foreign Traders Index is shown in Figure 6.18.

OTHER SOURCES OF COMPANY DATA

All of the bibliographic databases dealing with business and industry topics contain abstracts or provide references to articles about specific companies, their products and services—or both. Scientific and technical research and development databases, including patents files (see Chapter 8), contain valuable information about a company's current R&D efforts. And the news databases, covered in Chapter 5, are always a valuable source of news items and stories about companies.

Figure 6.18: A Record from Foreign Traders Index (Dialog)

```
176709
  MUELLER, ALBERT    7911
  EPPLESTR. 19
  D-7000 STUTTGART 70     GERMANY (WEST)
  EXECUTIVE: HORST SCHRAEPLER    BUSINESS MANAGER/OWNER
  PHONE: 711/764003     CABLE: NA      TELEX: NA

  RELATIVE SIZE: MEDIUM    EMPLOYEES: 20    ESTABLISHED: 1835

  (27310) BOOKS :    (1) RETAILER OF ; (5) IMPORTER OF
  (27210) PERIODICALS :    (1) RETAILER OF ; (5) IMPORTER OF
```

Seeing "the numbers" is often important when researching a company. As we have shown, some of the databases discussed as "directories" in this chapter also contain financial and statistical data in the form of numeric tables. The next chapter gives further information on these databases and describes others that offer essential company financial and statistical data, along with investing and economic forecasting.

7

Balance Sheets, Quotes and Forecasts

A majority of business-oriented online information services and databases are numeric; that is, the data and information contained in and presented by them are in the form of numbers rather than text. The numbers are usually shown in charts or tables and represent financial data (such as corporate balance sheets, income statements and profits), securities prices over time, and economic and demographic statistics. Sometimes the numbers are supplemented by textual notes and descriptive summaries or analyses.

APPLICATIONS FOR FINANCIAL DATABASES

Numeric online services are obviously meant for people who do a lot of work with numbers, such as financial, investment and statistical analysis, economic forecasting, and so forth. The users of numeric database services are frequently professional analysts—economic, financial and marketing researchers—who are trained in the statistical manipulation of numeric data and who serve as intermediaries between the database services and the end users of the information. Librarians and technical information specialists—traditional intermediaries in the retrieval and transfer of bibliographic data—are becoming more frequent users of numeric data services, too, usually in large corporate information centers.

However, many services have recently introduced software and services to attract the more general business user. Any professional or business person can now access and manipulate numeric data on his or her personal computer. Some of the many possible applications in a business setting include:

- investment analysis

- credit analysis

- competitive analysis

- mergers and acquisitions analysis

- market share analysis

- industry analysis

- portfolio management and analysis

- securities performance analysis

- trends analysis

- forecasting

- corporate planning

- diversification studies

Many of these applications can be done offline—after disconnecting from the online service—by downloading data to your personal computer into financial spreadsheet programs like VisiCalc or Lotus 1-2-3 (see Chapter 10).

NUMERIC DATABASE SERVICES

Several commercial online services—many of them timesharing service companies—deal almost exclusively with numeric databases. In addition to providing data, they generally offer various statistical and computational functions online so the user can manipulate the numbers into comparative charts, graphs and ratios. With graphic plotters, the user can create bar, line and pie charts from the data. Generally, high annual subscription fees characterize these services (with the exception of I.P. Sharp), and there are charges for computational units used, as well.

Four of these services are of particular interest to business users. ADP Network Services and I.P. Sharp Associates were discussed in Chapter 4. As noted, ADP offers more than 30 databases in six categories of economic, financial and securities information. These are accessible to IBM Personal Computer users with ADP's Datapath software. I.P. Sharp has more than 95 databases of financial, demographic, economic, securities and statistical data. More than 15 of these databases are available through Sharp's Infomagic service for personal computer users with Sharp's Micromagic software.

Data Resources, Inc. (DRI) provides access to more than 70 databases supporting financial, economic and securities investment analysis. For personal computer users, DRI offers DataKits and VisiLink software. Chase Econometrics/Interactive Data Corp. (CE/IDC) has about 55 databases of financial, economic and securities data and offers several software packages to be used with various personal computers.

These services are listed in Appendix C. More about some of their specific applications software packages for personal computers is presented in Chapter 10.

SELECTED NUMERIC DATABASES

As we have seen in earlier chapters, numeric databases may be found on almost any service. Dow Jones News/Retrieval Service, CompuServe Information Service, The Source, Dialog Information Service, Bibliographic Retrieval Services (BRS), and SDC Orbit Search Service all have numeric databases among their offerings, or at least bibliographic or text databases that contain tabular numeric data.

In the following sections, we will look more closely at a number of databases that emphasize, or are entirely composed of, numeric data. These can be divided into three categories. First are databases offering corporate financial data:

- Disclosure II

- Compustat II

- Value Line Data Base II

- PTS Annual Reports Abstracts

The second category includes stock quotes and other securities data:

- Dow Jones Current Quotes

- Dow Jones Historical Quotes

- Stockcheck

- MicroQuote

- Business Update Market Indicators

- Corporate Earnings Estimator

- Media General Database (Stockvue)

The third category covers economic statistics and forecasts:

- Money Market Services

- Citibase

- BI/Data

- BI/Data Forecasts

- PTS Forecasts

- PTS Time Series

- U.S. Bureau of Labor Statistics (BLS) Consumer Price Index

- BLS Producer Price Index

- BLS Employment, Hours and Earnings

- BLS Labor Force

- U.S. Exports

- U.S. Economic (USECON)

These databases are summarized in Table 7.1.

CORPORATE FINANCIAL DATA

The information contained in corporate annual and other reports is of obvious value to business people. Databases of corporate financial information compile these facts for a wide range of companies. You can use the information to do financial analyses of one or more companies, or an entire industry. You can evaluate profitability, price performance and a variety of other financial ratios.

Table 7.1: Selected Financial, Securities and Economic Databases

Producer and Database Title	Vendor	Type of Numeric Data			Online Computation
		Financial	Securities	Economic	
Disclosure, Inc. Disclosure II	ADP, Dialog, Dow Jones, DRI, I.P. Sharp	X			X
Standard & Poor's Corp. Compustat II	ADP, CE/IDC, CompuServe, DRI	X			X
Value Line Data Service Value Line Data Base II	ADP, CE/IDC, CompuServe, DRI	X			X

Dow Jones, Inc.
    Dow Jones Current Quotes
    Dow Jones Historical Quotes
	Dow Jones		X
			 X		

United Press International, Inc. Stockcheck	The Source		X		
CompuServe, Inc. MicroQuote	CompuServe		X		X
The Source Business Update Market Indicators	The Source		X		
Zack's Investment Research, Inc. Corporate Earnings Estimator	Dow Jones	X	X		
Media General Financial Services, Inc. Media General Database (Stockvue)	Dow Jones, The Source		X		X
Money Market Services, Inc. Money Market Services	Dow Jones			X	
Citibank Economics Department Citibase	CompuServe, I.P. Sharp			X	X

Business International Corp.
    BI/Data Forecasts
    BI/Data
	Dialog, I.P. Sharp			X
				 X	

Predicasts, Inc.
    PTS Annual Reports Abstracts
    PTS Forecasts
    PTS Time Series
	BRS, Dialog	X		X
				 X	

(continued on next page)

Table 7.1: Selected Financial, Securities and Economic Databases (cont.)

Producer and Database Title	Vendor	Type of Numeric Data			Online Computation
		Financial	Securities	Economic	
U.S. Bureau of Labor Statistics	Dialog				
BLS Consumer Price Index				X	
BLS Producer Price Index				X	
BLS Employment, Hours and Earnings				X	
BLS Consumer Labor Force				X	
U.S. Bureau of the Census	Dialog				
U.S. Exports				X	
ADP Network Services, Inc.	ADP				
U.S. Economic (USECON)				X	

Among the most useful databases of corporate financial information are Disclosure II, Compustat II and Value Line Data Base II. (The textual content of Disclosure II was discussed in Chapter 6.) Another important source, PTS Annual Reports Abstracts from Predicasts, Inc., also offers financial abstracts, which were included in the description of this database in Chapter 6.

Corporate financial databases are available on Dow Jones and CompuServe as well as on numeric services.

Disclosure II

Disclosure II, from Disclosure, Inc., is a database of corporate information derived from reports filed with the Securities and Exchange Commission (SEC) by more than 9400 public companies. The financial section of a complete corporate record in Disclosure II consists of the following:

- corporate balance sheet (assets and liabilities statements) for the two most recent fiscal years, shown in Figure 7.1

- quarterly income statements for the first three quarters of the current fiscal year

- annual income statement for the three most recent fiscal years

Figure 7.1: An Annual Assets and Comments Record from Disclosure II (Infomagic)

```
ANNUAL BALANCE SHEET - ASSETS (000S)
------------------------------------------------
SOUTHERN PACIFIC CO          1983          1982
------------------------------------------------
CASH                      697,600       183,200
MRKTABLE SECURITIES            NA            NA
RECEIVABLES               635,700       406,300
INVENTORIES               103,900        97,200
RAW MATERIALS                  NA            NA
WORK IN PROGRESS               NA            NA
FINISHED GOODS                 NA            NA
NOTES RECEIVABLE               NA            NA
OTHER CURRENT ASSETS       35,900        62,000
TOTAL CURRENT ASSETS    1,473,100       748,700
PROP, PLANT & EQUIP     6,688,000     7,062,400
ACCUMULATED DEP         2,406,000     2,500,600
NET PROP & EQUIP        4,282,000     4,561,800
INVEST & ADV TO SUBS      176,900       438,400
OTH NON-CUR ASSETS             NA            NA
DEFERRED CHARGES               NA            NA
INTANGIBLES                    NA            NA
DEPOSITS & OTH ASSET       70,800        48,300
TOTAL ASSETS            6,002,800     5,797,200
------------------------------------------------
REPORTING DATES          12/31/83      12/31/82

COMMENTS:
1982  FINANCIAL STATEMENTS AND 1981 INCOME STATEMENT RESTATED;CASH INCLUDES
TEMPORARY CASH   INVESTMENTS;OTHER  ASSETS   INCLUDE  DEFERRED  CHARGES;TOTAL
OPERATING EXPENSES TREATED AS SELLING,  GENERAL AND ADMINISTRATIVE EXPENSES
(10-Q 03-31-83)  (10-Q 06-30-83)  (10-Q 09-30-83)  (10-K  12-31-83)   (10-Q
03-31-84);EXTRAORDINARY ITEM IS INCOME OF DISCONTINUED OPERATIONS;FIVE YEAR
SUMMARY OMITTED
```

- five-year summary report of sales, net income and earnings per share, shown in Figure 7.2

- industry segment data showing sales and operating income for standard industrial segments, also in Figure 7.2

Additional data, such as various financial ratios (see Figure 7.3), may be

Figure 7.2: Five-Year Summary Report and Industry Segment Data from Disclosure II (Infomagic)

```
                    5 YEAR SUMMARY
        ------------------------------------------------
                    EARNINGS         NET          NET
        GTE CORP    PER SHARE      SALES       INCOME
        ------------------------------------------------
           1982       4.70    12,066,000      805,000
           1981       4.32    11,026,000      691,000
           1980       2.95     9,979,000      589,000
           1979       4.30     8,898,000      638,000
           1978       3.99     7,736,000      551,000
        ------------------------------------------------

        SEGMENT DATA
        ------------

        12/31/82                  SALES REVENUE    OPERATING INCOME
        ELECTRICAL PRODUCTS        1,614,000,000       126,000,000
        COMMUNICATIONS PRODUCTS    2,514,000,000       151,000,000
        TELENET COMMUNICATIONS       137,000,000       -24,000,000
```

available for some corporations. The financial data in Disclosure II may be statistically manipulated by using MicroDisclosure, a software package for the IBM Personal Computer, available from Disclosure, Inc., Like other software packages, this will be discussed in Chapter 10.

Disclosure II is updated weekly and is available on ADP, Dialog, Dow Jones, DRI, and I.P. Sharp/Infomagic.

Compustat II

Compustat II, from Standard & Poor's Compustat Services, Inc., is more a numeric data service than a database. Compustat II is a massive compilation of corporate financial data arranged in several individual databases. S&P does not operate an online service itself, but makes it available through the following online service vendors: ADP, CE/IDC, CompuServe and DRI. The minimum annual subscription fee is $5000, the maximum is $50,000, and there are various options available within that range.

Figure 7.3: Financial Ratios from Disclosure II (Infomagic)

```
                              RATIOS
-------------------------------------------------------------
GTE CORP                      1982       1981       1980
-------------------------------------------------------------
QUICK RATIO                   0.64       0.50
CURRENT RATIO                 0.98       0.95
TOTAL LIABILITIES TO TOTAL AS 0.68       0.70
TOTAL LIABILITIES TO INVESTED 1.02       1.06
TOTAL LIABILITIES TO COMMON E 2.60       2.91
PCT PRE TAX INCOME TO NET SAL 11.38     12.01      11.69
PCT PRE TAX INCOME TO TOTAL A 6.16       6.32
PCT PRE TAX INCOME TO INVESTE 9.24       9.63
PCT PRE TAX INCOME TO COMMON  23.62     26.37
PCT NET INCOME TO NET SALES   6.92       6.55       4.81
PCT NET INCOME TO TOTAL ASSET 3.75       3.44
PCT NET INCOME TO INVESTED CA 5.62       5.25
PCT NET INCOME TO COMMON EQUI 14.37     14.38
NET SALES TO WORKING CAPITAL  -142.09   -61.90
NET SALES TO NET PROP;PLANT+E 0.66       0.65
NET SALES TO TOTAL ASSETS     0.54       0.53
NET SALES TO RECEIVABLES      6.45       6.03
RECEIVABLES IN DAYS SALES     56.58     60.56
NET SALES TO INVENTORIES      9.87       8.18
INVENTORIES IN DAYS SALES     36.99     44.60
-------------------------------------------------------------
```

Compustat II contains financial, economic and business statistical data describing corporations (both public and private), banks, utilities and other industries. The data are updated weekly. All of the data are numeric and may be manipulated statistically online, using the computational applications programs of the service vendors. In Compustat II you may select the following types of numeric and statistical data:

• corporate income statements

• corporate balance sheets

• sources and applications of funds

• supplemental income statements

- operating statistics and ratios

- lines of business data

- market data

- company annual reports

- SEC 10-K and 10-Q reports

- Uniform Statistical Report

- company descriptions and direct contacts

The major Compustat II databases and files are composed of the following:

- Industrial File: annual data for up to 20 years and quarterly data for up to 10 years

- Bank File: up to 20 years of annual and up to 12 years of quarterly data on commercial banks

- Utility File: annual data for up to 20 years and quarterly data for up to 12 years on utilities

- Telecommunications Compustat II: a special database of annual and quarterly data on more than 90 Class A telephone companies

- Price/Dividends/Earnings File: 10 key market items and 120 indexes, including Dow Jones, Standard & Poor's, and American and New York stock exchanges for more than 4200 industrial and nonmanufacturing companies

- Industrial Research File: 60 annual items for the 20 previous years for companies that have been deleted from Compustat II because of bankruptcy, suspension of stock trading, merger or acquisition

- Aggregate Files: composite financial and market data on about 175 industry groups

Compustat II is one of the most heavily used of all numeric databases. Figures 7.4 and 7.5 illustrate some of the statistical displays of company data that are possible with Compustat II.

Value Line Data Base II

Founded by Arnold Bernhard in the 1930s, the Value Line is a respected name among mutual funds. Today, Value Line Data Services publishes more than 400,000 time series on more than 1700 public companies. The annual and quarterly data cover more than 200 variables including:

Figure 7.4: Computer Companies with Price to Earnings Ratios between 17% and 25% from Compustat II (ADP)

COMPUTER COMPANIES

TICKER	COMPANIES	TORLA	TORAT	PE
APM	APPLIED MAGNETICS	24.100	81.650	24.254
CBU	COMMODORE INT'L	129.500	235.400	24.235
BGH	BURROUGHS CORP.	1082.470	4123.120	23.727
M	MANAGEMENT ASSIST	113.390	214.950	21.479
PRM	PRIME COMPUTER	NA	NA	21.250
PDN	PARADYNE CORP.	NA	NA	20.729
BAR	BARRY WRIGHT	20.530	98.040	20.673
DEC	DIGITAL EQUIPMENT	859.550	4024.010	20.022
STK	STORAGE TECHNOLOGY	606.680	1072.690	17.130
MDS	MOHAWK DATA	142.430	299.300	16.944
TC	TELEX CORP.	96.470	157.640	15.250
IBM	INT'L BUSINESS MACH.	12581.000	32541.000	14.844
CDA	CONTROL DATA CORP.	5186.900	6911.900	13.913
NCR	NCR CORP.	1436.470	3373.050	13.503
HON	HONEYWELL INC.	2327.500	4470.900	13.477
EA	ELECTRONIC ASSOC.	9.080	30.900	13.462
SY	SPERRY CORP.	2958.600	5343.00	11.786
	NUMBER OF COMPANIES	15	15	15
	AVERAGE	1904.978	4198.978	18.040
	TOTAL	28574.671	28574.671	306.786

Figure 7.5: Telecommunications Companies with Earnings per Share Ratios Greater than Three from Compustat II (ADP)

| | | EPS>3 | |
TICKER	COMPANIES	EPS	EMPL
T	AMERICAN TELE & TELEGRAPH	7.870	821.532
SNG	SOUTHERN NEW ENG TELEPHONE	6.120	13.449
GTE	GTE CORP	4.730	200.000
CSN	CINCINNATI BELL INC	4.480	5.200
CNT	CENTEL CORP	3.930	13.343
RTC	ROCHESTER TELEPHONE CO	3.180	2.742
	NUMBER OF COMPANIES	6	6
	AVERAGE	5.502	176.044
	TOTAL	30.310	1056.266

- financial histories
- earnings estimates
- projections
- target price forecasts
- quarterly results
- industry composites
- risk measures
- earnings predictability measures
- stock price histories
- restated sales and earnings
- trading volume figures

The companies covered include major industrial, utility, transportation, banking, insurance, savings and loan, and retail firms. All of the major firms on the New York Stock Exchange are covered, along with selected companies from the American and over-the-counter (OTC) exchanges.

Value Line Data Base II is available on ADP, CE/IDC, CompuServe, DRI and several other numeric database services. The frequency of updating varies according to the vendor. Various pricing options are available, including annual subscriptions, quarterly fees or charge per item accessed online. For example, on CompuServe, an annual subscription is $5500; a quarterly subscription is $1750, and various individual reports are available for $0.80 or $1.60 each. Annual data are available from 1955, and quarterly data from 1963. Figure 7.6 shows a series of market price and per share data from 1978 through 1982.

STOCK QUOTES AND OTHER SECURITIES DATA

One of the most popular uses of business online services is for daily stock price quotes and quotes for other securities and commodities. Two kinds of quotation services are available: 15-minute delayed and real-time tickers. Price quotations on the popular information utilities—CompuServe, Dow Jones and The Source—are delayed at least 15 minutes, as required of the exchanges by the Securities and Exchange Commission (SEC). Real-time services, direct from the exchange tickers, are far more expensive and are used by professional market brokers, analysts and others—annual subscriptions are usually required. These services are not included in this discussion.

Each service displays price queries a little differently; which one you use depends on personal preferences. Quotes are displayed in response to stock ticker symbols, and current quotes are, of course, updated continuously during the business day.

Dow Jones Current Quotes and Historical Quotes

The Dow Jones Quotes database is the most popular database on Dow Jones News/Retrieval. In includes Current Quotes and Historical Quotes. All companies trading on the New York, American and OTC exchanges are included. Current prices are displayed by Current Quotes 15 minutes or more after new prices are posted by the exchanges. Historical Quotes gives high, low and closing prices and volume traded for the most recent 12 days

Figure 7.6: Market and per Share Data from Value Line Data Base II (ADP)

```
MARKET PRICE AND PER SHARE DATA                    5/25/83
(Share Prices and Turnover on CALENDAR Year Basis)

      DIGITAL EQUIPMENT                  YEAR ENDING: June 30
      3573 ELECTRONIC COMPUTING EQUIP
```

Price as of 5/20/83	108.500				
YTD High Stock Price	132.125				
YTD Low Stock Price	61.750				
EPS - 12 Mon Trail	5.700				
P/E Recent/12 Mon EPS	19.035				
Recent Ind Ann Divd	0.000				
Recent Divd Yield					
BETA	1.345				
ALPHA					
5 Year Growth in EPS	23.198				
5 Year Growth: Sales	29.046				

FISCAL YEAR	1978	1979	1980	1981	1982
Share Price-High	54.875	69.500	98.750	113.250	115.000
Share Price-Low	38.500	48.625	59.250	80.250	61.750
Share Price-Close	53.625	68.875	95.000	86.500	99.500
Primary EPS	3.400	4.100	5.450	6.700	7.530
Diluted EPS	3.400	4.100	5.450	6.700	7.530
Diluted EPS-Incl Ext	3.400	4.100	5.450	6.700	7.530
P/E Prim EPS-High	16.140	16.951	18.119	16.903	15.272
P/E Prim EPS-Low	11.324	11.860	10.872	11.978	8.201
P/E Prim EPS-Close	15.772	16.799	17.431	12.910	13.214
P/E Dilut EPS-Close	15.772	16.799	17.431	12.910	13.214
Cash Flow/Share	4.825	5.814	7.015	8.196	10.317
Work Cap/Share	22.247	26.520	36.390	37.348	39.495
Com Equity/Share	22.691	27.588	36.248	49.306	57.299
Tang Book Val/Shr	22.691	27.588	36.248	49.306	57.299
Trading Turnover %	78.073	57.629	80.219	75.270	150.680
Shares Traded	31130	23401	36554	40908	83216
Number of Shares Out	39873	40606	45568	54348	55227
Total Market Value	2138190	2796738	4328960	4701102	5495087
Shares Out-Prim EPS	43225	44941	47171	52567	55429
Shares Out-Dil EPS	NA	NA	NA	NA	NA

and the 12 days preceding that, as well as on a monthly or quarterly basis; it is updated daily.

Neither current nor historical price data may be manipulated statistically online. Dow Jones does offer several software packages for offline portfolio management and investment analysis on your personal computer. A 12-day historical price series is displayed in Figure 7.7, and a current price display appears in Figure 7.8, where it can be compared with the display for Stockcheck.

Stockcheck

In 1984 United Press International (UPI) introduced a new interactive price quote service, called Stockcheck, which is available on The Source. Previously, The Source offered the old UPI Unistox reports, designed for newspapers; these were not interactive and were updated only four times

Figure 7.7: A 12-day Historical Price Series from Dow Jones Historical Quotes (DJNRS)

```
DOW JONES HISTORICAL
STOCK QUOTE REPORTER SERVICE


STOCK 1TXN  [Texas Instruments, Inc.]*
```

DATE	HIGH	LOW	CLOSE	VOL(100/S)
07/03/84	129 7/8	127 3/4	128	755
07/05/84	128 1/2	126 3/4	126 3/4	427
07/06/84	126 1/4	124 3/4	125 5/8	1266
07/09/84	126	123 3/4	125	807
07/10/84	125 1/2	123 1/2	123 3/4	1009
07/11/84	123 1/2	122 1/4	122 5/8	836
07/12/84	122 7/8	117	119	2654
07/13/84	119 3/4	117 1/4	118 5/8	933
07/16/84	118 3/4	116	118	807
07/17/84	118 5/8	117	117 3/4	885
07/18/84	119 3/8	118 1/4	119 3/8	972
07/19/84	119 7/8	118 1/2	119 3/8	664

*Bracketed company name added by author.

Figure 7.8: Stock Price Quotes as Displayed by Dow Jones Current Quotes (DJNRS) and Stockcheck (The Source)

```
ENTER QUERY
  txn

DOW JONES STOCK QUOTE REPORTER SERVICE.
STOCK QUOTES DELAYED OVER 15 MINUTES.
*=CLOSE PRICE ADJUSTED FOR EX-DIVIDEND

STOCK      BID       ASKED
           CLOSE     OPEN      HIGH      LOW       LAST      VOL(100'S)
TXN        122 1/4   123 1/4   123 1/4   118       119       2469


* UPI STOCKCHECK - The Source


Enter Stock/Bond Symbols or Press Return for Previous Menu
TXN
                            Sales
  Date   Time  Symbols  P-E (hds)  High   Low     Close    Chg.
09/18/83 16:35 TXN       *   1332   124   121 5/8 122 1/4  -1
```

daily. Stockcheck is continuously updated and delayed 15 minutes, like Dow Jones Quotes

Neither UPI nor The Source offers statistical manipulation online for stock price data, but The Source does have a portfolio management utility program as part of the Stockvue database (see below).

A typical display of a quote from Stockcheck appears in Figure 7.8 and can be compared with the Dow Jones display for the same issue. Note that Stockcheck includes the time and date.

MicroQuote

Some investors prefer CompuServe's MicroQuote database and computational service over the stock quotation services available from Dow Jones and The Source because of its sophisticated portfolio management and analysis features. MicroQuote gives current high, low and closing prices and trading statistics for more than 32,000 stocks, bonds and options. Historical prices and volumes are available for most issues over the last 10 years.

Dividend history with dates is available back to 1968. Additional information includes earnings per share, ratings and shares outstanding. Bonds show
yield and maturity data, along with Moody's ratings. Options data include
exercise prices, expiration dates and underlying stock prices. MicroQuote
users can search for stocks by ticker symbol or full name of the issuing
company.

Several programs are available online with MicroQuote to manipulate and
display various items and to create reports. There is a program to help
download securities data to your personal computer, and one to create and
analyze your own portfolio. A display of a sample portfolio valuation is
shown in Figure 7.9.

Figure 7.9: A Portfolio Valuation from MicroQuote (CompuServe)

```
               SECURITIES VALUATION   10/13/81

                    PRICE MKT-VAL              %OF
       TICKER  AMT    COST ORI-VAL P/E  %YLD  TOT
       ------------------------------------------
                ---  EQUITY ISSUES  ---
       HRB     400  32.50   13000  11  5.91   19
                    19.25    7700

       IBM     250  55.50   13875   9  6.20   21
                    35.25    8813

       WTHG    100  21.75    2175  11  2.76    3
                    20.00    2000

                --- DEBT ISSUES  ---
       T 85  50000  75.00   37500      5.83   55
                    49.00   24500

                --- OPTIONS  ---
       GE CL   500   2.19    1094              2
       ------------------------------------------

        TOTAL MKT VALUE: $     67,644

        TOTAL ORI VALUE: $     43,013

        GAIN OR LOSS     $     24,631
                          ===========
```

Market Indicators

A part of The Source Business Update database, which was discussed in Chapter 5, is the current Market Indicators feature. This gives the Dow Jones, New York Stock Exchange and Standard & Poor's market indexes, updated several times daily. The opening, high, low, closing and changes for the Dow Jones Closing Averages are available, for example. A partial display is shown in Figure 7.10.

Figure 7.10: Stock Closing Reports from Market Indicators (The Source)

```
MARKET AT 1630 ON MONDAY, SEPT.19

DOW JONES CLOSING AVERAGES

     Stock   Open     High     Low      Close    Change
30 Indus  1227.64  1242.68  1221.24  1233.94   up   8.23
20 Trans   574.23   588.02   571.86   582.84   up  10.11
15 Utils   131.45   132.32   130.64   131.45  off   0.44
65 stock   489.90   469.90   487.04   493.17   up   4.29
Transactions in stocks used in averages:
              Monday          Friday
Indus      7,784,400      7,307,400
Trans      3,048,000      3,349,900
Utils      2,729,200      1,682,000
65 Stock 13,561,600     12,339,300

--MORE--

NEW YORK STOCK EXCHANGE CLOSING INDEXES

Composite         97.09   up 0.92
Industrial       113.05   up 1.10
Transportation    96.69   up 1.80
Utility           48.36   up 0.19
Finance           98.26   up 1.22
    Equivalent to a gain of 35 cents in the average price of an
N.Y.S.E. common share.
    Volume 85,630,000 shares.

--MORE--
```

Corporate Earnings Estimator

Available on Dow Jones is the Corporate Earnings Estimator, from Zacks Investment Research, Inc. This database provides weekly forecasts of earnings per share, arrived at by consensus of about 1000 investment market analysts from more than 60 brokerage houses nationwide. The database is updated weekly and forecasts earnings based on historical data. A typical display for a company is illustrated in Figure 7.11.

Figure 7.11: Earnings per Share Estimates from Corporate Earnings Estimator (DJNRS)

```
IBM
--FISCAL YEAR ENDS   12/84

EARNINGS PER SHARE ESTIMATES
--MEAN    10.59
--HIGH    11.00
--LOW     10.25
NUMBER OF ANALYSTS   28
P/E RATIO (ESTIMATED EPS)   10.04

PAST EARN PR SH ESTIMATES (MEAN)
--WEEK AGO    10.59
--13 WEEKS AGO   10.49
--26 WEEKS AGO   10.39

IBM
--FISCAL YEAR ENDS   12/85

EARNINGS PER SHARE ESTIMATES
--MEAN    12.34
--HIGH    13.00
--LOW     11.80
NUMBER OF ANALYSTS   22
P/E RATIO (ESTIMATED EPS)    8.62

PAST EARN PR SH ESTIMATES (MEAN)
--WEEK AGO    12.34
--13 WEEKS AGO   12.13
```

Media General Database (Stockvue)

Media General Financial Services, Inc. produces an extensive database of corporate financial and stock issue statistics. The complete database is available only on Control Data Corp.'s Business Information Services, a numeric service available on Control Data's private telecommunications network. However, portions of this database are available on Dow Jones News/Retrieval (as Media General Databank) and on The Source (as Stockvue).

Figure 7.12 illustrates typical information on fundamental revenues, earnings per share, dividends, ratios and shareholdings as offered by Dow Jones. Data can be manipulated using special Dow Jones software (see Chapter 10). Stockvue, on The Source, analyzes performance of more than 3200 common stocks traded on the New York, American and OTC exchanges. Stockvue lets you analyze specific stock issues, industry groups, and personal or corporate portfolios. More than 50 categories of data are available for making analytical comparisons. The Media General databases are updated weekly.

ECONOMIC STATISTICS AND FORECASTS

Business people are naturally interested in the state of the economy. There are many sources of statistical data on every facet of the domestic U.S. and international economies. The federal government is the primary source of economic statistics, and both the federal government and private companies produce databases of economic data as historical and projected time series. Forecasting and trend analysis are major applications of historic data, and virtually every numeric database service provides historic time series and forecasts. Some economic databases are available on the popular information utilities and library research services. We'll look at a few of the more heavily used databases.

Money Market Services

Money Market Services, a database from Money Market Services, Inc., is available on Dow Jones. It is a weekly economic survey of forecasts by economists and money market analysts from about 50 leading financial institutions around the U.S. The database is divided into Commentary and Analysis, Median Forecasts of Monetary and Economic Indicators, and bar charts illustrating median forecast distribution. Figure 7.13 shows typical charts of a money market forecast.

Figure 7.12: Stock Performance Data from the Media General Database (DJNRS)

```
NORFOLK SOUTHERN CP                  NORFOLK SOUTHERN CP
-FUNDMNTL DATA- 07/13/84 (710)       -PRICE & VOLUME- 07/13/84(710)

REVENUE              (1)             PRICE CHANGE          (1)
-LAST 12 MOS $3,297 MIL              -LAST TRDNG WK -2.2%
-LAST FISCAL YEAR $3,148 MIL         -LAST 4 WKS 0.0%
-PCT CHANGE LAST QTR 20.3%           -LAST 13 WKS -12.2%
-PCT CHANGE YR TO DATE 20.3%         -LAST 52 WKS -8.6%
EARNGS 12MOS $402.9Q MIL             -YR TO DATE -20.0%
EARNINGS PER SHARE                   CHANGE VS. S & P 500
-LAST 12 MONTHS $6.40                -LAST TRDNG WK 99%
-LAST FISCAL YEAR $5.67              -LAST 4 WKS 99%
-PCT CHANGE LAST QTR 80.2%           -LAST 13 WKS 92%
-PCT CHANGE FY TO DATE 80.2%         -LAST 52 WKS 100%
-PCT CHANGE LAST 12MOS 2.4%          -YR TO DATE 87%
-FIVE YR GROWTH RATE -7.0%

                                     PRICE RANGE           (2)
DIVIDENDS            (2)             -LAST CLOSE $50.50
-CURRENT RATE $3.20                  -52 WEEK HIGH $70.63
-CURRENT RATE YIELD 6.3%             -52 WEEK LOW $50.00
-5 YR GROWTH RATE 5.0%               -5 YEAR HIGH $70.63
-PAYOUT LAST FY 49%                  -5 YEAR LOW $40.25
-PAYOUT LAST 5 YEARS 32%             RELATIVE PRICE
-LAST X-DVD DATE 04-30-84            -P/E RATIO CURRENT 7.9
RATIOS                               -P/E RATIO 5 YR AVG HI 10.7
-PROFIT MARGIN 12.2%                 -P/E RATIO 5 YR AVG LOW 7.3
-RETURN ON COMMON EQUITY 8.5%        -PRICE TO COMMON EQUITY 76%
-RETURN ON TOTAL ASSETS 4.9%         -PRICE TO REV PER SHARE 96%
-REVENUE TO ASSETS 40%               -RELATIVE PRICE INDEX 65%
-DEBT TO EQUITY 23%
-INTEREST COVERAGE 8.5
-CURRENT RATIO 2.1                   PRICE ACTION          (3)
                                     -BETAS UP      NC
                                     -BETAS DOWN      NC
SHAREHOLDINGS        (3)             VOLUME
-MARKET VALUE $3,175 MIL             -THIS WK SHRS 650,000
-LTST SHR OUTSTND 62,875,000         -THIS WK DOLLAR $33,079,000
-INSIDER NET TRADING 0               -THIS WK % SHRS OUTSTND 1.03%
-SHORT INTEREST RATIO 0.8 DYS        -LIQUIDITY RATIO 3,569,000
-FISCAL YEAR ENDS 12 MOS             -ON BALANCE INDEX 33
```

Figure 7.13: Economic Forecast Charts from Money Market Services (DJNRS)

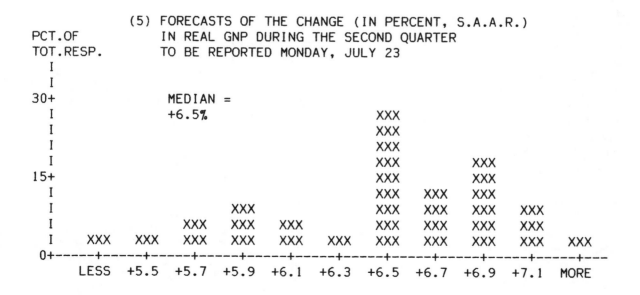

```
                    (1) FORECASTS OF THE CHANGE (IN BLN OF DOL.)
PCT.OF                  IN M1 DURING THE WEEK ENDED JULY 16
TOT.RESP.               TO BE RELEASED THURSDAY, JULY 26
  I                             XXX
  I                             XXX                    MEDIAN =
20+                         XXX XXX                    +$.7 BLN
  I                         XXX XXX XXX
  I                         XXX XXX XXX
  I                         XXX XXX XXX
  I                     XXX XXX XXX XXX
10+                     XXX XXX XXX XXX
  I             XXX XXX XXX XXX XXX XXX
  I             XXX XXX XXX XXX XXX XXX
  I XXX XXX XXX XXX XXX XXX XXX XXX
  I XXX XXX XXX XXX XXX XXX XXX XXX XXX
 0+-----+-----+-----+-----+-----+-----+-----+-----+-----+---
 -1.5  -1.0  -0.5    0   +0.5  +1.0  +1.5  +2.0  +2.5  +3.0
```

```
                    (5) FORECASTS OF THE CHANGE (IN PERCENT, S.A.A.R.)
PCT.OF                  IN REAL GNP DURING THE SECOND QUARTER
TOT.RESP.               TO BE REPORTED MONDAY, JULY 23
  I
  I
30+             MEDIAN =
  I             +6.5%                        XXX
  I                                          XXX
  I                                          XXX
  I                                          XXX         XXX
15+                                          XXX         XXX
  I                                          XXX XXX XXX
  I                     XXX                   XXX XXX XXX XXX
  I                 XXX XXX XXX               XXX XXX XXX XXX
  I     XXX XXX XXX XXX XXX XXX               XXX XXX XXX XXX XXX
 0+-----+-----+-----+-----+-----+-----+-----+-----+-----+-----+---
        LESS +5.5  +5.7  +5.9  +6.1  +6.3  +6.5  +6.7  +6.9  +7.1  MORE
```

Citibase

The Citibank Economics Department produces the Citibase economic database, offering more than 4500 time series of data on industrial and economic indexes and indicators, and consumption and production statistics. Through data gathered from various government and other sources, Citibase monitors the most frequently cited U.S. economic indicators. Citibase data are most often used for econometric forecasting and financial trends analysis.

Categories of economic time series in Citibase include:

- national income and product

- foreign exchange rates

- money supply

- interest rates

- business enterprise and profits

- imports and exports

- manufacturing and trade

- industrial production index

- construction and housing starts

- producer and consumer price indexes

- demographics, employment and earnings

- selected forecasts

Major suppliers of data for Citibase include the Bureau of Economic Analysis *Business Conditions Digest* and *Survey of Current Business*, the Bureau of Labor Statistics (BLS, see below) and the Federal Reserve. Citibase is available on CompuServe and I.P. Sharp/Infomagic, as well as several other timesharing numeric database services. Updating varies among vendors, but new information is compiled daily.

Figure 7.14 shows a time series of gross national product data. A printout of business cycle indicators is displayed in Figure 7.15.

BI/Data and BI/ Data Forecasts

Business International Corp. produces two economic databases. BI/Data provides one of the most extensive available collections of numeric data on the world economy. More than 20,000 annual time series of current and historical data for 135 countries cover:

• national accounts

Figure 7.14: A Time Series of Gross National Product Data from Citibase (Infomagic)

1 JUL 1983

```
                        GROSS NATIONAL PRODUCT
          BILLIONS OF CURRENT DOLLARS AND RATES OF CHANGE
                 SEASONALLY ADJUSTED AT ANNUAL RATES
```

		2ND/82	3RD/82	4TH/82	1ST/83
GNP-	GROSS NATIONAL PRODUCT	3045.2	3088.2	3108.2	3170.6
GC-	PERSONAL CONSUMPTION EXP.	1947.8	1986.3	2030.8	2052.9
GPI-	GROSS PRIV. DOM. INVESTMENT	431.5	443.3	391.5	421.7
GIF-	FIXED INVESTMENT	444.7	438.6	439.9	458.1
GIN-	NONRESIDENTIAL	352.2	344.2	338.4	337.1
GIR-	RESIDENTIAL	95.5	94.3	101.4	121.0
GV-	CHANGE IN BUSINESS INVENTORIES	-16.2	4.7	-48.3	-36.3
GNET-	NET EXPORTS OF GOODS AND SERVICES	34.9	6.9	9.1	19.6
GGE-	GOVERNMENT PURCH. GDS AND SERVICES	630.9	651.7	676.8	676.3

```
          *** PERCENT CHANGE - ANNUAL RATE  ***
```

		2ND/82	3RD/82	4TH/82	1ST/83
GNP-	GROSS NATIONAL PRODUCT	6.8	5.8	2.6	8.3
GC-	PERSONAL CONSUMPTION EXP.	6.1	8.1	9.3	4.4
GPI-	GROSS PRIV. DOM. INVESTMENT	17.1	11.4	-39.2	34.6
GIF-	FIXED INVESTMENT	-2.4	-7.9	-6.6	-1.5
GIN-	NONRESIDENTIAL	-5.3	-8.8	-6.6	-1.5
GIR-	RESIDENTIAL	9.3	-4.9	33.7	102.8
GGE-	GOVERNMENT PURCH. GDS AND SERVICES	0.5	13.9	16.3	-0.3

SOURCE: CITIBASE

Figure 7.15: Business and Economic Indicators from Citibase (Infomagic)

```
15 JUL 1983                    BUSINESS CYCLE INDICATORS
                            1967=100 - SEASONALLY ADJUSTED
------------------------------------------------------------------------

                                              MAR/83 APR/83 MAY/83 JUN/83
------------------------------------------------------------------------

DLEAD -COMPOSITE INDEX OF LEADING INDICATORS-910   150.5  152.6  154.5
DCOINC-COMPOSITE INDEX OF COINCIDENT INDICATORS-910 134.6 135.8  137.3
DLAGG -COMPOSITE INDEX OF LAGGING INDICATORS-930   113.6  112.6  110.6
DRATE -RATIO - COINCIDENT TO LAGGING INDEX-940     118.5  120.6  124.1

COMPONENTS OF LEADING INDEX :
LPHRM -AVG WORKWEEK PRODUCTION WORKERS/MFG (HRS)-1  39.5   40.1   39.9   40.1
LUINC -AVG WEEKLY INITIAL CLAIMS FOR UNEMPLOYMENT
          /STATE INSURANCE PROGRAMS(000)-5         479.0  470.0  453.0
MOCM72-VALUE OF MFGS' NEW ORDERS FOR CONSUMER GDS
          AND MATERIALS (BIL 72$)-8                 31.8   32.2   33.7
FSPCOM-STOCK PRICE INDEX(1941-43=10-NSA)-19        151.9  157.7  164.1  166.4
MPCON2-CONTRACTS/ORDERS FOR PLANT/EQUIP(BIL 72$)-20 12.7   13.8   13.9
HSBP  -NEW PRIVATE HOUSING AUTHORIZED (1967=100)-29 118.5 124.1  132.1
IVPAC -VENDOR PERFORMANCE-PCT COMPANIES REPORTING
          SLOWER DELIVERIES (NSA)-32               50.0   52.0   52.0
PSMC99-CHANGE IN SENSITIVE MATERIALS PRICE-99       2.1    0.1    0.9
SBCUC-CHANGE IN CREDIT OUTSTANDING-
          BUSINESS AND CONSUMER BORROWING-111      -1.4   -0.6   -1.7
BUS   -NET BUSINESS FORMATION - BCD12              112.7  111.2  114.9
IVMUT2-NET CHANGE IN INVENTORIES ON HAND/ON
          ORDER/72$(SMOOTHED)-36                   -9.4   -4.7
FM2D72-M2--MONEY SUPPLY (BIL 72$ SA)-106          883.4  880.5  885.1

           *** MONTH TO MONTH PERCENT CHANGE ***

DLEAD -COMPOSITE INDEX OF LEADING INDICATORS-910    2.0    1.4    1.2
DCOINC-COMPOSITE INDEX OF COINCIDENT INDICATORS-910 0.8    0.9    1.1
DLAGG -COMPOSITE INDEX OF LAGGING INDICATORS-930   -1.1   -0.9   -1.8

COMPONENTS OF LEADING INDEX :
LPHRM -AVG WORKWEEK PRODUCTION WORKERS/MFG (HRS)-1  0.8    1.5   -0.5    0.5
LUINC -AVG WEEKLY INITIAL CLAIMS FOR UNEMPLOYMENT
          /STATE INSURANCE PROGRAMS(000)-5          0.2   -1.9   -3.6
MOCM72-VALUE OF MFGS' NEW ORDERS FOR CONSUMER GDS
          AND MATERIALS (BIL 72$)-8                 1.2    1.0    4.7
FSPCOM-STOCK PRICE INDEX(1941-43=10-NSA)-19         3.5    3.8    4.1    1.4
MPCON2-CONTRACTS/ORDERS FOR PLANT/EQUIP(BIL 72$)-20 10.5   9.3    0.2
HSBP  -NEW PRIVATE HOUSING AUTHORIZED (1967=100)-29 -0.8   4.7    6.4
FM2D72-M2--MONEY SUPPLY (BIL 72$ SA)-106           0.8   -0.3    0.5
------------------------------------------------------------------------
SOURCE: CITIBASE AND BUSINESS CONDITIONS DIGEST
```

- balance of payments

- demographics

- industrial production

- labor force

- wages

- foreign trade

- production and consumption

- price indexes

BI/Data Forecasts gives macroeconomic forecasts for 35 countries.

Data are obtained from the United Nations, the Organization for Economic Cooperation and Development (OECD), the International Labor Organization (ILO), the International Monetary Fund (IMF) and the World Bank and are updated quarterly. BI/Data and BI/Data Forecasts are available through Dialog and I.P. Sharp. Part of the narrative summary and the numeric record of a forecast are shown in Figure 7.16.

PTS Forecasts and Time Series

Predicasts, Inc., publishes databases of economic time series as well as PTS Annual Reports Abstracts (see Chapter 6) and PTS Promt (see Chapter 8). The economic forecast databases are compiled by Predicasts economists and are published in print as *Predicasts* and *Worldcasts*.

Numeric data are available on both BRS and Dialog, as two separate databases, PTS Forecasts and PTS Time Series. These are massive files, containing more than 650,000 statistical summaries including:

- 450,000 projections, from published data (PTS Forecasts)

- 150,000 annual historical time series dating from 1957 (PTS Time Series)

- 60,000 U.S. Census of Manufacturers series (PTS Time Series)

Figure 7.16: Part of the Text and Numeric Records from a BI/Data Forecasts Report (Dialog)

```
01234567
BI/DATA FORECAST REPORT

JAPAN,  MAY 14, 1984
                              PART I
```

JAPAN SHOULD CONTINUE TO REGISTER AMONG THE HIGHEST REAL ECONOMIC GROWTH
RATES IN THE OECD ON AVERAGE DURING THE NEXT FIVE YEARS. THE PACE OF
ECONOMIC GROWTH SHOULD ACCELERATE TO AN AVERAGE RATE OF 4% DURING 1984
AND 1985 DUE TO AN UPSWING IN THE US AND OTHER MAJOR MARKETS, AN
IMPROVEMENT IN PRIVATE CONSUMER AND CAPITAL SPENDING, AND THE POSITIVE
EFFECTS OF CRUDE OIL PRICE REDUCTIONS AND LIQUIDATION. AN EXPECTED
DOWNTURN IN MAJOR WORLD ECONOMIES PROBABLY WILL CONTRIBUTE TO A FALLOFF
IN GROWTH RATES IN 1986-87.

GOVERNMENT POLICIES WILL CENTER ON REVAMPING THE NATION'S ADMINISTRATIVE,
INDUSTRIAL, AND FISCAL STRUCTURE, AND MOVING GRADUALLY TOWARD A MORE
ACTIVE AND INDEPENDENT FOREIGN AFFAIRS AND DEFENSE ROLE -- PARTICULARLY
IN ASIA. DESPITE THE RULING LIBERAL DEMOCRATIC PARTY'S (LDP) LOSS OF AN
ABSOLUTE MAJORITY IN THE LOWER HOUSE, RESULTING IN A COALITION WITH THE
SPLINTER NEW LIBERAL CLUB, BASIC POLICIES AND THE PRO-BUSINESS LDP'S
LEADERSHIP ROLE SHOULD REMAIN INTACT. HOWEVER, NEW LDP-LED COALITIONS
          .
          .
          .
JAPANESE OFFICIALS WILL ATTEMPT TO ACCELERATE THE REDUCTION OF TARIFF AND
NONTARIFF BARRIERS AND REGULARIZE MECHANISMS FOR MEDIATING TRADE DISPUTES.

THE GRADUAL EASING OF THE LARGELY INFORMAL RESTRICTIONS ON FOREIGN
INVESTMENT WILL INCREASE OPPORTUNITIES FOR FOREIGN FIRMS TO FORM JOINT
VENTURES AND WHOLLY-OWNED SUBSIDIARIES, EXPAND EXISTING OPERATIONS, OR
ACQUIRE LOCAL COMPANIES. COMPANIES SHOULD FIND A BROADER RANGE OF
FINANCING SOURCES AS JAPAN GRADUALLY EASES FINANCIAL RESTRICTIONS AND
INTERNATIONALIZES THE YEN. HOWEVER, FINANCIAL OFFICIALS WILL REMAIN
RELUCTANT TO PERMIT FULL LIBERALIZATION AND THUS RISK LOSING CONTROL OVER
THE FINANCIAL SYSTEM.

PROSPECTS FOR HEALTHY TRADE AND PAYMENTS SURPLUSES, RELATIVELY LOW
INFLATION, AND GENERALLY SOLID OVERALL ECONOMIC FUNDAMENTALS SHOULD
CONTRIBUTE TO A STRONG YEN DURING MOST OF THE FORECAST PERIOD --
AVERAGING IN THE NEIGHBORHOOD OF Y210:US$1. HOWEVER, FLUCTUATIONS WILL
OCCUR IN RESPONSE TO US INTEREST RATE CHANGES AND INTERNATIONAL POLITICAL
UNCERTAINTIES.
```
```

Figure 7.16: Part of the Text and Numeric Records from a BI/Data Forecasts Report (Dialog) (cont.)

```
                                    PART II
                              JAPAN, MAY 14, 1984

EXPENDITURE ON THE GDP
----------------------
TRILLIONS OF YEN                CURRENT PRICES              % CHANGE

                        1983      1984      1985      1983    1984    1985
                      --------  --------  --------   ------  ------  ------
NATIONAL INCOME         234.5     254.0     276.0      3.5     8.3     8.7
GROSS DOMESTIC PRODUCT  274.5     297.0     323.0      3.7     8.2     8.8
PRIVATE CONSUMPTION     163.0     175.0     191.0      4.9     7.4     9.1
GOVERNMENT CONSUMPTION   28.0      30.0      32.0      4.1     7.1     6.7
TRADE, PRODUCTION AND PRICES
----------------------------
TRILLIONS OF YEN                CURRENT PRICES              % CHANGE

                        1983      1984      1985      1983    1984    1985
                      --------  --------  --------   ------  ------  ------
EXPORTS OF GOODS         34.9      40.0      44.0      1.4    14.6    10.0
IMPORTS OF GOODS         30.0      33.5      36.5     -8.1    11.6     9.0
BALANCE OF TRADE          4.9       6.5       7.5

                                   1980=100                  % CHANGE

CONSUMER PRICES (AVG.)  109.7     113.0     119.0      1.9     3.0     5.3
INDUSTRIAL PRODUCTION   104.9     112.0     115.0      3.6     6.8     2.7

YEAR-END PRIME RATE       5.5       5.5       6.0
EXCHANGE RATE AVG.     237.52    231.30 *


MEDIUM TERM FORECAST
--------------------
                                                             % CHANGE

                        1986      1987      1988      1986    1987    1988
                      --------  --------  --------   ------  ------  ------
GROSS DOMESTIC PRODUCT  346.0     364.0     395.0      7.1     5.2     8.5
REAL GDP                234.0     242.0     252.0      2.6     3.4     4.1
CONSUMER PRICES         124.0     127.0     132.0      4.2     2.4     3.9
INDUSTRIAL PRODUCTION   115.0     120.0     128.0      0.0     4.3     6.7
```

- 3000 historical and projected time series for major economic indicators (PTS Time Series)

PTS Forecasts records are drawn from published forecasts in trade journals, business, financial and other publications and include bibliographic citations. They are updated monthly. The time series data come from the U.N., IMF, OECD, the European Economic Community (EEC), the Food and Agricultural Organization (FAO) and other sources. They are updated quarterly. A composite time series and forecast record is displayed in Figure 7.17.

Bureau of Labor Statistics Databases

Dialog provides four statistical databases supplied by the U.S. Department of Labor Bureau of Labor Statistics (BLS) in various publications:

Figure 7.17: An Economic Time Series and Forecast from PTS Time Series (Dialog)

```
247066  Predicasts  08/09/23  (MEX821)  Mexico
  Automobiles per 000 capita.  Equipment Use.
            YEAR
            1960      13.21
            1961      14.57
            1962      14.79
            1963      15.31
            1964      16.68
            1965      17.83
            1966      18.40
            1967      20.08
            1968      21.16
            1969      23.16
            1970      24.53
            1971      25.51
            1972      28.01
            1973      28.74
            1974      33.52
            1975      39.92
            1976      42.37
            1977      42.96
            1978      44.97
            1979      46.84
            1980      48.75
            1985      60.28
            1990      73.66
            1995      86.16

        GROWTH RATE= 4.2%
        cc=3MEX    PC=3700000    EC=442
```

- BLS Consumer Price Index (see Figure 7.18)

- BLS Producer Price Index

- BLS Employment, Hours and Earnings (see Figure 7.19)

- BLS Labor Force

The time series in these databases are numeric only and do not contain

Figure 7.18: A Consumer Price Index from BLS Consumer Price Index (Dialog)

```
0114417
CWU51040080103    CONSUMER  PRICE  INDEX FOR URBAN WAGE EARNERS AND CLERICAL
WORKERS SUBFILE
ALL ITEMS LESS MEDICAL CARE;
WEST;
UNADJUSTED DATA

YEAR                    INDEX(DECEMBER 1977=100)

1984  JAN    NA         FEB    162.3       MAR    NA
      APR    162.9
1983  JAN    NA         FEB    155.9       MAR    NA
      APR    156.8      MAY    NA          JUN    158.0
      JUL    NA         AUG    159.3       SEP    NA
      OCT    161.1      NOV    NA          DEC    161.7
1982  JAN    NA         FEB    156.6       MAR    NA
      APR    157.3      MAY    NA          JUN    158.8
      JUL    NA         AUG    159.1       SEP    NA
      OCT    158.9      NOV    NA          DEC    156.1
1981  JAN    NA         FEB    143.4       MAR    NA
      APR    146.0      MAY    NA          JUN    148.0
      JUL    NA         AUG    151.3       SEP    NA
      OCT    155.0      NOV    NA          DEC    154.8
1980  JAN    NA         FEB    130.0       MAR    NA
      APR    133.5      MAY    NA          JUN    136.3
      JUL    NA         AUG    136.2       SEP    NA
      OCT    138.5      NOV    NA          DEC    141.3
1979  JAN    NA         FEB    111.0       MAR    NA
      APR    114.2      MAY    NA          JUN    117.2
      JUL    NA         AUG    119.9       SEP    NA
      OCT    122.4      NOV    NA          DEC    125.5
1978  JAN    NA         FEB    101.3       MAR    NA
      APR    102.9      MAY    NA          JUN    105.3
      JUL    NA         AUG    106.5       SEP    NA
      OCT    108.3      NOV    NA          DEC    108.4
1977  JAN    NA         FEB    NA          MAR    NA
      APR    NA         MAY    NA          JUN    NA
      JUL    NA         AUG    NA          SEP    NA
      OCT    NA         NOV    NA          DEC    100.0

SOURCE: U.S. BUREAU OF LABOR STATISTICS    DIALOG FILE 175
DATES AVAILABLE:(DEC. 1977-APR. 1984)
```

citations to their original printed publication from BLS, or narrative summaries or abstracts. These data series, especially the consumer and producer price indexes, are also available in other economic databases produced by various timesharing numeric services. They are updated monthly.

U.S. Exports Database

Dialog also provides a database, called U.S. Exports, from Census Bureau copies of shippers export declarations data. This file contains about 300,000 time series of statistics on exports from the U.S. to other nations. The file is entirely numeric, without narrative abstracts or summaries, and is updated annually. A typical time series is illustrated in Figure 7.20.

U.S. Economic Database

ADP Network Services produces the U.S. Economic database (USECON) of more than 20,000 time series of data from several government agencies and private sources, including BLS, the Bureau of Economic Analysis,

Figure 7.19: A Quarterly Time Series from BLS Employment, Hours and Earnings (Dialog)

```
0200560
SAU4266803999155   STATE AND AREA EMPLOYMENT, HOURS, AND EARNINGS SUBFILE
AVERAGE WEEKLY HOURS OF PRODUCTION WORKERS
OTHER DURABLE GOODS
DIV. OF INDUSTRY: MANUFACTURING, DURABLE GOODS
READING PA
UNADJUSTED DATA

                    HOURS
```

YEARS	Q1	Q2	Q3	Q4
1981	38.6	38.6	38.6	39.1
1980	39.0	39.2	38.7	39.3
1979	39.1	40.5	39.2	40.6
1978	36.5	39.1	39.1	39.8
1977	39.3	39.6	38.6	38.7
1976	39.7	40.1	41.1	40.2
1975	39.6	40.6	40.5	41.0

```
SOURCE: U.S. BUREAU OF LABOR STATISTICS      DIALOG FILE 178
DATES AVAILABLE:(JAN. 1972-DEC. 1981)
```

Figure 7.20: A Time Series from U.S. Exports (Dialog)

```
0000177
TURKEYS, LIVE,  IN THE DOWNY STAGE (BC=1000260)
U.S. Exports: All Countries (CC=000)

   Year       Quantity in NO    Value in $

   1980       34,148,956        44,683,355
   1979       30,423,931        38,293,632
   1978       32,855,402        33,182,618

Source: U.S. Bureau of the Census   DIALOG File 126
```

Federal Reserve Board, the Census Bureau, Moody's Investors Service, Standard & Poor's, Townsend-Greenspan & Co., Inc., the U.S. Department of the Treasury and *The Wall Street Journal.* A wide range of economic data, from bank reserves to wholesale inventories and sales, is available and is updated daily.

USECON users pay a monthly subscription fee of $200 to ADP. As with most statistical databases, information on USECON can be output to graphics printers and plotters as line, bar and pie charts, or graphs. Multicolored, presentation quality charts may be created with color pen plotters. Color charts and graphs can also be displayed on a color monitor or a graphics printer on your personal computer system, after downloading data into a spreadsheet program (see Chapter 10).

SUMMARY

Numeric databases are one of the largest categories of online information. Databases of statistics on the economy and financial data are the most numerous, and securities price quotation services are probably the most widely used. Many online numeric services also provide computational programs to manipulate and analyze the information online.

If your computational needs are not complex or if you wish to avoid online charges, a number of software packages are available that permit download-ing of numeric data and manipulating it offline for applications like portfolio management and analysis.

In Chapter 8, we will look at the largest category of non-numeric databases, the bibliographic databases offered by library research services.

8

Library Research at Your Desk

In terms of sheer volume of online information, the library research, or bibliographic, services have no equal. As noted in Chapter 4, Dialog Information Services, Inc. is the world's largest vendor of online information in numbers of characters, or bytes, stored for access online. Most of Dialog's approximately 200 databases are bibliographic and represent close to 100 million references to articles from about 60,000 journals and other publications over the past decade. These include publications in more than 40 languages, from every country in the world (with references supplemented by abstracts or summaries in English). Most of this volume of information is current to within one to two months.

The other library research services duplicate Dialog to some extent and also supplement Dialog's databases with others. Dialog and the other bibliographic vendors are currently adding full-text, directory, and business and financial databases to their offerings.

This massive amount of online information means that you can have nearly the equivalent of the world's major business and technical research libraries as close as the telephone and computer sitting on your desktop. You can research virtually any topic within minutes; truly exhaustive research might take several hours of online time.

The major customers of the bibliographic services are technical research libraries and information centers of "Fortune 500" corporations, government agencies and academic institutions. While these organizations will continue to be the major source of revenue, there is a vast market of business end users of personal computers developing. As discussed in Chapter 4, some of the library research vendors are working to tap this market by creating easier-to-use subsets of their primary services. Examples include BRS/After Dark and Dialog's Knowledge Index. In addition, some vendors, database producers and independent software companies offer microcomputer-based interface communications and search software that simplify the use of the library research services (see Chapter 10).

SOPHISTICATED SEARCH AND RETRIEVAL

The vast number, diversity and size of bibliographic and reference databases offered by library research services make it essential that there be ways to ensure precise retrieval of items on the desired topic. A single word like "apple" entered as a search keyword will retrieve all references to Apple computers and Apple Computer Inc. and, depending on the database, may also retrieve items about fruit, insects, "apples and oranges" comparisons, orchard farming and more.

To prevent retrieval of large numbers of non-relevant records, especially when working with databases of more than a million records, the online service vendors have developed extremely powerful and sophisticated retrieval methods. All bibliographic and reference databases are searched using carefully constructed search strategies, keyword phrases in which individual keywords are combined with logical and positional "operators." These operators indicate whether the keywords occur in the same sentence, title, paragraph, field or entire record, and whether they occur next to each other or in some other relation.

It is common in using the large technical databases to deal with requests like: "Find any patents issued or applied for in the last year in West Germany or the United States describing the manufacture or production of derivatives of amitriptyline or related tricyclic antidepressant drugs." Chemical names, formulas, Chemical Abstract Service registry numbers, country names and codes, event names and codes (manufacture or production), and date ranges all figure into this search. The actual form for the search request above, to be entered into CA Search on SDC Orbit, might look something like this: (/rn 50-49-7 or 50-48-6 or 50-47-5) (1) deriv and (manuf or prodn) and (/pc ger. or ger. offen. or us) and (84-84).

It can take considerable knowledge of both subject matter and information retrieval techniques, as well as experience, to manipulate a database effectively and efficiently to extract the desired information. The average business person may find that learning the skills required is beyond what he or she is willing to invest in order to utilize these services.

However, the range of information available on the library research services is so great that, once you are introduced to them, you will be tempted to take advantage of them. Whether you search them yourself, have someone else in your office do the searching, or use the services of a library or information broker, you will find that having the world's libraries electronically available at your fingertips can provide much information valuable to your major business decisions.

CURRENT AWARENESS AND DOCUMENT DELIVERY SERVICES

Library research services offer two other services that can be especially helpful to the business user.

All of the library research vendors provide automatic alerting, or current awareness, services, formally known as selective dissemination of information (SDI). Your search "profile" is automatically matched against weekly or monthly database updates, and you are automatically notified of any new records matching the profile. There are nominal fees for SDI service, which allows you to keep abreast of any new developments in your fields of interest. SDI current awareness is available for most of the bibliographic databases discussed in this and earlier chapters. NewsNet's NewsFlash service (Chapter 5) permits similar updating on its full-text newsletter databases.

In addition, full-text hard (paper) copy of many records is available through document delivery services, provided by information brokers such as Information on Demand. Other information brokers are listed in Appendix C. You can place orders through Dialog and SDC Orbit for hard copy to be delivered to you through the mail.

SELECTED BIBLIOGRAPHIC AND REFERENCE DATABASES

There are almost 250 bibliographic and reference databases on five major commercial online vendor services Bibliographic Retrieval Services (BRS), Dialog, SDC Orbit Search Service, Pergamon InfoLine and Medlars (National Library of Medicine). The first three are of greatest interest to the average business executive, so this chapter will concentrate on them. For details on databases not covered here, refer to the service vendors listed in Appendix C or to one of the database directories listed in Appendix B.

The databases we will survey are in three categories:

• bibliographic databases in business, industry, law and government

• bibliographic databases in science and technology

• reference databases on general and special topics

BIBLIOGRAPHIC DATABASES IN BUSINESS, INDUSTRY, LAW AND GOVERNMENT

The 13 databases listed in Table 8.1 cover a wide range of topics in business management, trade and industry activity, legal issues and government activity.

ABI/Inform

ABI/Inform (Abstracted Business Information) indexes and abstracts selected articles from more than 500 journals on management and administration and includes more than 200,000 records from August 1971 to date. This database is updated monthly and is available on BRS, Dialog and SDC Orbit. ABI/Inform is produced by Data Courier, Inc., a subsidiary of the *Louisville* (KY) *Times Courier*. A sample record is shown in Figure 8.1.

Accountants Index

The Accountants Index database is produced by the American Institute of Certified Public Accountants and corresponds to a printed index of the same name. Accountants Index indexes articles from more than 300 English-language publications covering all aspects of accounting, financial reporting, auditing, taxation, investments and securities, and related business areas. It contains more than 125,000 records from 1974 and is updated quarterly. This database is available on SDC Orbit.

Adtrack

Adtrack database, from Corporate Intelligence, Inc., indexes all advertisements of ¼-page or larger that have appeared in more than 150 U.S. consumer magazines since October 1980. Ads may be retrieved by company name, product or service name, and the contents and characteristics (e.g., size, color or black-and-white) of the ad. The ads in Adtrack represent over 98% of consumer magazine advertising revenues in the categories of airline inflight, automotive, business, family, entertainment, men's, women's and several special interest magazines. Figure 8.2. shows three Adtrack records. Adtrack is available on Dialog.

Arthur D. Little/Online

The consulting firm of Arthur D. Little, Inc. is known for its Industry Outlook Reports, Marketing Index Reports, Management Reports, and other reports and newsletters. Topics such as industry and economic

Table 8.1: Selected Bibliographic Databases Indexing Publications and Other Documents Covering Business, Industry, Law and Government

Database Title Publisher	Topics Covered	Publications Covered	Approximate Number of Records per Update	Online Service Vendors
ABI/Inform Data Courier, Inc.	Business management and administration	Journals and other	1900 monthly	BRS* Dialog† SDC Orbit
Accountants Index American Institute of Certified Public Accountants	Accounting, finance, securities, taxation	Journals, books	3000 quarterly	SDC Orbit
Adtrack Corporate Intelligence, Inc.	Advertisements in consumer magazines	Magazines	13,000 monthly	Dialog
Arthur D. Little/Online Arthur D. Little, Inc.	Non-exclusive reports on research, outlooks	Arthur D. Little publications	10 monthly	Dialog
The Computer Database Management Contents, Inc.	Electronic data processing	Magazines, journals	3000 biweekly	Dialog†
Congressional Record Abstracts Capitol Services, Inc.	Congressional bills, resolutions, reports, etc.	*Congressional Record*	1000 weekly	Dialog SDC Orbit
Federal Register Abstracts Capitol Services, Inc.	Federal rules, regulations, hearings, etc.	*Federal Register*	700 weekly	Dialog SDC Orbit
Harvard Business Review Online John Wiley & Sons, Inc.	Strategic management information	*Harvard Business Review*	Latest articles bimonthly	BRS* Dialog
Industry Data Sources Information Access Co.	Marketing and financial information on 65 major industries	Multiple sources	2000 monthly	BRS Dialog
Legal Resources Index Information Access Co.	Law and law-related literature	Law journals	3000 monthly	Dialog†
Management Contents Management Contents, Inc.	Business management and administration	Journals and other	2000 monthly	BRS* Dialog SDC Orbit
PTS Defense Markets & Technology Predicasts, Inc.	Defense industry	Defense journals	2000 monthly	BRS Dialog
PTS PROMT Predicasts, Inc.	Products and services markets	Journals and other	3000 monthly	BRS Dialog

*Available on BRS/After Dark.
†Available on Knowledge Index.

Figure 8.1: A Record from ABI/Inform (Dialog)

```
84011311
Keys to Success
  Dyson, Esther
  ICP  Business  Software  Review  v3n1  PP:  58-61  Feb/Mar 1984  ISSN:
0744-2602  JRNL CODE: ISB
    DOC TYPE: Journal Paper  LANGUAGE: English  LENGTH: 3 Pages
    AVAILABILITY: ABI/INFORM
  A number of companies,  both public and private,  illustrate or  lead  an
important trend of 1984 and beyond.   One of these is Apple Computer Corp.,
producer of the newly introduced Macintosh computer and the newly  enhanced
Lisa.   Although the firm will likely realize low earnings in 1984,  Apple's
position in 1985 will be strong.   The  firm  needs  to  bring  independent
software vendors (ISV) on board,  but this will be difficult because of the
constricting Macintosh/Lisa development environment.    Dun  &  Bradstreet
(D&B)   offers DunsPlus,  a system made up of components from International
Business Machines Corp.   (IBM),  Softword,  and Lotus  Development.   The
system  gives  the  user  a  personal  computer  able  to  address  outside
databases.   Federal Express plans to offer a faster  way  of  transmitting
information   through  a nationwide document facsimile transmission service.
Menlo Corp.'s In-Search enables people to get information out of Dialog,  a
subsidiary   of   Lockheed   that  offers  200  databases  to  about  50,000
subscribers.  Table.  Graph.
    DESCRIPTORS:  Product  development;   Software;   Vendors;   Information;
Services; Computer industry; Information retrieval; Online (DP); Data bases
; Trends; Stock prices; Manycompanies
    CLASSIFICATION  CODES:   8651  (CN=Computer industry);  8300  (CN=Service
industries  not  elsewhere  classified);   7500   (CN=Product  planning  &
development)
```

---

forecasts and market research, which are covered in its publications, are indexed and abstracted in Arthur D. Little/Online, available on Dialog. The full text of the executive summaries of these reports is also available. The database covers all reports from January 1983 to date—more than 400 records. The record of a research report is illustrated in Figure 8.3.

The Computer Database

Management Contents, Inc., producer of the Management Contents database (see below) also publishes the Computer Database, an index with

Figure 8.2: Records Referencing Magazine Advertisements from Adtrack (Dialog)

```
358793
TOYOTA
VAN WAGON, 1984 VAN
LIFE,    8312,   ISSN 0024-3019
12/83    Page: 22    1 Page
FULL COLOR
PRESENTED AS NEW
VAN TRUCKS EX CAMPERS .(37112372)


358781
TOYOTA
TERCEL WAGON, 1984 CAR
BUSINESS WEEK,   8312,   ISSN 0007-7135
12/05/83    Page: 3C    1 Page
FULL COLOR
AUTOMOBILES .(37111119)


354499
TOYOTA MOTOR SALES USA
COROLLA, 1984 CAR
PEOPLE,   8311,   ISSN 0093-7673
11/07/83    Page: 2C    4 Page
BLACK & WHITE AND COLOR IN MULTI-PAGE AD
GATEFOLD; NEW OR IMPROVED
AUTOMOBILES .(37111119)
```

abstracts to articles in more than 500 magazines and journals as well as numerous other publications, including books. The Computer Database covers all topics relating to the computer and data processing industries, including telecommunications and related electronics industries. Coverage is from 1983, and the database contains more than 75,000 records, with about 3000 new records added every two weeks. This database is on Dialog; a typical record is shown in Figure 8.4.

Congressional Record Abstracts and Federal Register Abstracts

Capitol Services, Inc., publishes two printed publications, *Congressional Record Abstracts* and *Federal Register Abstracts,* and produces two

Figure 8.3: A Record of a Research Report from Arthur D. Little/Online (Dialog)

```
1000055      CN=MN00006
World Markets for Information Processing Products to 1993
Withington, Ted; Rothenbuecher, Oscar
PUBLISHER: Arthur D. Little Decision Resources
AVAILABILITY: Arthur D. Little Decision Resources, Dept. V,  17 Acorn Park,
Cambridge, MA 02140, Tel: (617) 864-5770 x 4461
DOCUMENT TYPE: Meeting Notice


        In this series of meetings,  Ted Withington,  Vice  President  of
Arthur  D.  Little, Inc.,  and Oscar Rothenbuecher,  senior member of the
Information Systems Section, will update and expand their 20-year series of
industry studies.   They will assess the phases of market maturity in 1983,
1988, and 1993, as well as forecast order-of-magnitude regional revenues in
the  United  States,  Europe,  and  Japan,  for  general-purpose  and
special-purpose  computers,  plug-compatible  computers,  small  business
systems, desktop computers,  terminals and word processors,  software,  and
peripherals.   They will also identify key trends in each equipment market,
and  will  evaluate  the  strategic  positions  of the 20 leading companies
worldwide by product class and technology.  In addition,  the study authors
will   prepare   a   special   section   focusing   on  advanced  computers:
supercomputers,  fifth-generation computers,  and  expert  systems.   For
registration information, refer to the availabilty field above.

DESCRIPTORS: Computers;  Computer software;  Personal computers;  Markets;
Corporate strategy; Artificial intelligence

Copr. Arthur D. Little, Inc. 1983
```

corresponding databases by the same names. Congressional Record Abstracts covers congressional bills from January 1981. Federal Register Abstracts covers federal government activities from September 1977. The databases together contain over 250,000 records, about evenly split; both are updated weekly. These databases are available on Dialog and SDC Orbit; a record of discussion on a Senate bill from Congressional Record Abstracts is shown in Figure 8.5.

Harvard Business Review Online

One of the most respected journals on strategic business management and

Figure 8.4: A Record of an Article from the Computer Database (Dialog)

```
153772    CRW84D0946
  MicroPro Begins Shipments of $195 Spelling-Checker Package.
  Anon
  Computer Retail News  April 9, 1984, P. 46.
  Country of Publication: U.S.A.    Language: English
  ISSN: 0744-673X
  Document Type: Tabloid    Article Type: Product Announcement
  MicroPro  International Corp.  has begun the shipment of CorrectStar,  a
spelling-checker product,  which it developed jointly with Houghton-Mifflin
Co. of Boston.  The new product runs under the PC-DOS on the IBM PC and the
XT.  A new release for machines that run under  MS-DOS  will  be  out  next
month.   The  product has 65,000 entries and covers ninety-nine per cent of
the most commonly misspelled words in the English language.  It  sells  for
$195.
  Product  Name:   CorrectStar,  ,  MicroPro Int'l Corp.,  Word Processing
Software
  Descriptors: Spelling Verification; Dictionaries;  Word Processing;  New
Product; Software; Microcomputers
```

Figure 8.5: Reference to a Senate Discussion from Congressional Record Abstracts (Dialog)

```
  173251
  *  S.  2691 C.LEVIN (GRASSLEY),  deduction for additions to reserves for
beverage container deposit  refunds;   C/Finance;   stmt,  text  S6054  re
reversing  IRS  ruling  that  deposits  are  taxable  income when received;
GRASSLEY stmt S6055.
  Source: 98-066   Page  S6054
  MAY 18, 1984
  Subfile: SENATE PROCEEDINGS
  Descriptors: ENVIRONMENT-RECYCLING .(2617);  TAXES-BUSINESS &  CORPORATE
.(4506)
  NEW BILL
```

administration is the *Harvard Business Review*. The publisher, John Wiley & Sons, Inc., now produces this journal as a full-text database—Harvard Business Review Online (HBRO)—and distributes it via BRS and Dialog. The complete text plus abstract for every article is available from 1976 to date; abstracts and indexing are available back to 1971, along with selected earlier articles. HBRO contains over 2100 articles and is updated every two months.

Industry Data Sources

Industry Data Sources, formerly from HARFAX Database Publishing, is now produced by Information Access Co. (IAC). It provides access to extensive information on 65 major industries from a wide variety of publications. Source publications include reports on market research, statistics, finance and the economy, as well as forecasts, trade journals, newsletters, dissertations, conference papers and other bibliographic databases. Industry Data Sources contains more than 50,000 records from 1979 to date and is updated monthly with about 2000 new records. Search and retrieval data include SIC codes. The database is available on BRS and Dialog. A sample record appears in Figure 8.6.

Legal Resources Index

Legal Resources Index is another one of the family of databases produced by Information Access Co. (Others are discussed in Chapter 5.) Legal Resources Index (LRI) indexes more than 700 law journals and newspapers completely and indexes selectively from other publications. LRI covers the years 1980 to date and is updated monthly with about 3000 records. The record in Figure 8.7 is shown as it appears on Dialog.

Management Contents

The Management Contents (MC) database is published by Management Contents, Inc. MC contains indexes and abstracts for more than 150,000 articles on business management and administration from more than 500 English-language journals and other publications. The period covered is from September 1974 to the present. MC is updated monthly with about 2000 new records. MC and ABI/Inform are similar; they overlap about 50% in coverage. MC tends to have more concise abstracts. This file is available on BRS, Dialog and SDC Orbit. (A subset of this database is available on The Source as Management Contents, Ltd., as noted in Chapter 4.)

Figure 8.6: A Record from Industry Data Sources (Dialog)

```
073496     CN=84-004878
Paine Webber Mitchell Hutchins Inc.: Status Report: 1983 Winter Comdex.
Isgur, Barbara S.
December 27, 1983  Irregularly  3 pg.
PUBLISHER: Paine Webber Mitchell Hutchins, Inc. 140 Broadway, 25th Fl.  New
York NY 10005
United States of America
TELEPHONE: (212)437-2121
DOCUMENT TYPE: Directory, Investment Report (dire, invt)
RECORD STATUS: Primary Source
LANGUAGE: English
GEOGRAPHIC COVERAGE: United States of America (usa)

     Reports on new microcomputer technology exhibited at the  1983  Winter
Comdex  Show  in  Las  Vegas.   Table compares features of the IBM personal
computer and IBM compatible transportable computers. Indicates stock prices
of companies mentioned.

DATA DESCRIPTORS: New Technology, 1983; New Products, 1983;  Manufacturers,
1983; Technical Specifications, 1983; Prices, 1983; Stock Prices, 1983

SIC CODES: 3573, Electronic computing equipment
INDUSTRY DESCRIPTORS: Computers
```

Figure 8.7: A Record from Legal Resources Index (Dialog)

```
1968779    DATABASE: LRI File 150
  Westlaw  challenges  Lexis  pricing  in ad.   (includes other law practice
items)
  DeBenedictis, Don J.
  L.A. Daily J.   v97  p5  April 25  1984
  col 1    020 col in.
  JURISDICTION: United States; Massachusetts
  GEOGRAPHIC CODE: NNUS; NNUSNMA    SIC CODE: 8111
  DESCRIPTORS:  legal  research-prices;  Westlaw  (information  retrieval
system)-advertising;    Lexis  (information  retrieval  system)-prices;
information storage  and  retrieval  systems-law;  clients'  funds-usage;
lawyers-legal status, laws, etc.
```

PTS PROMT and Defense Markets & Technology Databases

The Predicasts Terminal Service (PTS) of Predicasts, Inc. produces two databases of abstracts on markets for new and existing technologies: PTS PROMT (PRedicasts Overviews of Markets and Technologies) and PTS Defense Markets & Technology (DMT). Source publications include more than 1500 industry and trade journals, worldwide, for PROMT and more than 100 international defense journals for DMT. PROMT indexes more than 700,000 records, dating from 1972. DMT contains more than 30,000 citations from 1982. Figure 8.8 shows a record from DMT. Both databases are available on BRS and Dialog.

Figure 8.8: A Record from PTS Defense Markets & Technology (Dialog)

```
0123566
Censored
Helicopter International, April, 1984, Vol. 7, Issue 5, p. 160

     The US government has tightened export controls to Iran.  It now bans
aircraft costing $3 mil+  each,  and helicopters with  a  10,000  lb  empty
weight. Exports to Cuba,  Lybia,  Yemen and Syria are similarly restricted.
The  Italian  government  has  requested  US  permission  to  purchase   11
Agusta/Boeing Vertol CH-47C Chinooks that were destined for Iran.
Tradename: CH-47C Chinook; CH-47C Chinook

*1USA; *United States; *9103263;  *Export Controls-Military;  *95;  *Export
    Controls; 8IRB; Iraq
1USA;  United States;  9103263;  Export  Controls-Military;  95;   Export
    Controls; 7LIY; Libya
1USA;  United  States;  9103263;  Export Controls-Military;  95;   Export
    Controls; 8YEM; Yemen Arab Republic
1USA;  United States;  9103263;  Export  Controls-Military;  95;   Export
    Controls; 8SYR; Syria
1USA;  United  States;  9103263;  Export Controls-Military;  95;   Export
    Controls; 3CUB; Cuba
4ITA; Italy; 3721142; Transport & Utility Helicopters; 61; Contract Sought;
    4ITA; Italy; Agusta (Giovanni)
1USA; United States; 3721142; Transport & Utility Helicopters; 61; Contract
    Sought; 4ITA; Italy; Boeing Vertol
```

BIBLIOGRAPHIC DATABASES IN SCIENCE AND TECHNOLOGY

The largest bibliographic databases (and the largest databases of any type) contain abstracts and indexes to the scientific and technical research literature. The largest of these are the files of chemical, biomedical and patent literature. (Some were among the very first bibliographic databases, designed to organize and control the huge masses of research reports which created the so-called "information explosion" beginning in the late 1950s.) Several databases that can be important to business product research and development are surveyed below and are summarized in Table 8.2.

Apilit

The Central Abstracting and Indexing Service of the American Petroleum Institute (API) produces the Apilit (American Petroleum Institute LITerature) database of references to the literature on petroleum refining and the petrochemical industry. Coverage also includes alternative (to fossil fuels) energy sources and the environmental effects of the energy industries. Apilit contains more than 350,000 records from 1964 to date and is updated monthly with about 1500 records. Apilit and its companion file on petrochemical patents, Apipat, are available on SDC Orbit. A sample record appears in Figure 8.9.

BIOSIS Previews

Biological Abstracts, published by BioSciences Information Service, is available online as the BIOSIS Previews database on BRS and Dialog. This database covers all aspects of the biomedical and life sciences, including medicine and agriculture. It contains more than 3.5 million records of international life sciences research literature, covering the period from 1969 to date, and is updated every other week with about 14,000 records per update.

CA Search

Chemical Abstracts Service (CAS) of the American Chemical Society has published *Chemical Abstracts* continuously since early in this century. Since 1967, parts of this publication have been available online as the CA Search (Chemical Abstracts Search) database. CA Search indexes journal literature, conference papers, patents and other literature sources worldwide. The total database from 1967 contains over 5.5 million records of document references and in-context subject indexing. CA Search is available on BRS, Dialog,

Table 8.2: Selected Bibliographic Databases Indexing Publications and Other Documents Covering Scientific and Technical Research and Development

Database Title Publisher	Topics Covered	Publications Covered	Approximate Number of Records per Update	Online Service Vendors
Apilit and Apipat American Petroleum Institute	Petrochemical research	Journals and patents	1500 monthly	SDC Orbit
BIOSIS Previews BioSciences Information Service	Agriculture and biomedicine	Journals	14,000 biweekly	BRS* Dialog†
CA Search Chemical Abstracts Service	Chemical science and technology	Journals and patents	17,000 biweekly	BRS* Dialog Pergamon SDC Orbit
Compendex Engineering Information, Inc.	Engineering and technology	Journals and other	8500 monthly	BRS Dialog SDC Orbit
Conference Papers Index Cambridge Scientific Abstracts	All areas of science and technology	Conference and symposium papers	10,000 monthly	Dialog BRS
Dissertation Abstracts Online University Microfilms International, Inc.	All areas of academic research	Doctoral dissertations	3500 monthly	BRS Dialog
DOE Energy Database U.S. Department of Energy	Energy research	Multiple sources	6000 biweekly	Dialog
Medline National Library of Medicine	Medicine, dentistry and nursing	Journals and other	20,000 monthly	BRS* Dialog† Medlars
NTIS National Technical Information Service	Applied science and technology	Technical reports	2500 biweekly	BRS* Dialog† SDC Orbit
SciSearch Institute for Scientific Information	All areas of science and technology	Journals	25,000 biweekly	BRS Dialog
Standards & Specifications National Standards Association	Industrial and military standards and specs	Standards and specs	50 monthly	Dialog
U.S. Patents Derwent Publications, Inc.	All areas of science and technology	U.S. patents	1300 weekly	SDC Orbit
World Patents Index Derwent Publications Ltd.	All areas of science and technology	International patents	6000 weekly	SDC Orbit

*Available on BRS/After Dark.
†Available on Knowledge Index.

Figure 8.9: A Reference and Indexing for a Trade Journal Article from Apilit (SDC Orbit)

```
ACCESSION NUMBER        3150501
TITLE                   PROGRAMMABLE CONTROLLERS ((PC'S)) BOOST PRODUCT
                        PIPELINE EFFICIENCY
AUTHORS                 NAVAJO PIPELINE CO; MIDLAND-LEA PIPELINE CO; GENERAL
                        ELECTRIC CO
SOURCE                  PIPE LINE IND. (ISSN 00320145) V59 N.6 22,24 (DEC.
                        1983) IN$ ENGLISH
CATEGORY CODE NAME      PIPELINE COMMUNICATION-CONTROL
CATEGORY CODE NAME      TRANSPORTATION AND STORAGE
INDEX TERMS             CAPACITY; CARGO; COMMERCIAL; CONTROL CENTER; CONTROL
                        EQUIPMENT/*1; DATA RECORDING; DATA STORAGE MEDIUM;
                        DENSITY; DISTRICT 3; ECONOMIC FACTOR; EFFICIENCY;
                        ELECTROMAGNETIC WAVE; FLUID FLOW; INCOME; MICROWAVE;
                        MODULAR; MONITORING; NEW MEXICO; NORTH AMERICA; ONE;
                        OPERATING CONDITION; OPERATOR; PERSONNEL; PETROLEUM
                        FRACTION; PHYSICAL PROPERTY; PIPELINE/*1; PRESSURE;
                        PROCESS CONTROL/*1; PROGRAMING; PUMP STATION/*1;
                        PUNCHED CARD; RADIATION; RADIO WAVE; REMOTE;
                        SHUTDOWN; STARTUP; TEMPERATURE; TEXAS; THROUGHPUT;
                        TOPOGRAPHY; USA; VALVE
LINKED TERMS            CARGO; PETROLEUM FRACTION
LINKED TERMS            CONTROL EQUIPMENT; MODULAR
LINKED TERMS            ECONOMIC FACTOR; ONE; OPERATOR; PERSONNEL
LINKED TERMS            PUMP STATION; REMOTE
```

Pergamon and SDC Orbit. Although abstracts are not available on CA Search, records include the abstract number, which can be seen as the number following "AN" in the sample record shown in Figure 8.10. On CAS Online, Chemical Abstracts' own online service, you can retrieve abstracts and chemical structure diagrams.

Compendex

The Compendex (COMPuterized ENgineering InDEX) database is produced by Engineering Information, Inc. and is the online equivalent of the printed *Engineering Index*. Compendex contains more than 1.3 million records of indexing and abstracts of journal articles and other publications on engineering and applied technology. Patents are not included. The file covers from 1970 to date, is updated monthly with about 8500 records and is available on BRS, Dialog and SDC Orbit.

Figure 8.10: A Reference and Indexing to a Research Article from CA Search (SDC Orbit)

```
AN - CA97-137119(16)
TI - An automatic X-Y scanning controller for laser annealing of ion-implanted
     semiconductors
AU - Lue, Juh Tzeng
OS - Inst. Ang. Kernphys., Kernforschungzent. Karlsruhe G.m.b.H., Karlsruhe,
     Fed. Rep. Ger., D-7500
SO - J. Phys. E (JPSIAE), V 15 (7), p. 705-7, 1982, ISSN 00223735
DT - J (Journal)
LA - Eng
CC - SEC76-3; SEC73
IT - Annealing: (laser, of ion-implanted semiconductors, automatic scanning
     controller for)
IT - Laser radiation, chemical and physical effects: (annealing by, of
     ion-implanted semiconductors, automatic scanning controller for)
IT - Semiconductor materials: (wafers, laser annealing of ion-implanted,
     automatic scanning controller for)
ST - microcomputer; implantation
```

Conference Papers Index

Conference Papers Index (CPI) is a database devoted to indexing scientific and technical research papers presented at more than 800 conferences, symposia and other meetings of various scientific organizations, worldwide. Conference Papers Index covers the period from 1973 to date and includes more than 1.2 million records. CPI, produced by Cambridge Scientific Abstracts, is updated with about 10,000 new records monthly and is available on BRS and Dialog. A sample record is shown in Figure 8.11.

Dissertation Abstracts Online

Dissertation Abstracts Online (DAO) corresponds to the printed *Dissertation Abstracts International*. It covers all academic disciplines but emphasizes science and technology. DAO indexes and abstracts all doctoral dissertations (excluding professional degrees such as M.D., L.L.D., etc.) awarded by accredited U.S. academic institutions since 1861. DAO includes more than 800,000 records, is updated monthly and adds about 3500 new records with each update. The database is produced by University Microfilms International, Inc.

Figure 8.11: A Record from Conference Papers Index (Dialog)

```
84009583    V12N2
  Control software for a vision-directed welding robot system
  Kuo, M.H.; Sutherland, H.A.; Sweet, L.M.
  Gen. Electr. Co., USA
  Second International Conference on Advanced Automation ICAA    8345019
Taipei, R.O.C.    19-21 Dec 83
   Institute of Information Science; Academia Sinica, R.O.C.
   Proceedings in: "Advanced Automation", Jul 1984, Philip J.    Alvarez,
Plenum Publishing Corp., 233 Spring St., New York, NY 10013, USA
   Languages: ENGLISH
   Descriptors: GENERAL ENGINEERING AND TECHNOLOGY; MATHEMATICS
   Section Heading:   GENERAL  ENGINEERING  AND  TECHNOLOGY  ;  MATHEMATICS
   Section Class Codes: 5000; 6500
```

DOE Energy Database

The U.S. Department of Energy's Technical Information Center (TIC) produces the DOE Energy Database (DOE) of references to and abstracts of the world's scientific and technical literature dealing with all aspects and forms of energy research and production. All unclassified materials processed by the TIC are included in this database, which is available on Dialog. Materials included in the file are journal articles, patents, conference papers, technical reports, books and monographs, theses and dissertations, and other engineering materials. DOE covers the period from 1974 to date and contains over 1.1 million records, with about 12,000 being added monthly. A sample record is shown in Figure 8.12.

Medline

One of the original online databases, Medline is produced by the National Library of Medicine (NLM) and indexes and abstracts the research and clinical literature of the biomedical sciences. Medline contains almost 4.3 million records from 1966 to the present. Approximately 20,000 new records are added each month. This database corresponds, in part, to the printed *Index Medicus,* the abstract journal also published by the NLM. Medline is offered by BRS, Dialog and NLM's own online service, Medlars.

NTIS

NTIS, from National Technical Information Service, a division of the

Figure 8.12: A Record from DOE Energy (Dialog)

1249119   EDB-84:041624
  Vulnerability to closing of Hormuz
  Energy Detente (United States)   5:5   1-5 P.   7 Mar 1984   Coden: EDETD
  Journal Announcement: EPA8403
  Document Type: Journal Article; Numerical data
  Languages: English and Spanish
  Subfile: EPA .(Energy Abstracts for Policy Analysis)
  Work Location: United States
  Tankers carrying roughly 8-million barrels per day (mmb/d) of crude oil,
or some 16% of the non-communist world's oil supply,   pass   through the
Strait of Hormuz. Experts agree that just 3-mmb/d of that could be exported
through alternate routes. If the war between Iran and Iraq should result in
their completely halting each other's production, this relatively limited
supply curtailment would reduce world oil production by over 3.4-mmb/d.
Since the two have not caused such mutual disaster during four years of
war, many observers believe there has been a deliberate avoidance of the
jugular squeeze. Nevertheless, the two combatants appear capable not only
of cutting off their oil production, but escalating fighting to the point
where Gulf traffic would be impeded. Potential results from a prolonged
Iran-Iraq crisis are viewed in three scenarios. Also included in this issue
are brief summaries of: (1) Mexico's new energy plan, internationalism, and
OPEC; (2)   update on Argentina's energy resource developments;   (3)
Venezuela: belt tightening; (4) Western Hemisphere oil production declines;
(5) (6) days of oil supply for Canada, USA, Japan, France, Italy, and UK;
and (6) US Department of Defense fuel consumption. The Energy Detente fuel
price/tax series and principal industrial fuel prices are included for
March for countries of the Eastern Hemisphere.
  Descriptors: *ARGENTINA----ENERGY POLICY;   *COAL----PRICES;   *MARITIME
TRANSPORT----VULNERABILITY;   *MEXICO----ENERGY   POLICY;   *MIDDLE EAST;
*NATURAL GAS----PRICES; *PETROLEUM----DOMESTIC SUPPLIES; *PETROLEUM----MAR-
ITIME TRANSPORT; *PETROLEUM PRODUCTS----PRICES; *STRAIT OF HORMUZ;   *US
DOD----FUEL CONSUMPTION;   *VENEZUELA----ECONOMIC POLICY ; IRAN;   IRAQ;
STATISTICAL DATA; TAXES
  Special Terms: ARABIAN SEA;   ASIA;   CARBONACEOUS MATERIALS;   DATA;
DEVELOPING COUNTRIES; ENERGY CONSUMPTION; ENERGY SOURCES; FLUIDS; FOSSIL
FUELS; FUEL GAS; FUELS; GAS FUELS; GASES; GOVERNMENT POLICIES; INDIAN OCEAN
; INFORMATION;   LATIN AMERICA;   MATERIALS;   MIDDLE EAST;   NATIONAL
ORGANIZATIONS; NORTH AMERICA; NUMERICAL DATA; PERSIAN GULF; SEAS; SOUTH
AMERICA; SURFACE WATERS; TRANSPORT; US ORGANIZATIONS
  Class Codes: 020700*; 294002

U.S. Department of Commerce, is another federally produced database. NTIS indexes and abstracts technical reports on research resulting from U.S. government grants. The file covers all of the sciences and technologies and represents documents not usually published elsewhere.

NTIS contains indexing, abstracts and original publication availability information for over 1 million reports from 1964 to date. Approximately 5000 new reports are indexed with every month's update. The reports of the Department of Defense, Department of Energy and the National Aeronautics and Space Administration, plus many other agencies, are cataloged. NTIS may be searched on BRS, Dialog and SDC Orbit. Figure 8.13 illustrates a report of research done for the Department of Education.

Figure 8.13: A Record from NTIS (Dialog)

```
921211   ED-200 216
  Data Input for Libraries: State-of-the-Art Report
  Buckland, Lawrence F.
  Inforonics, Littleton, MA.
  Corp. Source Codes: 075799000
  1 Aug 80    9p
  Available from ERIC Document Reproduction Service (Computer Microfilm
International Corporation), Arlington, VA 22210.
  Languages: English
  NTIS Prices: Not available NTIS     Journal Announcement: GRAI8221
  Country of Publication: United States
  This brief overview of new manuscript preparation methods which allow
authors  and  editors  to  set  their own type discusses the advantages and
disadvantages of optical character recognition (OCR),  microcomputers  and
personal  computers,  minicomputers,  and word processors for editing and
database  entry.  Potential  library  applications  are  also  indicated,
including  such  special  problems as converting back files,  and available
commercial services are mentioned.
  Descriptors: Cataloging; Cost  effectiveness;  Input  output  devices;
Library  catalogs;  *Library technical processes;  Minicomputers;  *Online
systems; Optical scanners
  Identifiers: Word processing; NTISHEWERI
  Section Headings:  5B (Behavioral and Social Sciences--Documentation  and
Information Technology); 88GE (Library and Information Sciences--General)
```

SciSearch

SciSearch, from the Institute for Scientific Information, is unique in that it is searched using the cited author or cited reference technique to research a topic, rather than the subject indexing method adopted by most abstract databases. SciSearch covers all scientific and technical disciplines. This database includes more than 5.6 million citations or references to articles from about 4100 major worldwide scientific and technical journals from 1974 to date. It adds 25,000 new citations every two weeks—an indication of the enormous amount of scientific publication. SciSearch is available on Dialog and BRS.

Standards & Specifications

Standards & Specifications (S&S), from the National Standards Association (NSA), is an online index to all standards and specifications accumulated by the NSA with the help of the National Bureau of Standards and the Department of Defense (DOD). S&S contains references to:

- all U.S. military standards from the DOD (more than 39,000)

- U.S. federal General Services Administration (GSA) standards and commercial item descriptions (about 5100)

- all U.S. industrial standards developed by such organizations as the American Society for Testing and Materials (ASTM), the American National Standards Institute (ANSI) and the Underwriters Laboratories (UL) (about 27,000)

New and revised standards are added monthly. A military standard is shown in Figure 8.14. The database is available on Dialog.

Figure 8.14: A Reference to a Military Standard from Standards & Specifications (Dialog)

```
033040     MIL-M-38510/490    NSA CARD NO: 102H
  Microcircuits,   Digital,   N-channel,  Silicon Gate,  Monolithic,   8-BIT
Microcomputer
  DOD  (DEPARTMENT OF DEFENSE)
  5962  (MICROCIRCUITS, ELECTRONIC)
  1981  DEC 01
  ENGLISH
```

U.S. Patents and World Patents Index

U.S. Patents (USP) is produced in the U.S. by Derwent Publications Inc. World Patents Index (WPI) is produced in the U.K. by Derwent Publications Ltd. Both are available on SDC Orbit. (Dialog and Derwent announced a license agreement in early 1984.)

Patents represent a huge body of scientific and technical literature, about 75% of which is never published elsewhere. The USP database contains indexing, abstracts and the full text of all claims for all patents issued in the U.S. since 1970. WPI indexes and abstracts all basic (original issue) patents and their equivalents (additional patents on the same invention in other countries) issued by 26 industrial countries, as well as European and Patent Cooperation Treaty (PCT) patents. More than 3.3 million patent families (basics plus equivalents) are included, dating from 1963. Both USP and WPI are updated monthly. Part of a patent record from U.S. Patents is shown in Figure 8.15.

REFERENCE DATABASES

Reference databases may be bibliographic databases covering a wide range of topics, encyclopedias containing full text, directories of people and organizations, and other databases on general or special topics. Most of the databases of company data covered in Chapter 6 fall in the reference category. In the paragraphs following, some additional reference databases are surveyed; these are summarized in Table 8.3.

Academic American Encyclopedia

The Academic American Encyclopedia (AAE) is a full-text general online encyclopedia of more than 29,000 entries on all topics. Tables, "fact boxes," bibliographies, cross references and "see also" references are included with most of the entries. The AAE is published by Grolier Electronic Publishing, a division of Grolier Publishing, Inc., the world's largest encyclopedia publisher. The AAE is updated twice a year and is available on BRS, Dialog and Dow Jones.

Biography Master Index

The Biography Master Index (BMI) database, from Gale Research Co., a leading reference book publisher, is a complete index to biographies of more than 1.9 million individuals in many fields. BMI indexes biographies

Figure 8.15: An Abstract Record from U.S. Patents (Dialog)

PATENT NUMBER	US4383286
TITLE	Cooling and power input assembly
INVENTOR	Hicks, Roy T., 566 Irelan, Buellton, CA, 93427
PUBLICATION DATE	83.05.10
APPLICATION NUMBER	367009, Filed 82.04.09
NOTES	11 Claims, Exemplary Claim 1, 2 DRAWINGS, 6 Figures
	Examiner: Tolin, G. P.
	Atty/Agent: poms, Smith, Lande & Rose
PATENT CLASSIFICATION	361/384, Cross Refs: 165/47 X, 361/357 X
FIELD OF SEARCH	174/15R, 174/16R, 361/381, 361/383, 361,384, 361/393, 361/394, 361/356, 361/357, 165/80B, 165/80D, 165/122, 165/128, 165/129, 165/47, 200/153G, 200/293, 200/294, 200/302, 200/306
DOCUMENT TYPE	INVENTION PATENT
CITATIONS(REFERENCES)	US3396780, 8/1968, Koltuniak, 361/384
	US3735807, 5/1973, Hunt, 165/47
	US3962608, 6/1976, Forster, 361/384
	US4027206, 5/1977, Lee, 361/384
	US4084213, 4/1978, Kirchner, 361/384
	US4084250, 4/1978, Albertine, 361/384
	US4126269, 11/1978, Bruges, 361/384
	US4237521, 12/1980, Denker, 361/384
ABSTRACT	A cooling and electrical control assembly is provided for an electrical equipment such as a computer which is normally provided with venting slots for the dissipation of heat by the normal flow of ambient air. The ventilation slots on certain computers, such as an Apple computer, are located on the upper sides of the housing for the computer, with the slots extending into the top panel of the electrical equipment and also down the sides thereof. The cooling and electrical control assembly disclosed in the present sepcification includes a housing having an open side, and protruding fingers for engaging the ventilation slots of the electrical equipment and for holding the housing into engagement with the side and top of the electrical equipment with the open side of the housing in sealing engagement with the ventilation openings. A fan is provided in the housing to exhaust air fom the electrical ...

Table 8.3: Selected Reference Databases, Including Directories, Library Catalogs and Full-text Publications

Database Title Publisher	Topics Covered	Database Type	Number/Type of Entries	Updating Frequency	Online Service Vendors
Academic American Encyclopedia Grolier Electronic Publishing	All topics	Full text	29,000 articles	Twice yearly	BRS* Dialog Dow Jones
Biography Master Index Gale Research Co.	Famous persons	Bibliographic citations	1,900,000 biographies	Periodically	Dialog
Books in Print R.R. Bowker Co.	All topics	Directory	700,000 books	Monthly	BRS* Dialog†
Encyclopedia of Associations Gale Research Co.	All topics	Directory	15,000 organizations	3 times yearly	Dialog
IRS Publications U.S. Internal Revenue Service	IRS tax rules	Full text	65 IRS publications	Yearly	BRS
LC/Line LC MARC U.S. Library of Congress	All topics	Catalog	1,800,000 books	Monthly	SDC Orbit Dialog
Marquis Who's Who Marquis Who's Who, Inc.	Notable persons	Directory	75,000 biographies	Quarterly	Dialog
.Menu-ISD International Software Database Corp.	Computer applications	Directory	15,000 computer programs	Monthly	Dialog
National Foundations The Foundation Center	All topics	Directory	21,000 private foundations	Yearly	Dialog
REMARC Carrollton Press, Inc.	All topics	Catalog	5,000,000 books	Monthly	Dialog
Trademarkscan Thomson & Thomson	Registered trademarks	Directory	615,000 trade/ service marks	Biweekly	Dialog
Ulrich's International Periodicals Directory R.R. Bowker Co.	All topics	Directory	112,000 serial publications	Every 6 weeks	BRS Dialog

*Available on BRS/After Dark.
†Available on Knowledge Index.

appearing in about 375 biographical dictionaries, directories and encyclo-pedias. Each reference includes the person's name, birth and death dates, when known, and citations to the source where the complete biographical sketch is available. BMI is available on Dialog.

Books in Print

Books in Print (BIP), from R.R. Bowker Co., is used by virtually every bookstore in the U.S. BIP is a current index to more than 760,000 books currently in print and planned for publication within the next six months from about 12,000 publishers. Information about out-of-print books is also available, and data are updated monthly. The books indexed cover every topic, and BIP was used to verify the books listed in Appendix C. The record for this book is illustrated in Figure 8.16. BIP is offered by BRS and Dialog.

Encyclopedia of Associations

In addition to the Biography Master Index, Gale Research also publishes the Encyclopedia of Associations (EA), both in print and online. The database provides entries on more than 15,000 professional societies, trade associa-tions, labor unions, cultural, religious and special interest groups, and many other American associations. EA is revised and updated twice yearly and is available on Dialog. Figure 8.17 shows a sample record.

Figure 8.16: The Record for the Book You Are Reading from Books in Print (Dialog)

```
0935847    1005150XX     Subfile: PC; ST
  The Executive's Guide to Online Information Services
  Hoover, Ryan E.
  Series: Information & Communications Management Guides Ser.
  175p.
  Knowledge Indus  09/1984
  Trade $32.95 professional; pap. $24.95 professional
  ISBN: 0-86729-090-0; 0-86729-089-7
  Status: Active entry
  Illustrated
  SUBJECT HEADINGS: ON-LINE DATA PROCESSING (00550103); INFORMATION STORAGE
AND RETRIEVAL SYSTEMS-BUSINESS (00636320)
```

Figure 8.17: A Record from the Encyclopedia of Associations (Dialog)

```
01112
  INFORMATION INDUSTRY ASSOCIATION (Data Processing)  (IIA)
  316 Pennsylvania Ave., S.E., Suite 400, Washington, DC 20003
  (202)544-1969
  Paul G. Zurkowski Pres.
  Founded:  1968.   Members:   170.   Trade  association  of "for-profit
information companies whose business it is to identify specific information
needs and to produce cost-effective,  timely and reliable products to  meet
those  needs;   companies  are  not  tied  to  any  particular  information
technology but are concerned with the information commodity." Conducts new
technology,  business  operations,  and  information  user  workshops and
seminars.  Presents annual Hall of Fame  Awards.   Committees:  Business
Operations; Future Technology and Innovation; Policy and External Affairs.
  Publications:   (1)   Friday Memo (newsletter),  weekly;  (2)  Information
Sources (directory),  annual;  also publishes The Business  of  Information
Report,   Understanding  U.S.  Information  Policy,  Planning  Product
Innovation,  and Strategic Market Planning.  Convention/Meeting:  annual -
1983 November, New York City.
  Section Heading Codes: Trade, Business and Commercial Organizations (01)
```

IRS Publications

IRS Publications is a unique database from the Internal Revenue Service, containing the full text of approximately 65 frequently requested IRS tax publications. It is updated annually to reflect changes and revisions in the tax law and filing rules. This database is ideal for a quick check of an IRS rule or tax form without bothering your tax accountant. The IRS Publications database is available on BRS.

Library of Congress Databases

Almost the entire catalog of books and other documents processed by the Library of Congress (LC) is available online in one of three databases: LC/Line, LC MARC or REMARC.

The LC/Line database on SDC Orbit and the LC MARC (MAchine Readable Cataloging) database on Dialog are similar in that both are produced from LC-generated tapes used to phototypeset printed catalog cards. These two databases contain records for over 2.5 million documents cataloged by LC and, on LC/Line, the Canadian National Library since 1968.

The REMARC (REtrospective MARC) database on Dialog is being produced by the Carrollton Press, Inc. from records of documents cataloged by LC from 1897 through 1978, including those not covered by MARC from 1968-78. REMARC contains references to about 5 million items.

Together, these three databases represent almost 7.5 million documents and provide a definitive record of almost every book ever published in the U.S.

Marquis Who's Who

The Marquis Who's Who database, from Marquis Who's Who, Inc., contains about 75,000 detailed biographical sketches of notable professional people in all fields. It currently lists all individuals in the printed *Who's Who in America*; planned updates will add persons listed in other Who's Who directories. Records may be searched by name, birth date, current address and several other items of information, including career milestones, civic or political activities, awards and interests. Marquis Who's Who is on Dialog and is updated quarterly. A sample record is shown in Figure 8.18.

.Menu-ISD

.Menu-ISD, from International Software Database Corp., is a directory of

Figure 8.18: A Record from Marquis Who's Who (Dialog)

```
1110187  FS01    BIOG UPDATE: 19830601; *
  Jobs, Steven Paul
  OCCUPATION(S): computer corporation executive
  BORN:   1955
  PARENTS: Paul and Clara J
  SEX: Unavailable
  EDUCATION:
  Student Reed Coll
  CAREER:
  With Hewlett-Packard, Palo Alto, CA, US, summers while high-sch. student;
  designer video games Atari Inc, 1974;
  now chmn bd Apple Computer, Inc, Cupertino, CA, US
  RESEARCH SPECIALTIES: Electronics (3233020);  Computer company management
(2199999)
   ACHIEVEMENTS:  Co-designer (with Stephen Wozniak)  Apple I microcomputer,
introduced 1976
  OFFICE: Cupertino, CA US
```

about 50,000 computer programs that are currently available commercially for all types of computers and applications and that have been produced since 1973. .Menu-ISD is searchable by computer type, operating system, application, vendor and price. Special conditions, such as licensing fees or availability of source code, are also included. The database is reloaded monthly with new and revised entries. A sample record is shown in Figure 8.19. .Menu-ISD is available on Dialog.

Figure 8.19: A Record from .Menu-ISD (Dialog)

```
005796    26725100
  DOW JONES MARKET ANALYZER V 1.0
  DOW JONES & CO
  PO BOX 300
  PRINCETON, NJ   08540
  (609)452-2000
  APPLE II/5-1/4-inch disk/48K/349.00$
  APPLE II+/5-1/4-inch disk/48K/349.00$
  APPLE II E/5-1/4-inch disk/48K/349.00$
  APPLE III/5-1/4-inch disk/48K/349.00$
  IBM PC/5-1/4-inch disk/64K/349.00$
  PC DOS 1.1 (IBM)/5-1/4-inch disk/48K/349.00$
  Country of Currency: USA
  Source Code Available: NO
  Integrated Packaging: NO
  Updates: YES
  Class of Computer: MICRO
  Special  Configuration:   CONTACT  DOW  JONES FOR SPECIFIC INFORMATION OF
REQUIREMENTS.
  Date of Release: 820700   Warranty: LIMITED
  Performs technical analysis  with  historical  stock  data  automatically
retrieved  from  Dow  Jones  News/Retrieval.   The MARKET ANALYZER collects
historical and daily market quotes from Dow Jones News/Retrieval and stores
the information for later viewing. Then you can construct relative strength
and analysis charts or individual  price  and  volume  charts  with  moving
averages, straight line constructions, price/volume indicators,  oscillator
charts and other functions.  It features automatic entry  of  one  year  of
daily historical data on stocks,  bonds,  mutual funds and options,  allows
for input of special indicators, and stores data on 104 stocks for 128 days
or 52 stocks for 256 days on one disk.
  182 COMMERCIAL/STOCK MARKET/COMMODITIES
```

National Foundations

More than 21,000 American private foundations which award grants for charitable purposes are listed in the National Foundations (NF) database, produced by The Foundation Center. The foundations listed in NF award grants in such fields as education, health, welfare and the sciences. Foundations may be searched by their primary fields of interest, names and geographical locations. NF has a companion database, Foundation Directory, which provides more complete data on the larger foundations included in NF. Both databases are updated annually and are available on Dialog.

Trademarkscan

Another unique database, Trademarkscan, produced by Thomson & Thomson, indexes all registered and pending U.S. trademarks used on every commercial product or service. Data are provided by the U.S. Patent and Trademark Office (PTO). This database is ideal for companies reviewing trademarks for new products and services and wishing to avoid conflict with names and designs already in use. Both names and designs or logos are included. Trademarkscan is available on Dialog. About 615,000 active and pending trademarks are included, with 2800 new and 4500 revised trade and service marks added biweekly. Figure 8.20 shows two trademark records. (SDC has announced a separate contract with the PTO to design a system to display graphics of logo designs online in addition to names.)

Ulrich's International Periodicals Directory

R.R. Bowker Co. publishes *Ulrich's International Periodicals Directory* and *Irregular Serials and Annuals* in both print and electronic forms. The online database, Ulrich's International Periodicals Directory, combines both publications and contains information on more than 115,000 international periodical, serial and irregularly issued publications of all types. Searchable data items include title, publisher, subject information, and ordering and buying information. Ulrich's is updated every six weeks, with about 5000 new titles being added annually. It is available on both BRS and Dialog.

SUMMARY

The almost 250 bibliographic and reference databases represent nearly 100 million international documents and other information sources published in the last 10 to 20 years and comprise by far the largest available source of online information. With the equivalent of nearly all the world's library

Figure 8.20: Trademark Records from Trademarkscan (Dialog)

```
          0610653
COMPUSTAT
          CLASS: 101 .(Advertising and Business)
          GOODS/SERVICES: SYSTEMIZING STATISTICAL & FINANCIAL INFORMATION &
          PREPARING DATACARDS &  TAPES BASED ON SUCH INFORMATION FOR USE BY
          OTHERS (IC35)
          SERIES CODE: 3    SERIAL NO.: 426754
          STATUS: Pending
          STATUS DATE: May 20, 1983   DATE OF USE: December 05, 1963
          OWNER: STANDARD & POOR'S CORP NEW YORK NY


          0590151
COMPUSTAT II   AND DESIGN
          CLASS: 101 .(Advertising and Business)
          GOODS/SERVICES:   COMPUTERIZED  FINANCIAL DATA REPORTING SERVICES
          (IC35)
          SERIES CODE: 3    SERIAL NO.: 052895    REG. NO.: 1072562
          STATUS: Registered;Multiple Class
          STATUS DATE: September 06, 1977   DATE OF USE: December 05, 1963
          OWNER: INVESTORS MANAGEMENT SCIENCES INC NY NY
```

catalogs and indexes as close as your telephone, you may do research on virtually any topic for current or historical information—and even for future information, using automatic SDI alerting features.

In addition to the representative sample of databases presented here and in Chapters 5 and 6, you can find many more by checking with service vendors, listed in Appendix C, or consulting database directories, listed in Appendix B. New databases are becoming available monthly; if the one you need is not yet available, it probably will be in the near future.

So far, we have reviewed selected database offerings of the popular information utilities, full-text news vendors, numeric services, and bibliographic and reference vendors. These databases are available on multi-faceted services that provide a wide range of information and other features on many different topics. There are also specialized online information utilities dedicated to one type of information for specific purposes. We will look at a few of these of interest to business people in the next chapter.

9

Specialized Information Services

In Chapters 4 through 8, we looked at several online information services that offer databases on a wide range of subjects, from business administration to general news. All of those services provide access to information that is of interest to people in almost any business or industry and, in some cases, to the general population.

There are also a number of commercial information services dedicated to meeting specific, specialized information needs. Many are not available on other online service vendors' systems. Most are oriented toward business managers and executives or professional people.

In this chapter, we'll examine five specialized commercial online information services:

- Official Airline Guide Electronic Edition

- Lexis

- Interactive Marketing Services

- BRS/Medical Colleague

- Comp-U-Store

Table 9.1 summarizes important information about these five services.

OFFICIAL AIRLINE GUIDE ELECTRONIC EDITION

Official Airline Guides, Inc., a Dun & Bradstreet company, is an old and respected publisher of domestic and international airline schedules. Almost every business person who travels is familiar with the printed *Official Airline Guide* and its pocket guide version. The Official Airline Guide Electronic Edition (OAGEE) service began in 1983 and offers all domestic airline flight schedules and fares online. OAGEE has announced future plans to include international schedules and fares.

Using OAGEE at your desk, you can:

Table 9.1: Selected Online Service Vendors Offering Specialized Information

Service Name Parent Company	Subject Specialty	Ease of Use*	Data Networks	Available on Other Services	Micro Software	Electronic Mail	Start-up Fee	Annual Subscription†	Lower Night Rates	Credit Card Billing†
OAG Electronic Edition Official Airline Guides Inc. Dun & Bradstreet Corp.	Airline schedules	2	Telenet Tymnet	CompuServe Dow Jones			■		■	■
Lexis Mead Data Central Mead Corp.	Full-text legal research	1	Telenet Leased		■		■	■		
Interactive Market Systems Interactive Market Systems, Inc.	Media and market	3	Telenet Tymnet				■	■		
BRS/Medical Colleague Bibliographic Retrieval Services, Inc.	Full-text medical research	2	Telenet Tymnet Uninet			■	■	□		□
Compu-U-Store Comp-U-Card International, Inc.	Shopping and buying	1	Telenet Tymnet	CompuServe Dow Jones The Source			■	■	■	■

*Ease of use on a scale of 1 (very easy for novice) to 5 (difficult for novice).
†■ = required   □ = option

- select the lowest possible available fare to your destination and return

- find the most convenient schedules for your favorite airline or any carrier

- identify the airport closest to your point of doing business and select flights and fares accordingly

- choose one or more return flights to hold in reserve in case there are delays in your business transactions or by the airline

- make travel plans for business or pleasure

OAGEE is not a substitute for travel agents, since you cannot make reservations, but it does give you freedom to schedule your own air travel and present your agency with a printout of desired schedules and fares.

The OAG system is extremely easy to use after a few minutes of reviewing the user guide provided to new subscribers. Figure 9.1 shows the online welcome screen and main command menu. The OAGEE is largely menu-driven, with self-help prompts and an online tutorial with instructions on how to use the system.

Information Available

You may search for and display three distinct types of information in the OAGEE:

- flight schedules (direct and connecting)

- fares (one way, round trip and special)

- fare limitations and conditions

Flight Schedules

Currently, all domestic flights originating in the continental U.S. are listed in this database. Flights are listed beginning with the earliest in the day through the latest.

When you select flight information from the menu, you are prompted for a departure and destination city. If there is not an airport at one or both locations, you are shown a list of the nearest airports and asked to choose the

Figure 9.1: The Welcome Screen, Bulletin and Main Command Menu from the Official Airline Guide Electronic Edition (OAGEE)

```
WELCOME TO THE OFFICIAL AIRLINE GUIDE
(OAG), COPYRIGHT 1984, OFFICIAL AIRLINE
GUIDES, INC., OAK BROOK, ILLINOIS 60521
PRESS RETURN FOR SUBSCRIBER BULLETIN
        (LAST ISSUED 18 JUN)

ENTER /M FOR A LIST OF OAG EE COMMANDS
OR ENTER /I, /F, /S OR /U


   S U B S C R I B E R   B U L L E T I N
     IMPORTANT NEWS FOR ALL OAG EE USERS
*******************************************
*               " DUNSNET "               *
*   NEW NETWORK FOR EAST COAST ACCESS      *
*           ENTER 1 FOR DETAILS            *
*                                          *
*ALL NEW "HOW TO USE" INSTRUCTIONS NOW*
*             INSTALLED                    *
*           ENTER 2 FOR DETAILS            *
*                                          *
* TELEPHONE TRAINING STILL AVAILABLE  *
*           ENTER 3 FOR DETAILS            *
*******************************************
ENTER /F, /S, /M, /I, /U (/Q=EXIT OAG)
        /m

        ** OAG COMMAND MENU **
ENTER:/I FOR INFORMATION AND ASSISTANCE
      /F FOR FARES DISPLAYS
      /S FOR SCHEDULE DISPLAYS
      /M TO RETURN TO THIS MENU
      /U FOR USER COMMENTS AND
           SUGGESTIONS BOX
      /Q TO EXIT FROM THE OAG EE
NOTE:YOU MAY USE CITY NAMES OR 3-LETTER
     CODES. EXAMPLES:
          /S MIA;DALLAS 1SEP 3P
          /F MIAMI;DALLAS 1SEP
     IF YOU OMIT ANY PART OF THE ENTRY,
     THE SYSTEM WILL PROMPT YOU FOR IT.
ENTER THE COMMAND OF YOUR CHOICE
        /f
```

one you prefer. If you choose a departure city or destination with more than one airport, you are shown the available choices and are asked to list your preference. You are next asked to enter the time of day you wish to depart and return. The available flights are displayed. At that point, you have the choice of viewing return schedules or looking at fares for the flight(s) you have selected. A display of schedules appears in Figure 9.2.

Fare Information

Once you have selected the flight(s) of your choice, you may ask to have the fares for that flight displayed. Fares are always listed starting with the least expensive and progressing through the most expensive. The lowest fares are usually special excursion rates that have limitations and conditions attached; the highest fares generally represent first class travel.

Figure 9.2: Sample Airline Schedules for OAGEE

```
ENTER  DEPARTURE  CITY  NAME  OR  CODE
       dallas

ENTER  DESTINATION  CITY  NAME  OR  CODE
       new york

ENTER  DEPARTURE  DATE
OR  PRESS  RETURN  TO  USE    04  JUL
       05  jul

              DIRECT  FLIGHTS        THU-05  JUL
SELECTED  FROM  AA  FARE  DISPLAY
FROM-DALLAS;FT.WORTH,TX,USA
#  TO-NEW  YORK,NY;NEWARK,NJ,USA
  NO  EARLIER  DIRECT  FLIGHT  SERVICE
1    700A    DFW   1107A    EWR  AA  120  M80  B  0
2    700A    DFW   1108A    LGA  AA  244  72S  B  0
3    840A    DFW   1255P    LGA  AA   82  D10  B  0
4    100P    DFW    513P    LGA  AA  316  D10  L  0
5    100P    DFW    523P    JFK  AA  164  72S  L  0
6    100P    DFW    659P    LGA  AA  446  767  L  1
ENTER  R  FOR  RETURN  AA  SCHEDULES
ENTER  +,X#,L,R,F,RF        (#=LINE  NUMBER)
       r
```

You may also begin by looking at the available fares for travel between your departure and destination points and then ask for a list of schedules available at those fares. A fares screen is shown in Figure 9.3.

Fare Limitations and Conditions

Special conditions and limitations usually apply to the lowest fares listed in the OAGEE. For any fare displayed for which limitations are indicated, you may ask to see the special terms that apply. The most common limitations

Figure 9.3: The Fares Menu and Sample Air Fares from OAGEE

```
                    FARE  MENU
FARES  FOR                          FARES  FOR
DIRECT FLIGHTS              DIRECT FLIGHTS
AND CONNECTIONS                        ONLY
---                                     ---
1   COACH CLASS AND EQUIVALENT FARES    6
2   FIRST CLASS AND EQUIVALENT FARES    7
3   BOTH COACH AND FIRST CLASS FARES    8
4   ADVANCE-PURCH AND EXCURSION FARES   9
5        ALL OF THE ABOVE FARES         10

PLEASE ENTER A NUMBER
        6

FARES IN US DOLLARS              THU-05 JUL
SELECTED FOR DFW-NYC

#   ONE-WAY   RND-TRP ARLN/CLASS FARECODE
 NO LOWER FARES IN CATEGORY
1*   144.00    288.00     EA/L       LZ6
2*   154.00    308.00     ML/M       M6
3*   160.00    320.00     AA/M       MSAT
4*   160.00    320.00     BN/M       MSA
5*   160.00    320.00     PI/H       H6
6*   160.00    320.00     DL/M       MSAT
7*   160.00    320.00     UA/M       MD6
8*   169.00    338.00     PI/Q       Q
 *  ENTER L# TO VIEW LIMITATIONS
ENTER +,L#,X#,S#,R#,M,RF(#=LINE NUMBER)
        s3
```

are that you must book in advance by a certain margin, that you may travel only in specified months on certain days and/or at certain times, or that you must stay at the destination for a certain period.

Regardless of the limitations, business people can frequently find special low fares with conditions that fit their travel schedules, and it is possible to save 30% to 50% off regular coach fares. OAG claims savings of up to 70% in its literature. A typical limitations and rules screen is illustrated by Figure 9.4.

Figure 9.4: Fare Limitations Information from OAGEE

```
LIMITATIONS DISPLAY              SUN-08 JUL
NYC-DFW      CLASS:Q  FARECODE:QFS
AMERICAN AIRLINES
FARE DESCRIPTION: SUPER COACH FARES
BOOKING CODE: Q/QN.

FARE IS ONLY AVAILABLE FOR TRAVEL FROM
 08:45P THRU 09:45P ON ANYDAY.
APPLIES FROM LA GUARDIA AIRPORT.
 * END OF LIMITATIONS DISPLAY *
ENTER S TO VIEW SELECTED AA SCHEDULES
ENTER F TO RETURN TO FARES DISPLAY
      /q
```

Subscription and Cost

The cost of the OAGEE service is very reasonable. The average online connect hour charge is $32 during prime time and $21 during non-prime time. OAGEE is available by direct subscription ($50) from Official Airline Guides, Inc. or through CompuServe Information Service or Dow Jones News/Retrieval Service. See the listings in Appendix C for addresses and telephone numbers.

LEXIS

In Chapters 4 and 5 we discussed the general-interest services of Mead Data

Central (MDC), particularly the Nexis news service. However, MDC's first and largest online service is Lexis, a full-text service devoted specifically to legal research.

Most large law firms in the U.S. use the Lexis legal research service. An increasing number of smaller firms are also turning to Lexis to find case records and decisions relevant to pending cases. Lexis is menu-driven and requires no knowledge of computers, information retrieval or data processing. Information may be retrieved by keywords (judges, courts, dates) and key phrases used in decisions, text of counsel, and sections of statutes or regulations.

Information Available

The Lexis database contains libraries of laws and cases of the U.S. Supreme Court, all of the lower federal courts, the supreme and lower state courts of all 50 states plus the District of Columbia. The full text of The Federal Register is also available online. A recent service addition, Lexpat, provides the full text of U.S. patents issued from 1975 to date.

Lexis' specialized law libraries cover the topics of taxes, securities, trade regulation, bankruptcy, patents, trademarks and copyright, communications, labor, public contracts and Delaware corporations. The complete text of the constitution and bylaws, codes of conduct, and informal opinions of the American Bar Association are included. Selected legal publications from Matthew Bender are available. Many law libraries from the United Kingdom and France are offered.

Lexis also permits citation searching through Shepard's Citations, AutoCite and Lexis itself.

In addition, Lexis provides access to the online Encyclopaedia Britannica, the Nexis news service, an accounting library and the Associated Press Political Service. Subscribers to Dialog Information Services, Inc. can also access that service through Lexis. A summary of the Lexis law databases is presented in Table 9.2.

You can use Lexis to:

- obtain the text of opinions not yet available in print

- obtain court decisions not included in any case law reporter

Table 9.2: Selected Full-text Law Databases Available on Lexis

Database Title	Subject/Content
Federal Law Libraries	
United States Code	U.S. public laws
Federal Register	New laws and regulations
Code of Federal Regulations	All federal regulations
Supreme Court Decisions 1925+	Supreme Court decisions
Supreme Court Briefs	Supreme Court briefs
Presidential Documents	Orders, decrees, etc.
Internal Revenue Codes	IRS tax code
Securities and Exchange Commission Administrative Determinations	SEC rulings and cases
Federal Trade Commission Reports	FTC rulings and cases
Patent, Trademark and Copyright Decisions	Copyright, patent cases
Federal Communications Commission Reports	FCC rulings and cases
National Labor Relations Board Reports	NLRB rulings and cases
Federal Energy Regulatory Commission Reports	ERC rulings and cases
Nuclear Regulatory Commission Reports	NRC rulings and cases
Public Contracts Cases	Contracts rulings and cases
Board of Contract Appeals Determinations	Board of Appeals rulings
State Law Libraries	
Supreme Court Decisions	State supreme courts, most states
Court of Appeals Decisions	State courts of appeals, 50 states, DC
Attorney General Opinions	State attorneys general, some states
Delaware Corporation Cases, Delaware	Delaware corporation rulings
Delaware Corporation Cases, Federal	Delaware corporation rulings
United Kingdom Law Libraries	
Statutes	British laws and regulations
Statutory Instruments	British laws and regulations
Cases	British government cases, most ministries
Double Taxation Agreements	British tax cases
Inland Revenue Publications	British tax publications
Industrial Relations Cases	British labor rulings
Intellectual Property Cases	Copyright, patents, etc.
Local Government Cases	British local cases
European Court Reports	European courts
European Commission Decisions	European government rulings

(continued on next page)

Table 9.2: Selected Full-text Law Databases Available on Lexis (cont.)

Database Title	Subject/Content
French Law Libraries	
Public Cases	French public law
Private Cases	French private law
Statutes and Regulations	French laws and regulations
International Cases and Regulations	International law
Miscellaneous	
Auto-Cite	Cited cases and law
Shepard's Citations	Cited cases and law
Matthew Bender Publications	Legal publications
Lexpat Patent Research Service	U.S. patents
American Bar Association	ABA organizational information

- identify opinions of a particular judge

- locate cases involving specific legal principles

- locate cases involving specific fact patterns

- locate cases involving two or more distinct fields of law

- locate cases or statutes containing particular terminology or phrases

- retrieve cases about which only limited information is known

- find the most recent cases citing earlier cases, statutes, articles or treatises

- double-check previous research or briefs by opposing counsel

The keyword search capability of Lexis makes it easy to do extensive legal research in a fairly short time. Figure 9.5 shows a reference retrieved by a KWIC (keyword in context) search. Figure 9.6 contains part of the full-text record for the same case.

Subscription and Costs

Lexis is available over MDC's custom UBIQ terminal with retrieval functions labeled on special keys. Lexis is also now available to users of a

Figure 9.5: The KWIC (Keyword in Context) Format of a Law Case from Lexis

```
                        LEVEL 1 - 1 OF 1 CASE

          SMITH, CORRECTIONAL SUPERINTENDENT v. PHILLIPS

                           No. 80-1082.

                 SUPREME COURT OF THE UNITED STATES

                         50 U.S.L.W. 4169

CONCURBY:                      January 25, 1982
   O'CONNOR

CONCUR:
   ... my view that the opinion does not foreclose the use of "implied bias" in
appropriate circumstances.

   I
   Determining whether a juror is biased or has prejudiced a case is difficult,
partly because the juror may have an interest in concealing his own bias and
partly because the juror may be unaware of it.  The problem may be compounded
```

Figure 9.6: A Portion of the Full Text of a Law Case from Lexis

```
   O'CONNOR                    50 U.S.L.W. 4169

CONCUR:
   JUSTICE O'CONNOR, concurring.

   I concur in the Court's opinion, but write separately to express my view
that the opinion does not foreclose the use of "implied bias" in appropriate
circumstances.

   I

   Determining whether a juror is biased or has prejudiced a case is difficult,
partly because the juror may have an interest in concealing his own bias and
partly because the juror may be unaware of it.  The problem may be compounded
when a charge of bias arises from juror misconduct, and not simply from
attempts of third parties to influence a juror.

   Nevertheless, I believe that in most instances a post-conviction hearing
will be adequate to determine whether a juror is biased.  A hearing permits
counsel to probe the juror's memory, his reasons for acting as he did, and
his understanding of the consequences of his actions.  A hearing also permits
the trial judge to observe the juror's demeanor under cross examination and
```

number of personal computers, using special software that duplicates the functions of the UBIQ terminal. The software costs about $225. A customer may choose between a leased dedicated phone line from Lexis or, for smaller firms that are less frequent users, dial access over the Telenet packet-switching network. There are subscription and connect hour price options for both heavy and casual users. Hourly rates generally range from $30 to $90. Contact MDC at its Dayton headquarters (Appendix C) or one of its sales offices in most major cities.

INTERACTIVE MARKET SYSTEMS, INC.

Interactive Market Systems, Inc. (IMS), founded in 1969, is a New York-based online service company providing access to more than 300 international numeric databases that relate to advertising and media marketing planning and research. Its primary customers are advertising agencies and media market research and planning firms. IMS will provide printouts for customers without personal computers or data terminals.

In addition to online databases, services include cost ranking, cost efficiency, advertising campaign modeling, market and media survey cross-tabulating, reach and frequency analysis, and optimization studies.

Information Available

IMS' extensive collection of media market analysis databases falls into three categories:

- United States broadcast media

- United States print media

- international media

Table 9.3 lists selected databases in each of these categories.

United States Broadcast Media

A number of databases are available in the category of U.S. broadcast media. Arbitron Network Programs by ADI (Area of Dominant Influence) analyzes average quarter-hour network and spot TV allocations. Arbitron Radio Ratings Reports analyzes spot radio audiences for all ADIs and SMSAs (Standard Metropolitan Survey Areas). Arbitron Television Coverage Study and Arbitron Radio's County Coverage measure television and

Table 9.3: Selected Media and Market Planning Databases from Interactive Market Systems, Inc.

Database Title	Subject/Content
United States Broadcast Media	
Arbitron Network Programs by ADI	Quarter-hour and spot TV allocations
Arbitron Radio Ratings Reports	Radio audience measures
Arbitron Radio's County Coverage	County radio listening measure
Arbitron Time Period	Spot TV allocation analysis
Arbitron Television Coverage Study	County TV audience measure
Nielsen Network Programs by DMA	Network TV allocation analysis
Nielsen Viewers in Profile	Average quarter-hour analysis
United States Print Media	
ACORN	Demographic cluster analysis
Mediamark Research (MRI)	Media measurement data
Mendelsohn Media Research	Media habits U.S. adults
Prizm	Consumer behavior by zip code
Roper Reports	Public opinion studies
Scarborough Market Study	Media market audience study
Simmons	Media market audience study
Simmons Teenage Research Study (STARS)	Teen magazine reader study
Values and Lifestyles	Consumer demographics
International Media	
Asian Profiles	Media reading/buying habits
Australian-Wide Survey of Readership	Continuous reader survey
British National Readership Survey	Adult readership patterns
Bureau of Broadcast Measurement	Canadian audience surveys
Dow Jones' Far East Economic Review	Executive preference survey
European Businessmen Readership Survey	Senior male executives
French National Readership Survey	Readership habits survey
German Business Readership Survey	Readership habits survey
National Business Readership Survey	British readership survey
Newspaper Audience Data Bank	Canadian readership survey
Toronto Business Executives and Careers	Demographics from Toronto

radio audiences, respectively, on a county-by-county basis nationwide. Nielsen Network Programs by DMA (Demographic Measurement Area) provides network TV allocation analysis of TV audience data for any measured demographic area. Nielsen Viewers in Profile measures average quarter-hours by station in individual markets. All of the above are useful in media and market planning.

United States Print Media

There are several market research databases which address the U.S. print media. ACORN (A Classification of Residential Neighborhoods) offers a cluster analysis study on the demographic profile of residents in 44 unique neighborhoods. Mediamark Research contains measurement data for magazines, cable TV and radio, compiled from questionnaires and interviews. Mendelsohn Media Research provides data on market and media habits of U.S. adults with household incomes of over $40,000. Prizm (Potential Rating Index by ZIP Markets) predicts consumer behavior by zip code groupings, each with a unique demographic profile.

Roper Reports contains public opinion studies on economic, business, political and social issues. Scarborough Market Study analyzes audiences of newspaper, magazine, TV and radio media by SMSA and ADI. Simmons is a national psychographic and demographic study of audiences for a wide variety of media including outdoor billboards and Yellow Pages. Values and Lifestyles studies the changing values and lifestyles of Americans classified by population into eight different consumer types. All of these databases are used in media and market planning.

International Media

Analytical databases studying media markets outside the U.S. cover the United Kingdom, Ireland, Australia, Canada, France, West Germany, the Netherlands, most other west European countries, the Far East and the Middle East. These databases include readership patterns and other demographic data. Dow Jones' Far East Economic Review, European Businessmen Readership Survey and Toronto Business Executives and Career Study specialize in information about executives.

Subscription and Costs

Advance subscriptions may be required to use IMS' services, and costs vary widely, depending on the database. Interested persons should contact the New York headquarters location (see Appendix C) or one of the regional offices, located in several major U.S. and overseas cities.

BRS/MEDICAL COLLEAGUE

BRS/Medical Colleague is a medical information service designed for medical professionals. Colleague helps physicians and other practitioners stay abreast of the medical literature by providing the full text of many major medical text and reference books. BRS/Medical Colleague is designed for the end user; it is menu-driven, using the same general format as BRS/After Dark (see Chapter 4).

Information Available

BRS/Medical Colleague includes the Medline bibliographic database (also available on the regular BRS library service, BRS/After Dark, Dialog and the NLM service), but what makes Colleague unique is that it contains the full text of the Critical Care Medical Library plus many other medical reference books. BRS calls this collection the Complete-Text Medical Library. BRS/Medical Colleague is a joint effort by BRS and W.B. Saunders Co., called BRS/Saunders Medical Knowledge Resources.

The available services provide for the physician what Lexis does for the lawyer. The Critical Care Medical collection includes 24 key books on emergency and critical care published by Saunders and by Churchill Livingstone, Inc., both major medical publishers. Selected titles (databases) offered in full text are listed in Table 9.4. Other databases include Epilepsyline, Excerpta Medica, Health Audio-Visual Online Catalog, Health Planning and Administration, International Pharmaceutical Abstracts, IRCS (full-text biomedical electronics journal) and all of the other bibliographic databases available on the regular BRS library service.

Because of the variety of bibliographic and full-text databases offered by BRS/Medical Colleague, this service is a combination of both a library research and a full-text online service. It is an example of a library research database vendor (BRS) expanding into other kinds of online database offerings to meet the needs of specialized markets. It is also the first new medical service vendor since the National Library of Medicine began its commercial service, based on Medline, in 1972.

Table 9.4: Selected Full-text Medical Databases from the Critical Care Medical Library on BRS/Medical Colleague

Book Title	Author(s)/Editor(s)	Publisher	Year of Publication
Current Therapy	Howard F. Conn	W.B. Saunders	1982
Textbook of Surgery, 12th Edition	David C. Sabiston, Jr.	W.B. Saunders	1981
Principles and Practices of Emergency Medicine	George R. Schwartz Peter Safar John H. Stone Patrick B Storey David K. Wagner	W.B. Saunders	1978
Birch's Emergencies in Medical Practice	Colin Ogilvie	Churchill Livingstone	1981
Emergencies in Obstetrics and Gynecology	Arnold W. Cohen	Churchill Livingstone	1981
Instructions for Patients	H. Werter Griffith	W.B. Saunders	1982
Triage Manual (Blue Book Series)	Michael Copass Mickey Eisenberg	W.B. Saunders	1981
The Manual of Admitting Orders and Therapeutics (Blue Book Series)	Eric B. Larsen Mickey Eisenberg	W.B. Saunders	1981
Emergency Medical Therapy (Blue Book Series)	Mickey Eisenberg Michael Copass	W.B. Saunders	1981
Manual of Antimicrobial Therapy and Infectious Diseases (Blue Book Series)	Mickey Eisenberg Clifton Furukawa C. George Ray	W.B. Saunders	1981
Physician's Book of Lists	David Margulies	Churchill Livingstone	1983
Gray's Anatomy, 36th British Edition	Peter L. Williams Roger Warwick	Churchill Livingstone	1980

(continued on next page)

Table 9.4: Selected Full-text Medical Databases from the Critical Care Medical Library on BRS/Medical Colleague (cont.)

Book Title	Author(s)/Editor(s)	Publisher	Year of Publication
Acid Base and Potassium Homeostasis	Barry M. Brenner Jay H. Stein	Churchill Livingstone	1978
Acute Renal Failure	Barry M. Brenner Jay H. Stein	Churchill Livingstone	1980
Acute Renal Failure	Antoine Chapman	Churchill Livingstone	1980
Brain Failure and Resuscitation	Alan Grevik Peter Safar	Churchill Livingstone	1981
Chronic Renal Failure	Barry M. Brenner Jay H. Stein	Churchill Livingstone	1981

Subscription and Costs

There are several Colleague subscription plans offered by BRS. The standard open access plan costs $50 to sign up, and hourly connect time access fees vary from $35 for the full-text Complete-Text Library to $47 for Medline. Special evening and weekend access rates of $16 and $14 per hour, respectively, are available in a separate plan. Monthly and annual subscription plans that offer some savings are also available. Contact BRS at its Latham, NY, headquarters (see Appendix C) or at one of its regional sales offices for further details.

COMP-U-STORE

Originally called Comp-U-Star, Comp-U-Store is a nationwide online discount shopping and buying service of Comp-U-Card International, Inc. of Stamford, CT. Comp-U-Store is available directly or through Compu-Serve, Dow Jones or The Source.

Information and Services Available

The Comp-U-Store database provides descriptive and discount price information on more than 50,000 brand-name products. Information includes features, brand names, model numbers, a general description and price quotations. Discounts of up to 40% off retail list prices are available.

Information about products and prices is available in the Comp-U-Store database for the following types of business and personal products:

- personal computers, peripherals and software

- electric and electronic typewriters

- telephones and accessory equipment

- calculators

- TV, video and stereo equipment

- cameras and photographic equipment

- watches

- appliances

- crystal and sterling

- new American cars (FOB Detroit)

There are other products, as well—generally hard goods that do not require measuring or fitting. (Thus such items as clothes, shoes, curtains, furniture and fabrics are not available.)

Most customers of Comp-U-Store use the service for comparison shopping, using the discount price quotes for bargaining with local wholesale outlets. Those who do order items directly through Comp-U-Store get factory-sealed, guaranteed merchandise delivered to their designated address from one of several regional distribution centers around the U.S. In most cases, the quoted price is the delivery price, including any applicable taxes.

The Comp-U-Store system is easy to use: it is menu-driven with online help tutorials. There are three modes of online activity available for users:

- browsing (ordering is not possible in this mode)

- membership enrollment, enabling a user to enter a membership subscription, charged to a bank card

- shopping and ordering (placing an order for items by members)

A typical online session is illustrated in Figure 9.7.

Figure 9.7: A Typical Online Session in the Comp-U-Store Shopping Service

```
                          SM
     WELCOME TO COMP-U-STORE

     QUESTIONS? CALL 800-843-7777

     ALL USERS ARE SUBJECT TO THE TERMS
     AND CONDITIONS AS STATED BELOW.
     COPYRIGHT 82-84 COMP-U-CARD.


     **************************************
     WERE YOU THE WINNER OF COMP-U-STORE'S
     SCAVENGER HUNT IN JUNE? FIND OUT ON
     MONDAY, JULY 2. THEN BE SURE TO TRY
     YOUR LUCK WITH THE NEW CLUES IN JULY'S
     SCAVENGER HUNT!
     **************************************

              MAIN MENU
     1. HELP & INFORMATION
     2. MEMBER SIGN-UP/ADDRESS CHANGE
     3. COMP-U-GRAM QUESTIONS/ANSWERS
     4. SCAVENGER HUNT
     5. COMP-U-STAKES AUCTION
     ---------------------------------
         SHOPPING & ORDERING
     ---------------------------------
     6. THE COMP-U-STORE
     7. BEST BUYS (DATABASEMENT)
     8. THE HOME FURNISHING STORE
     9. THE COMP-U-MALL
     ENTER AN ITEM #: 6

     ENTER:
      PRODUCT TYPE
      (LIST) FOR PRODUCT LISTING
     >list


       #            CATEGORIES
      ---     ------------------------
       1      APPLIANCES
       2      CAMERAS & OPTICAL EQUIPT.
       3      CARS & CAR STEREO
       4      TABLEWARE
       5      LUGGAGE
       6      SPORTING GOODS
       7      STEREO & AUDIO EQUIPMENT
       8      TV & VIDEO EQUIPMENT
       9      OTHER ELECTRONICS
       10     COMPUTERS & ACCESSORIES
       11     MISCELLANEOUS
     ENTER A CATEGORY # :10


     CODE        PRODUCT
     ----    -------------------------
     APAB    APPLE BUSINESS SOFTWARE
     APAG    APPLE GAME/EDUC. SOFTWARE
     APUS    APPLE UTILITY SOFTWARE
     ATAB    ATARI BUSINESS SOFTWARE
     ATAG    ATARI GAME/EDUC. SOFTWARE
     ATUS    ATARI UTILITY SOFTWARE
     COAB    COMMODORE BUS. SOFTWARE
     COAG    COMMODORE GAME/ED. SOFTWR
     COUS    COMMODORE UTIL. SOFTWARE
     CPAC    COMPUTER ACCESSORIES
     CPMD    MODEMS
     CPMM    MEM. EXPANSION & STORAGE
     CPPR    COMPUTER PRINTERS
     CPRS    RADIO SHACK COMPUTERS
     CPUT    COMPUTERS
     CPVM    COMPUTER VIDEO MONITORS
     DIAB    DEC BUSINESS SOFTWARE
     DIUS    DEC UTILITY SOFTWARE
     IBAB    IBM BUSINESS SOFTWARE
     IBAG    IBM GAME/EDUC. SOFTWARE
     IBUS    IBM UTILITY SOFTWARE

     ENTER A PRODUCT TYPE :ibus

     ENTER:
      BRAND NAME
      (NP) NO PREFERENCE
      (LIST) BRAND LISTING
     > list

     CODE     MANUFACTURER
     ----   -------------------------
     APHA    ALPHA
     APSF    APPLIED SOFTWARE
     ASHT    ASHTON TATE
     BCJM    BRUCE & JAMES
     BDBD    BRODERBUND
     CNTL    CONTINENTAL
     IRIS    IRIS COMMUNICATIONS
     MONO    MONOGRAM
     MUSE    MUSE
     PREQ    PERSONAL EQUITY
     SAM     SAM'S SOFTWARE
     SCAR    SCARBOROUGH
     SSYS    SOFTWARE SYSTEMS
     TTEC    TELETECH CORPORATION

     ENTER:
      BRAND NAME
      (NP) NO PREFERENCE
      (LIST) BRAND LISTING
```

Subscription and Costs

One year's membership in Comp-U-Store is $25, which gives you a member number and password with buying privileges. The hourly access fee for connect time and data communications is $18 in prime time and $5 in non-prime time. If you are a user of CompuServe, Dow Jones or The Source, you can see a demonstration online and sign up as a member using the browsing and enrollment modes. For further information, contact Comp-U-Card (see Appendix C).

SUMMARY

In this chapter we have taken a very brief tour of five specialized online information services. There are many others, covering a wide range of needs. Consult one of the database directories listed in Appendix B for services that may be appropriate for you.

In the next chapter we will look at some of the capabilities of personal computers and at special software that enables you to make the best use of the many available databases and services.

10

Special Applications with Personal Computers

In this chapter we will discuss some of the powerful capabilities you have at your disposal by using a personal computer, rather than a data terminal, to communicate with online information services. Some of these capabilities are made possible by the microprocessor and disk storage of a personal computer and by the data terminal software you use for online communication—for example, the ability to transfer information from another computer to your own (called downloading) or the reverse (called uploading).

Other capabilities require special software in addition to the computer's inherent powers. For example, access interface software permits you to use online databases more easily and effectively; to reformat and analyze retrieved information; and to integrate it into reports and other documents prepared by using common business applications programs.

Our discussion in this chapter begins with a brief review of the capabilities of personal computers and their advantages over dumb data terminals, including a look at some popular types of business software. The major focus of the chapter is on the three specific personal computer functions, or applications, for the use of online information: downloading and uploading of data; end-user system interface programs; and data manipulation or integration programs. The discussion of downloading also examines some of the legal and copyright issues involved. In describing the use of personal computers for interface and data manipulation, we will review some existing commercially available software packages.

THE ADVANTAGES OF PERSONAL COMPUTERS

In Chapter 2, we touched on the three types of terminals used to gain access to online information services: dumb data terminals, word processors and electronic typewriters with data communications capability, and microcomputers equipped with modems and data communications programs. It is appropriate, at this point, to review some of the characteristics of each type of terminal.

A data terminal simply allows communication with a remote computer over telephone lines. Using a dumb data terminal, you can enter data or instructions into the remote computer and display stored or processed information sent from that computer. Since it has no microprocessor, the terminal cannot "remember" what it receives for later recall and use; thus, it is "dumb." Like the telephone itself, it can be used only as a communicating device.

Personal computers, word processors and electronic typewriters all have microprocessors and so can store information and recall and process that information according to the instructions of various programs. When not operating as a data terminal, the computer, word processor or electronic typewriter can also perform other functions. However, electronic typewriters and word processors offer only a specialized single function.

Occasionally, you will see the term "smart terminal." This can refer to dumb terminals to which some sort of memory has been added to allow temporary storage of small amounts of data or to personal computers, which are "smart" when being used as terminals.

Until recently, microcomputers cost considerably more than dumb terminals; for libraries and other professional information centers where online information retrieval was to be the primary application, it was more economical to lease or buy terminals. Now that many personal computers are so reasonably priced, it makes less sense to buy a dumb terminal for online communication. A personal computer is a far more powerful tool and costs about the same as a high-quality, high-speed printing data terminal.

The business personal computer can also replace a typewriter, a calculator or adding machine, a filing cabinet and a data terminal, with appropriate software and accessory equipment. It can take the drudgery out of accounting, financial and business planning, record keeping and correspondence. With some of the special applications software described in later sections, it also can ease the complexities of using multiple online information services. First, let's review the common business office applications of microcomputers.

Business Applications Software for Personal Computers

The three applications most used for personal computers in an office setting are, in order of descending popularity:

- financial spreadsheets

- word processing

- database management systems

Financial spreadsheets, such as Lotus 1-2-3, VisiCalc and a host of others, let you do financial projections on sales, income, balance sheets and a myriad of "what if" models. With graphics capabilities added, you can produce line, bar and pie charts from the spreadsheet models. Word processing programs, such as WordStar, replace typing for letters, memos, reports and other documents. They allow easy manipulation and editing of text and can be used to produce multiple copies of a document. Database software—e.g., dBase II—replaces filing cabinets for some documents and enhances them in others by creating computerized indexes to all of your filed records and publications.

These applications can also be used to enhance the benefits of online services. There are times when it would be very convenient to be able to obtain data from an online database like Dow Jones Quotes or Disclosure II financial time series and use the information directly in a spreadsheet program for statistical manipulation and modeling. Or you might want to incorporate bibliographic references from a Dialog database into a report being written using a word processing program. Or you simply would like to use Dialog more often but you spend so much online time remembering what to do next and simultaneously trying to refer to the user manual that it isn't worth the time and money. Some of the applications reviewed in the following sections are designed for just these purposes.

Microcomputer Applications for Online Services

Finally, as noted above, microcomputer applications for handling data from online information services include:

- information downloading and uploading

- online system interface programs

- information manipulation and integration programs

Downloading and uploading can be done with any of the data communications software packages listed in Table 2.3 of Chapter 2. System interface and data integration require additional software, discussed below.

DOWNLOADING AND UPLOADING

"Downloading" means receiving online information into your computer's memory and disk storage. "Uploading" is transmitting data from your computer's storage and memory online to another computer. Most good TTY terminal communications software for microcomputers provides for this capability.

Applications

By downloading you can capture any information from any online service, store it on your disks, and then review it, reformat or otherwise manipulate it, and use it in any way you wish.

Uploading enables you to compose electronic mail letters and messages on your computer and get them perfect before sending them to another party. You can also work offline to prepare a strategy for searching the desired database (or databases), then dial an online service, upload your search strategy, download the results, go offline and review the output at your convenience. With dumb terminals, you must do all searching and reviewing while connected to the information service. By downloading and uploading you can save as much as 50% on hourly access and computer resource units interacting with an online system.

Most of the illustrations of online system output used in this book were downloaded using a TI Professional Computer, a Hayes 1200 baud Smart-Modem and PC-Talk II communications software, and then printed on a TI Omni 856 letter-quality printer with Gothic ASCII 96 typeface. Before printing, the records were cleaned up with WordStar word processing software to eliminate any extraneous data captured along with the desired information. The same procedure can be used with any online data to incorporate it in a report or other document being created with word processing or spreadsheet software.

Legal Implications

The widespread use of microcomputers as online communications terminals and the corresponding downloading of information are of major concern to the online information industry. Downloading is one of the most hotly debated topics among online information service vendors, database publishers and computer users. This concern is understandable. The primary sources of revenue for database producers and vendors alike are online connect-time charges and royalties. Downloading and uploading can greatly reduce the amount of time you are connected to the services and royalty payments can be avoided.

The downloading issue is somewhat analogous to the question of photo-copying and copyright. The online services' search and retrieval software is copyrighted. Most full-text and bibliographic databases are copyrighted by their producers. Vendors and producers fear that users will download significant portions of their databases, and then create their own local databases, eliminating the need to go online altogether, except for occasional updates.

Some publishers also fear that their databases can be downloaded, reformatted significantly to disguise their origins, and resold or widely distributed, cheating the publishers of their royalties. Although this could be done fairly easily with microcomputers, so far no lawsuits have surfaced where a database publisher contended that such was happening.

At least one database producer sells "pre-downloaded" diskettes of informa-tion for offline use. BioSciences Information Service, publisher of the huge BIOSIS Previews databases of biomedical research abstracts (see Chapter 8), offers B-I-T-S (BIOSIS Information Transfer Systems). This service provides references and abstracts on floppy diskette, which represent database updates matching the subscriber's current awareness profile.

The Copyright Act of 1976 is vague on the whole issue of software, online databases and other forms of digital information. Bibliographic data is also a shady area in copyright law. A bibliographic citation or reference to a publication which lists title, author, issue, page number, etc., is generally considered to be in the public domain. Creative effort put into indexing and original annotation and abstracting, however, are considered to be copyright-protected. Full-text articles and stories enjoy the same protection as their printed counterparts. Lists and tables of numeric data commonly found in the numeric data retrieval services are usually considered to be public.

Because no clear-cut landmark case has yet been tried on the issue of downloading, it is useful to follow the general principle stated in the copyright law with regard to photocopying. The "fair use" doctrine says that photocopying is not infringing on the rights of the copyright holder as long as the copies are intended for fair use—for example a one-time copy for personal use or for a once-only group purpose, such as a committee deliberation or a board meeting.

Despite the fears noted above, some online vendors, database publishers and third-party software companies actually encourage downloading and uploading. They themselves provide microcomputer programs that will download and upload. In addition, they provide end-user interfaces to the online search and retrieval systems that make the systems easier to use and that put them within reach of anyone who has a personal computer. Some of these programs also provide the mechanisms to facilitate reformatting the downloaded information and integrating it into popular business spread-sheet, word processing or database management software for further manipulation. We will review some of these special packages for utilizing online information services below.

INTERFACE AND DATA MANIPULATION PROGRAMS

As noted in earlier chapters, although some online service systems are fairly easy to use with a minimum of training, others were designed for professional information specialists and are difficult and time-consuming to learn to use effectively.

In order to reach the potentially huge markets of business and professional end users, the library research and numeric services, as well as database producers and third-party firms, are developing easy interface packages on diskette for their services. Even CompuServe and Dow Jones offer software to make their systems almost foolproof to use. Other packages provide both interface and facilities for reformatting and integrating retrieved online data into business software such as VisiCalc, Lotus 1-2-3, and dBase II or III. Some of the packages that are currently available are summarized in Table 10.1 and surveyed on the following pages. For information about how to obtain software, contact the producer.

Datapath/1-2-3

ADP Network Services, Inc. offers Datapath/1-2-3 software for the IBM Personal Computer (PC). Datapath provides communications to the ADP numeric databases and permits downloading of data into the Lotus 1-2-3 spreadsheet. Lotus 1-2-3 can then be used to manipulate the data for financial modeling.

Table 10.1: Selected Online System Interface, Downloading and Business Software Integration Programs

Software Producer or Vendor Software Package Name	Computer Required*	Function Description	List Price†
ADP Network Services, Inc. DataPath/1-2-3	IBM PC	Integration of online numeric data into Lotus 1-2-3 spreadsheet	$235 ($690 as package with Lotus 1-2-3)
CompuServe, Inc. Executive Information Service	IBM PC	Interface to CompuServe Executive Information Service	$49
Disclosure, Inc. microDisclosure	IBM PC	Interface and numeric data analysis for Disclosure II	$250
Dow Jones Software Dow Jones Market Analyzer	Apple IBM PC	Interface and analysis for Dow Jones Quotes database	$349
Dow Jones Market Manager	Apple IBM PC	Interface and stock market portfolio analysis	$299
Dow Jones Market Microscope	Apple IBM PC	Interface and analysis for Media General and Earnings	$699
Dow Jones Spreadsheet Link	Apple IBM PC	Integrates numeric data from Dow Jones into spreadsheet	$249
I.P. Sharp Associates, Ltd. Micromagic	IBM PC	Interface and downloading from databases into VisiCalc	$50
Informatics General Corp. PC/Net-Link	IBM PC	Interface and database guide to library research services	$650
Information Access Co. Search Helper	Apple IBM PC	Interface and strategy guide to IAC databases on Dialog	$200 per year (with search module $1950 per year)
Institute for Scientific Information Sci-Mate	CP/M-80 CP/M-86	Interface to BRS, Dialog, ISI	$440
Menlo Corp. In-Search	IBM PC	Interface, database selector and search for Dialog system	$400
SDC Information Services Orbit SearchMaster	IBM PC	Interface and strategy developer for SDC Orbit	N.A.
Texas Instruments NaturalLink	TI PC	Interface and natural language query for Dow Jones News Retrieval	$95

*IBM PC generally means the IBM and compatible MS-DOS models, e.g., Compaq, Columbia, TI Professional, etc. Apple means II, II+, IIe; some may also run on the IIc. CP/M-80 and CP/M-86 mean that you can use an Apple, IBM PC or any other microcomputer equipped with these operating systems.

†Manufacturer's list price as of July 1984.

CompuServe Executive Information Service

Although the CompuServe Executive Information Service (EIS), described in Chapter 4, is relatively easy to use, CompuServe offers special interface software for EIS subscribers who are IBM PC users. The software allows you to design your own menus to access information and includes autodial and automatic log-on as well as downloading and uploading capabilities.

microDisclosure

In Chapters 6 and 7, we described the Disclosure II database from Disclosure, Inc., of Bethesda, MD, containing information on more than 9400 public companies. Disclosure's microDisclosure software provides access and an easy-to-use interface to this information, as well as analysis programs so you can do "what if" financial forecast modeling.

The menu-driven microDisclosure interface comes with a program disk, an analysis disk and a database disk for storing downloaded information for later use. Figure 10.1 illustrates two menus from the microDisclosure program.

Dow Jones Software

Dow Jones & Co., Inc. has several software packages for use with Dow Jones News/Retrieval Service.

Dow Jones Market Analyzer

The Dow Jones Market Analyzer is a tool for technical stock market analysis designed for individual investors and professional investment advisors. You can log on automatically to Dow Jones News/Retrieval and download both daily and historical stock quotes from the Dow Jones Quotes databases. The Market Analyzer automatically enters one year's worth of daily price data and updates daily stock, bond, mutual fund and options data.

The program creates graphic line charts for comparison of up to five stock issues, relative strength charts to compare stocks to Dow Jones Averages and moving average charts to help you decide when to buy and sell. You can also chart price and volume performance with straight-line least-squares fits, trend lines and speed-resistance lines, several performance indicators and oscillator charts. Figure 10.2 shows the main menu screen.

Figure 10.1: Welcome and Main Menu Plus Search Criteria from microDisclosure

```
IBM Personal Computer              Version 1.0

                    microDISCLOSURE

      microDISCLOSURE Program and DISCLOSURE II
          Database Copyright 1983 Disclosure
            Partners. All rights reserved.

Do you want to..

1 - call the microDISCLOSURE host computer
2 - examine company data previously saved on your own database disk
3 - prepare a new database disk for saving future company data
4 - change your microDISCLOSURE access information
5 - leave microDISCLOSURE and return to DOS

Choice?

Which criteria do you want to search...

1 - Type of Business
2 - Geographic
3 - Income Statement Information (eg. Net Sales, Net Income)
4 - Balance Sheet Assets Information (eg. Cash, Total Assets)
5 - Balance Sheet Liabilities Information (eg. Notes Payable)
6 - Officers or Directors
7 - Shares/Employers
8 - Miscellaneous (eg. Auditor, Exchange)

Choice?
```

Dow Jones Market Manager

Formerly called the Dow Jones Investment Evaluator, the Market Manager is designed to help individual investors manage their portfolios. This menu-driven package provides automatic log-on to the Dow Jones Quotes databases on Dow Jones News/Retrieval and automatically evaluates your position in the stock market, based on your portfolio. You can create and edit portfolios containing up to 50 securities, each. The main editing menu screen appears in Figure 10.3.

Figure 10.2: Main Menu from the Dow Jones Market Analyzer

```
DOW  JONES  MARKET  ANALYZER
===  =====  ======  ========
            1.  MAINTENANCE

            2.  INDIVIDUAL  CHARTS

            3.  COMPARISON  CHARTS

            4.  DJN/RS  DAILY  UPDATES

            5.  DOW  JONES  EZ  TERMINAL

            6.  SETUP

            7.  QUIT

               SELECT  ===>

          (C)  1981  RTR  SOFTWARE,  INC.
     DOWLINK  (C)  1981  DOW  JONES  &  CO.,  INC.
```

The Dow Jones Market Manager has a "tax lot" accounting system to record all of your securities transactions and match your sell transactions to existing market positions to minimize your tax liability. You can generate individual account reports and an overall securities report of your holdings of stocks, bonds, mutual funds and stock options. With the Market Manager, you can see how your investments are doing on a daily basis, monitor investments in which you are gaining or losing money, chart long- and short-term unrealized gains and losses, and monitor the impact of daily financial and economic news on your portfolio. Purchase and use of this program may be tax deductible. (Ask your tax accountant or advisor.)

Dow Jones Market Microscope

Another securities analysis software package from Dow Jones is the Dow Jones Market Microscope, a complete stock market analysis program for professional money managers, business planners and securities analysts. It is menu-driven and features special keystrokes for analytical functions such as screening reports and summary matrixes for buying and selling.

Figure 10.3 Main Editing Menu from the Dow Jones Market Manager

```
EDITING FUNCTIONS                    Dow Jones

     There are 10 securities in DJNRS

     TYPE:   1   To ADD a security

             2   To CHANGE a security

             3   To DELETE a security

             4   To DISPLAY portfolio stocks

             5   To PRINT portfolio stocks

             6   To UPDATE a security

             7   For Main Edit Menu

                 SELECT (1-7) _
```

Market Microscope automatically collects fundamental data such as daily price and volume on more than 3100 public companies and 170 industries. Market Microscope automatically calls up and downloads data from the Media General database and Corporate Earnings Estimator (see Chapter 7). Up to 20 of 68 financial indicators may be downloaded and stored. Buy-and-sell screens automatically issue alerts when stock prices reach critical points you have specified. Figure 10.4 shows a personalized fundamental indicator list.

Dow Jones Spreadsheet Link

As its name suggests, Dow Jones Spreadsheet Link links your personal computer spreadsheet to "the big board." You can automatically log on to Dow Jones News/Retrieval and download daily or historical price and volume data, fundamental data from the Corporate Earnings Estimator and Media General databases, or corporate financial data from Disclosure II into Lotus 1-2-3, MultiPlan or VisiCalc spreadsheets. You can then do "what-if" analyses of this data. Spreadsheet Link is ideal for investment analysts, individual investors, credit and sales managers, and others who need to collect and analyze data. The main menu is illustrated in Figure 10.5.

Figure 10.4: Personalized Fundamental Indicator List from the Dow Jones Market Microscope

```
============================BUY SCREEN===================================

OIL REF. & MKTG.              (070)-01/28/83              02/04/83

A. %CHANGE VS S&P 500 LAST 52WKS... HIGH TO LOW  LIMIT: 100
B. CURRENT P/E RATIO............... LOW TO HIGH   LIMIT: 6.9
C. PRICE TO COMMON EQUITY RATIO%... LOW TO HIGH   LIMIT: 100
D. 5YR EPS %GROWTH RATE............ HIGH TO LOW   LIMIT: 15
E. %DIV PAYOUT LAST FISCAL YR...... HIGH TO LOW   LIMIT: 85
F. DEBT TO EQUITY RATIO %.......... HIGH TO LOW   LIMIT: ICF(29)
G. CURRENT RATIO.................. HIGH TO LOW   LIMIT: 2
H. SHARES OUTSTANDING (1000)....... LOW TO HIGH   LIMIT: ICF(5671302)
I. EST EPS PRESENT FISCAL YR....... HIGH TO LOW   LIMIT: ICF(NONE)
J. EST EPS %GROWTH NEXT FY......... HIGH TO LOW   LIMIT: ICF(NONE)
K. CURRENT PRICE - 02/04/83....... LOW TO HIGH   LIMIT: NONE
L. LAST DAY'S VOL(100S) - 02/04/83. HIGH TO LOW   LIMIT: NONE
```

Figure 10.5: Main Menu from the Dow Jones Spreadsheet Link

```
                DOW JONES SPREADSHEET LINK

                       MAIN MENU

        1.   RETRIEVE INFORMATION FOR SPREADSHEET

        2.   ESTABLISH TERMINAL CONNECTION

        3.   BEGIN SPREADSHEET PROGRAM

        4.   SET UP HARDWARE

        5.   SET UP SOFTWARE

        6.   SET UP COMMUNICATIONS

        7.   SET UP ENTIRE SEQUENCE (4-6)

        8.   QUIT


        SELECTION ===>
```

Micromagic

I.P. Sharp's Micromagic program downloads both numeric and textual data from I.P Sharp databases into VisiCalc spreadsheets for modeling and analysis. Micromagic consists of two components: Microcom and Microput. Microcom has the communications software to link your IBM PC to the Sharp database access system. Microput performs the downloading functions into VisiCalc.

PC/Net-Link

The Library Services Division of Informatics General Corp., Rockville, MD, offers an interface program called PC/Net-Link, which allows you to automatically log on to any of the library research services and to change to another service at the touch of a single key. A unique feature of this program is its subject catalog of all databases available from public online services, which can be edited and updated as new databases are added and old ones are dropped.

Search Helper

Search Helper software is a product of Information Access Co. (IAC), publisher of news indexing and full-text databases discussed in Chapter 5. IBM PC users can employ Search Helper to search IAC and Management Contents databases on Dialog. With Search Helper, you formulate your search strategies offline before logging on to Dialog. The software then logs on automatically to Dialog, performs the strategy against the IAC databases and permits you to download them, where you can analyze the results offline. Figure 10.6 shows the main menu screen of Search Helper.

You can license the interface software alone, on an annual basis, or license it with a search module at a special annual price that includes 700 online searches, telecommunications charges and up to 20 citations per search.

Sci-Mate

The Institute for Scientific Information (ISI), Philadelphia, publishes *Science Citation Index, Social Science Citation Index* and several other indexes of cited references. These indexes are available online as SciSearch (see Chapter 8) through ISI's own service, BRS and Dialog. ISI's Sci-Mate is a menu-driven software package that provides an automatic, user-friendly interface to the ISI databases on all these services. Sci-Mate has tutorials that let you interact with any of the services in natural English. You can

Figure 10.6: Title and Main Menu from Search Helper

```
This is SEARCH HELPER (tm)

     Copyright 1983 Information Access Company.
     Portions (C) Copyright Microsoft Corporation
         1979,1981.   All rights reserved.

To find magazine and newspaper references
    about items of interest, press RETURN...

        You may search the following sources:
            1) Magazine Index
            2) National Newspaper Index
            3) Legal resource Index
            4) Trade & Industry Index
            5) Management Contents
            6) NEWSEARCH (last 30 days of all 5)
            7)    A brief description of each
```

create search strategies offline before logging on, dial the services automatically and use the strategy in more than one service. You can also download textual data onto your disks for later analysis and reformatting.

ISI also has a personal data manager to create your own database of citations from records retrieved online; this may be purchased separately.

In-Search

Menlo Corp., an entrepreneurial firm in Santa Clara, CA, offers In-Search, an interface to all of the databases on the Dialog system. In-Search makes it simple for a novice to use Dialog without any prior training or experience. Within 30 minutes, anyone can construct search strategies that will retrieve relevant bibliographic references and abstracts from any of the Dialog databases.

In-Search is menu-driven and presents Dialog databases in a library catalog card format. The databases are arranged into four main categories: business, government and news; engineering, mathematics and physical sciences; biology and medicine; and arts, education and social sciences. The natural language interface asks you to choose a category and then lets you "flip" through the cards to find the database or databases you feel are most relevant. It then guides you through the process of formulating a search query.

Once you have entered your query, In-Search automatically logs on to Dialog, executes the search, retrieves the records, logs off and lets you browse through the results. If you want to refine your search or do another, you repeat the process.

Menlo offers a demonstration diskette of questions that can be answered using In-Search (see Figure 10.7). In-Search is available in some computer retail outlets.

Figure 10.7: Examples of Questions that Can Be Answered Using In-Search from the In-Search Demonstration Diskette

```
|           Select an item by typing its number           |
|                                                         |
| 1  Business Person       | 5  Doctor                    |
| 2  Market Researcher     | 6  Engineer                  |
| 3  Finance Person        | 7  Scientist                 |
| 4  Attorney              | 8  Educator                  |
|                                                         |
| 9  Database Tour                                        |
|                                                         |
| Q  Type Q to Quit the demo and return to DOS            |
```

```
            M A R K E T   R E S E A R C H E R

Select one of these sample searches to see how In-Search can
answer specific questions a market researcher might ask.
```

```
| 1 | Where has the Bank of America been advertising lately?        |
| 2 | What is the current and projected market for frozen orange    |
|   |   juice?                                                      |
| 3 | Where can I find market research reports on cellular radio?   |
| 4 | Which Brazilian companies are interested in importing         |
|   |   electronic components from the U.S.?                         |
```

```
          Select a question by typing its number.
                          -or-
          Type Esc to return to the first menu.
```

Orbit SearchMaster

SDC Information Services has announced Orbit SearchMaster—an interface and search strategy tool for its Orbit Search Service. SearchMaster will guide you through search strategy development offline, automatically log you on to Orbit, execute the search, download the results to your disk and log off. SDC plans a fall 1984 release.

NaturalLink

NaturalLink by Texas Instruments (TI) of Dallas, TX, is a natural language applications software development package for use on the TI Professional Computer. NaturalLink Access to Dow Jones News/Retrieval is a particular application that permits you to search the Dow Jones databases by formulating queries in natural English statements. NaturalLink does all of the translation necessary for the Dow Jones system. Even experienced Dow Jones searchers may find it helpful, since there is no need to look up commands that aren't used frequently.

Figure 10.8 presents a sample screen showing how a query is constructed.

Figure 10.8: A Sample Screen from NaturalLink

```
What is the current quote for Texas Instruments

is the current quote for        and              on the composite tape
is the option price for                          on the New York exchange
were the stock prices for                        on the Pacific exchange
is the price/volume info for                     on the Midwest exchange
is the fundamental data for
are the Dow Jones averages
happened on Wall Street Week
are the estimated earnings for
is the Disclosure II info for
are the headlines

concerning the company          for each month in
covering the topic of           for each quarter in
in the Economic Update          for the last 12 days
in the Wall Street Journal      for the last 13-24 days
in the World Report             calls in the month of

Press:  F10 to Back Up  SHIFT-F11 to Quit  F6 to Save    ENTER to Execute
```

NaturalLink is screen-oriented and menu-driven. It presents elements of search queries relevant to the database being searched in "windows," or boxes, on the screen, and you construct your query simply by positioning the screen cursor over the element you want and pressing the carriage return. Very little typing is required. If you aren't already a subscriber to Dow Jones, purchase of NaturalLink includes a subscription and one free hour of non-prime time access.

SUMMARY

In this chapter we have looked at the ways in which a personal computer can enhance your use of online information services. Many software packages can help you gain effective and efficient access to online service systems and then use the information in a variety of ways—e.g., to help you with personal or business financial management or to incorporate information into business reports.

New developments in computerized online services are occurring with increasing frequency. Some of these developments, including videotex, and some of the obstacles facing the online services industry are discussed in the next and concluding chapter.

11

Looking Ahead: Videotex and Other Online Trends

We have described only a small number of the more than 250 commercial online information services in operation worldwide, and a mere handful of the 2000 or so databases available. These mid-1984 figures represent a growth rate of about 75% since 1982, just for *information* services.

Besides information, there are many other types of computerized online services available or soon to be available. They include:

- computing services

- communication services

- transaction services

- education services

- entertainment services

- multipurpose services (videotex)

Some of these have been mentioned earlier. Because many of them are provided by the same companies that offer information services, and because you can use the same equipment (a personal computer, a modem and the telephone) to gain access to them, we will discuss them very briefly here. We will give special attention to multipurpose systems, often called videotex.

COMPUTING SERVICES

Computing services are provided by time-sharing companies to the customer who doesn't have his own large computer. They offer programs for various tasks, such as accounting, inventory control, payroll and statistical modeling. Of the services discussed in this book, CompuServe, The Source, ADP Network Services and I.P. Sharp Associates offer online computing services in addition to access to information databases.

COMMUNICATION SERVICES

Communication services include electronic mail, computer conferencing and other types of online communication between computers.

Electronic Mail

The most commonly used communication service is electronic mail (e-mail). Several of the online services we have looked at in this book offer some form of electronic mail. Some are simple systems for sending brief memos or messages, but do not permit you to compose actual letters online. A few services can send messages and queries to their customer service departments; replies may be sent back online, by phone or by conventional mail.

A small number of online service vendors offer full-fledged e-mail services, on which you can create perfect letters or other messages offline, log on to the system and upload your mail for electronic delivery. The Source and CompuServe have their own e-mail services. Dow Jones News/Retrieval Service and Bibliographic Retrieval Services (BRS) offer you the use of MCI Mail, a full e-mail service in conjunction with MCI Telecommunications, Inc. (In fact, a subscription to Dow Jones News/Retrieval includes a subscription to MCI Mail and vice versa.) Other major e-mail services are OnTyme from Tymnet and Telemail from GTE Telenet.

Computer Conferencing

Multiple party online conferencing allows two or more people to communicate in an interactive "live" conference session. All parties to the conference can simultaneously see on their display screens whatever anyone types from his or her keyboard. Conferencing is currently available on CompuServe and The Source.

TRANSACTION SERVICES

Transaction services cover a wide variety of online activities that result in a transaction of some sort, usually a monetary one. Electronic funds transfer (EFT) is a name commonly applied to financial transaction services. Automatic teller machines (ATMs) are specialized EFT terminals connected online to central computer systems that monitor your bank balance, dispense cash, transfer funds and adjust balances accordingly. CompuServe offers a home banking service that does everything an ATM does except dispense cash.

The Comp-U-Store service described in Chapter 9 is an example of another kind of online transaction that allows you to order products using your bank card. The Comp-U-Store service is available through CompuServe, Dow Jones and The Source. Ticketron credit card ticket buying machines, like ATMs, also allow online transactions.

Other transaction services being offered online now or expected in the near future are online airline reservations and ticket purchase, hotel reservations, rental car reservations and entire trip planning and payment services. Stock and other securities trading online will soon be a commonplace occurrence. Some trading services are already operational (both The Source and CompuServe have online brokerage services), and others are under development.

EDUCATION AND ENTERTAINMENT

Interactive educational systems and services are already available. Control Data Corp.'s (CDC) Plato service, available on CDC's own packet-switching network, is one example. Its "courses" include money management and other topics of interest to business and professional people as well as a wide range of subjects for both adults and children. Online games and quizzes are offered on CompuServe and The Source.

MULTIPURPOSE ONLINE SERVICES

Multipurpose online services offer a combination of some or all of the activities noted above. CompuServe is a prime example. Such services are menu-driven, appeal to all kinds of people, and can be used easily without any prior computer or typing experience. Meant for home as well as business use, multipurpose services are often called "videotex."

VIDEOTEX: THE ULTIMATE ONLINE UTILITY?

Many online industry observers and analysts are very vocal about videotex. Some claim that videotex is the online technology that will appeal to the masses and that will become as commonplace in homes by the year 2000 as television is today. Others say that it is a technology without a market and that it will not succeed except in narrow specialized applications. What, precisely, is videotex?

Videotex Defined

There are diverse opinions as to what videotex really is. The word originated as "videotext" (with the final "t") and meant the display of computerized text on a video display screen—either a television set or a computer monitor. By this definition, any online service that displays text on a video screen can be accurately called videotext or videotex. CompuServe, which calls itself a videotex service, certainly fits this definition. So do Dow Jones, The Source, Dialog and every other service we have talked about in this book with the possible exception of the numeric services. The commonly accepted definition, however, is somewhat narrower.

Most people in the online industry define videotex as the transmission and display of both text and color graphics for home/office television reception. Videotex offers menu-driven information, communication and transaction services designed to appeal to a wide audience.

The text characters displayed by a videotex service follow the ASCII standard used by all online services. The graphics code is commonly one of two general types—alphamosaic or alphageometric. Alphamosaic graphics, developed by the British in the 1970s and used in most European videotex services, are rather crude; pictorial representations look like they are built of blocks or mosaic tiles, thus the name. Alphageometric graphics, developed in Canada and used in North American videotex systems, offer much higher resolution and can depict actual objects far more accurately than can alphamosaic graphics.

Status of Videotex Services

There are videotex systems operating in Great Britain (Prestel), Canada (Telidon) and other countries. (The British term for videotex is "viewdata.") In the United States, however, videotex is still in the trial stage, with no large-scale systems in operation. One impediment to widespread adoption is the alphageometric standard.

The standard accepted in North America, based on the Canadian Telidon system, is called NAPLPS (North American Presentation Level Protocol Standard); it is being used by all operational U.S. videotex trials, as of mid-1984. The problem with these systems is that they require specialized retrieval equipment in order to decode the graphics signals for display on a television set or color monitor. The typical communicating personal computer is not compatible with videotex systems. Expensive graphics adaptors are required to link your computer to these systems, and special, costly decoders or terminals are needed. Many potential customers are reluctant to pay for these items, especially if they have already invested in a personal computer or plan to buy one.

The largest videotex system in operation in the United States is Viewtron in southern Florida, which started in late 1983 and aims to reach 5000 homes by the end of 1984. This is a project of the Knight-Ridder newspaper publishing firm, in cooperation with AT&T. Viewtron has met with limited success and currently serves about 2200 homes. AT&T has developed a NAPLPS graphics terminal called Sceptre, which costs more than most home computers and which Viewtron has been selling for $600, about half of retail cost, with marginal success.

A trial videotex service in southern California by Times Mirror (publisher of *The Los Angeles Times*) was completed in 1983; commercial service was scheduled to start in fall 1984. IBM, Time Inc., J.C. Penney and Sears are other companies doing development work in videotex.

The basic concept of videotex is sound—a multifunction home and business information, transaction and communications service that offers news, general information, business and financial services, entertainment, education, home banking, home shopping, electronic mail and many other services, supported in large part by advertising, as television is today. But before videotex will be widely adopted, it will have to adapt to the personal computers now used both in business and in the home. This, in turn, will require an inexpensive add-on to handle the graphics code.

THE FUTURE OF ONLINE SERVICES

Whether or not videotex survives in its current, largely experimental form, the concept of multipurpose online utilities is valid. These utilities will serve the online information, communication and transaction needs of the general public, while new specialized information utilities will meet the needs of narrower vertical business and professional markets. And just as present online services are tailored to the personal computer and its users, so too will future videotex-like super utilities be, if they are to find wide acceptance.

As we have seen, the amount and variety of business information available make online services an attractive resource for many business and professional people. Current trends suggest that the use of such services will continue to grow. There are, however, some obstacles to be overcome before online information services achieve their full potential.

Barriers to Wider Use

There are estimated to be between 5 million and 7 million microcomputers currently in use in U.S. businesses and homes. There are between 200,000 and 300,000 online information service users in the U.S.—a small percentage of the personal computer users. If the number of online users is to grow extensively, service vendors will have to meet certain criteria. These are:

- provide systems that are easier to use

- reduce costs to users

- standardize retrieval systems and formats

- find alternatives to the telephone for transmission

At present, each of these areas has problems. Let's examine some of them briefly.

Difficulty of Use

Before online information services become more widely used by business people or any other group, including the general public, they will have to become easier to use—in fact, essentially foolproof. Many of the services covered in this book claim to be "user-friendly," and a few of them are, by the current definition of the term. In other words, they are menu-driven, and they also offer on-screen help in the form of tutorials and "how-to-proceed" messages. CompuServe and the Mead Data Central services are among the friendliest of those surveyed in this book, although even they require a little effort and practice before you are completely comfortable with them. The command-driven library research and numeric services are very difficult for the end user, as we have seen.

Most online services require the use of an instruction or user manual, whether printed or online, and some practice or training, in order to make the most effective use of them. This goes for the videotex trials and services as well. Videotex is being touted as the medium that will bring interactive online services to the general public, but before it does, or can, it will have to be as simple as a television set or telephone to operate. The same is true for the "traditional" online services.

This means that voice input, i.e., asking the computer a question in plain English, will probably play a part in online services for a mass audience. Current videotex technology is menu-driven, but selecting items from up to ten levels of hierarchical menus is time consuming and cumbersome, and it is easy to get lost. Color graphics are pretty (and expensive) but don't always contain needed information.

High Costs

Online information services (including videotex) are very costly to provide, and vendors must charge fairly high subscription and/or use fees to make any money—both factors which discourage any but serious information users. For most business executives, the cost is not prohibitive, and the value of the information is well worth the price. However, in order to appeal to the public at large, online services must attract a huge following and be supported by advertising to keep costs at a level the average person will pay.

Videotex services are attempting to do this, but thus far, videotex is a technology in search of a market. Currently, the primary videotex users are small test groups of people in upper middle income areas—upwardly mobile "white collar" business and professional people whose videotex equipment and service are provided, or at least subsidized, by the vendors. As we have seen, the services require special decoders and terminals, and are largely incompatible with current computer communications technology.

There is a related problem. Videotex does not offer enough of any one thing to appeal to vertical interests; instead, it attempts to satisfy information and other interests of a large cross section of the population. Prestel, the British videotex service, has operated for five years with some 35,000 customers and has yet to make a profit. Videotex is not yet something that the average person "must have"—unlike television, for example, it is not yet low cost, easy to use and of widely accepted value.

Lack of Standards

All online service vendors have different retrieval protocols. That is, no two services are alike in the way the user interacts with the system to retrieve information. Each claims its own system is best, but that is a matter for conjecture that depends, in large part, on the purpose of the system and on the users it was designed for. Not even the experimental videotex services are standardized.

This lack of standardization reflects a major problem in the computer/data processing and electronic publishing industries as a whole: few standards are in force. Everyone does it his or her own way, and everyone has the "best" way. Very few personal computers are totally compatible in being able to share operating systems and software. To be compatible is to risk violating patents and copyrights.

Broadcasting is standardized. Newspaper and magazine publishing are standardized. But electronic publishing and online information systems are not standardized. (Fortunately, however, most computer communications use the ASCII alphanumeric character set and the serial RS-232-C asynchronous data transmission standard. Without these, effective online information systems could not exist at all.)

Graphics will be an important part of future online services, and, as we have seen, there is little standardization of computer graphics among videotex operators or in the computer industry as a whole. The recent adoption of the NAPLPS graphics protocol among North American videotex operators is a step in the right direction, despite its problems. There is talk of making NAPLPS the graphics standard for the entire North American computer industry. As it exists now, the computer graphics industry offers a bewildering array of formats, resolutions, and corresponding software and equipment to create, display and print graphics.

Transmission Methods

The telephone networks are not ideally suited to the transmission of digital data. The data communications industry has made the existing system work, but the increasing volume of online data transmission will place increasing burdens on a very busy voice network. Further data processing developments—including increased miniaturization and speed in microprocessors and the use of optical disks to store huge volumes of data in a small space—will continue to bring down the costs and increase the amounts of computer data and data communications, thereby placing even greater demands on current telecommunications networks.

Research in this area is promising. The telecommunications industry is developing new systems to simultaneously handle both voice and data transmission. Local area networks (LANs) are the subject of much research. These networks will tie computers together in relatively small local areas to transmit data without burdening the phone systems. Other technologies under development for data transmission were mentioned in Chapter 3: interactive cable systems, not yet perfected; satellite, being used with some success by news wires and others; and optical fiber transmission, which allows transmission of data in quantities and at speeds thousands of times faster than the copper cable systems presently in use.

The Potential of Online Services

In spite of present problems, online information services offer business users an extraordinarily cost-effective means of gathering critical information. As we have seen, online information services continue to grow, and new specialized services are arising for particular markets and professions. The number of online services your computer can connect to is increasing at an annual rate of between 25% and 30%.

Major changes in telecommunications and traditional online services will make information retrieval services easier and easier to use. In one visionary, but certainly feasible, scenario, libraries, shopping centers, convenience stores, airports and other locations will provide public access to a wide variety of online services through easy-to-use consoles, kiosks and terminals, either coin or credit card operated. These services will offer information or transactions on innumerable topics and activities, from getting cash to tracing obscure magazine articles to ordering tickets for the next flight.

CONCLUSION

Regardless of what form they ultimately take, online services are here to stay, and your personal computer can open up new worlds of business information. There will continue to be both general purpose services and many specialized information services to help you to make daily business decisions faster and more reliably.

Appendix A: Glossary*

Abstract: A concise summary of an article, book or other publication.

Acoustic Coupler: A *modem* designed to hold the telephone handset in rubber cups during transmission. A microphone converts the sound tones from the handset's receiver into *digital signals* that the computer or *terminal* can understand. Likewise, the acoustic coupler converts digital signals from the sending terminal or computer into *analog signals* for transmission over the phone lines. See also *direct connect modem*.

Alphanumeric: Data or information consisting of letters and numbers; 99% of online information service *databases* are alphanumeric. A few present graphics as well. See also *videotex*.

Analog Signal: A continuous signal that varies according to the strength of input. Telephones convert human voice signals (sound waves) into electrical analog signals for transmission. *Modems* convert discontinuous data signals (*digital signals*) to audible analog signals for telephone transmission.

ASCII: American Standard Code for Information Interchange; the commonly accepted international standard computer communications code adopted in 1968. ASCII is a seven-bit code that uses combinations of seven binary *bits* to represent 128 numbers, letters, symbols and control commands (characters). See also *EBCDIC*.

Asynchronous Transmission: A method of transmitting *ASCII* characters wherein each *character* is transmitted as a discrete unit in a start-stop fashion with arbitrary spacing between characters. See also *synchronous transmission* and *X.25*.

Auto Dialer: A feature found on "smart" *modems* and *terminals* which allows you to program them to automatically dial a data access number by pressing a single key. Auto dialers can also often be programmed to log you on to a particular *online service*.

Baud: A unit for measuring data transmission speed. Baud rate is essentially the same as *bits* per second (bps), thus, 300 baud is equivalent to 300 bps or 30 *characters* per second (cps). The common transmission rates using *packet-switching networks* and voice grade telephone lines are 300 and 1200 baud. Dedicated *leased lines* may transmit at speeds of up to 9600 baud or 960 cps.

Bell-compatible: *Modems* converting *digital signals* to audio tones which meet Bell Telephone standards are "Bell-compatible." Bell 103-compatible modems are the standard for 300 *baud* modems. Bell 212A-compatible modems are the standard for 1200 baud *full-duplex* modems.

Bibliographic: A *record* or citation containing essential information about a publication. It usually consists of the title of the publication, the author(s) or editor(s), the name of the page numbers (if an article) and the date of publication.

---

*Words that appear in italics are defined elsewhere in this glossary.

Bit: An acronym for binary digit, the smallest unit of data in computer communications. A bit has a value of either 1 or 0 (either "on" or "off" electrically). A combination of seven or eight bits represents a *byte*, or *character*.

Byte: A computer "word" (*bits* being "letters") which actually represents a *character*, i.e., a letter, number or other symbol.

Character: Any *alphanumeric* representation, i.e., a letter, numeral, punctuation mark or other symbol transmitted in data communications. A character is typically built from seven or eight *bits*, plus a start bit and a stop bit when transmitted, and is the same as a *byte*.

Communicating Word Processor: A word processor that is equipped for *online* computer communications with the addition of the necessary *communications hardware* and *software*.

Communications Hardware: Circuit boards or modules and *modems* added to a *personal computer* or word processor to permit *online* communications. This hardware is built into an *ASCII* data terminal.

Communications Software: Programs used with hardware to permit *personal computers* and word processors to communicate *online*. These programs are built into the circuits of an *ASCII* data terminal.

Computer Resource Unit (CRU): A unit for billing for use of *numeric online services*, such as financial and economic *database* services, which require computing to generate reports of data. See also *connect time*.

Connect Time: The time you are connected to an *online service*; the usual basis for billing for use of an online service, often measured in hundredths of hours, minutes or seconds. See also *computer resource unit*.

Database: A collection of related information in machine-readable form usually stored on magnetic disk or tape. Databases may be *numeric*, textual or both. A database can be reference (including *bibliographic*), which tells you where to get the complete information, or source, which contains the complete information. Source databases may be numeric or *full-text*.

Data Set: Another name for a *modem*, either *acoustic* or *direct connect*. Also, a telephone equipped with a modem for data communications.

Digital Signal: A series of electrical impulses, either "on" or "off," that carries information in the form of *bits* and *bytes* in computer circuits. Digital signals must be converted to audio signals (*analog signals*) for transmission over phone lines and data *networks*.

Direct Connect Modem: A *modem* that plugs directly into a standard telephone outlet or modular jack. See also *acoustic coupler*.

Download: To capture and store information from an *online service* or data communications channel on the storage device, e.g., floppy disks of a *personal computer* or *communicating word processor*. See also *upload*.

Dumb Terminal: A data terminal without a central processing unit and consisting of a typewriter keyboard and a printer or screen. A dumb terminal is capable of sending and receiving information but not of processing it. See also *intelligent terminal*.

EBCDIC Code: Extended Binary-Coded Decimal Interchange Code, an eight-*bit* code for letters, numbers and other characters, used primarily by IBM mainframe computers and 2700-series terminals. The IBM Personal Computer uses *ASCII*.

Full-Duplex: A method of data communications that allows you to send and receive information simultaneously, just as in talking on the telephone. See also *half-duplex*.

Full Text: A *database* that contains the full text of an article or other publication.

Half-Duplex: A method of data communications that allows transmission in only one direction at a time, as in citizens' band (CB) radio. See also *full-duplex*.

Handshaking: The protocol for exchange of signals between computers and terminals which ascertains that another device is present and that communications can begin. See also *asynchronous transmission* and *X.25*.

Host Computer: The computer used by an *online service* to store and transmit *databases* offered by the service; the computer you connect your *terminal* with to use online services.

IEEE-448 Interface: The Institute of Electrical and Electronics Engineers standard for defining signals for a parallel interface. Commodore *personal computers* use this interface for *modems* and printers. See also *RS-232-C interface*.

Information Provider: The organization that provides the information or *databases* offered by an *online service*. Also called database provider, database supplier or database publisher. Information providers may be publishers, wire services, stock exchanges or government agencies.

Intelligent Terminal: A data terminal that has limited computing capability, such as a *modem* and *auto dial* and auto answer features. A *personal computer* with these features is also an intelligent terminal. See also *dumb terminal*.

Interactive Service: See *online service*.

Keyword: A word or other term that defines the content of an online *record* and that can be used to define and retrieve information from a *database*.

Leased Line: A permanent dedicated telephone circuit for transmitting *digital signals*, which is leased from a telephone company. Permits higher data transmission speeds (up to 9600 *baud*) than a standard *voice-grade line*, which has a maximum capacity for 1200 baud.

Modem: A data signal MOdulator-DEModulator device permitting computers and terminals to communicate with each other by converting *digital signals* to *analog signals* and vice versa for transmission over telephone lines. A modem may be a separate device or be built into a terminal. See also *acoustic coupler* and *direct-connect modem*.

Network: A group of computers connected to one another by telephone lines or cable so that they can send and receive data among themselves. See also *packet-switching network*.

Node: A minicomputer in a *packet-switching* data communications *network* which relays data signals to other nodes in the network to get information to and from its destination.

Offline: The state when a computer is not communicating with other computers but is doing all of its work locally on its own processors. See also *online*.

Online: The condition when a person (through a *terminal*) or a computer is communicating with another computer via telephone, *leased line*, cable or other communications channels.

Online Service: A computerized information, transaction or communication service with which a user can communicate by telephone, cable, satellite or other communications channels. Also called interactive service. See also *host computer*, *system operator* and *vendor*.

Originate/Answer: A *modem* is either in an orginate or answer mode of operation. In a data communications arrangement, one modem must be set to originate and the other to answer.

Packet: A group of data and control *bits* transmitted and switched between computers by a *packet-switching network*. Packets are of a set length and may share communications channels with many other packets, all addressed to different designated destinations.

Packet-switching Network (PSN): A data communications network used to interact with *online services*. Computer information is grouped in *packets* and switched through the system with other packets to the appropriate recipient. The major PSNs in the U.S. are Autonet, GTE Telenet, Tymnet and Uninet.

Parallel Communications: Transmission of eight *bits*, or one *byte*, at a time, sequentially. See also *IEEE-448 interface* and *serial communications*.

Parity: A method of checking for errors in data communications that checks whether a control *bit* is either "even" or "odd."

Personal Computer: A small self-contained computer which is designed for use by one person, and which usually fits on a desk or a typing table. Also called a microcomputer. The simplest personal computers are called home computers and are designed for games and entertainment more than for serious computing. When equipped with data communications hardware and software, personal computers become *intelligent terminals*.

Polling: The method used by *online service* computers to serve all users simultaneously. The computer continually cycles through all online users to ascertain if they are sending data. If so, it processes the request and moves on to the next. If not, it skips that user momentarily and goes to the next, etc.

Record: A unit of information received from an *online service*. A record may be a few lines to several pages long, depending on the type of information represented. A *bibliographic* record is usually only a few lines long, while a *full-text* record may be quite long. *Numeric* records may be of any size.

RJ-11: A standard modular telephone jack for use with a standard telephone or *direct connect modem*. A direct connect modem must be RJ-11 compatible for use with a standard telephone modular jack.

RS-232-C Interface: A standard for *serial communications* defined by the Electronics Industry Association.

Most *personal computers* and *communicating word processors* use the RS-232-C serial interface for *modems* and printers. Some, like the IBM PC, provide the *IEEE-448 interface* as well.

Selective Dissemination of Information (SDI): A means of alerting users to the latest *records* of potential interest; also called current awareness or interest profile.

Serial Communications: Transmission of each bit separately and sequentially. See also *RS-232-C interface* and *parallel communications*.

Synchronous Transmission: Data communications method in which bits are transmitted at a set, controlled rate, usually used to send large amounts of data over *leased lines* and seldom used to communicate with commercial *online services*.

System Operator: An organization which operates the computer system and software that provide *online services*. See also *host computer*.

Terminal: A device used to communicate with a computer. Usually consists of a keyboard, a display device (screen or printer) and a serial or parallel port for a *modem*. See also *communicating word processor, dumb terminal, intelligent terminal and personal computer*.

Upload: To send information over telephone lines to another computer or terminal from your personal computer's storage devices, such as floppy disks. See also *download*.

Vendor: Another name for a *system operator* of an *online service*. A vendor offers many *databases* from different *information providers*.

Videotex: The interactive *online* display of *alphanumeric* and color graphics information on a video screen. Also called videotext or viewdata.

Voice-grade Line: A standard telephone line for voice communications. Can be used for data transmission at 300 or 1200 *baud*.

X.25: The American National Standards Institute (ANSI) standard protocol for online data communications *handshaking*, or connection between computers and terminals. Used by *packet-switching networks*.

Appendix B:
Sources of Additional Information

ARTICLES

Alber, Antone. "Videotex: Data Transmission for the Masses." *Interface Age,* December 1982, p. 112.

Asinof, Lynn. "Data Retrieval Services Are Used Increasingly by Brokers and Investors for News and Prices." *Wall Street Journal*, September 27, 1982, p. 36.

Bellasalmo, Gary. "On-line Data Bases for Professional Applications." *Interface Age*, March 1983, p. 137.

Benson, Terry. "Data Communications Today." *Interface Age*, March 1983, p. 60.

Bonner, Paul and James Keogh. "Connected! A Buyer's Guide on Modems." *Personal Computing*, April 1984, p. 122.

"Bringing You MCI Mail," *Dowline*, no. 7, p. 4.

"A Budding Mass Market for Data Bases." *Business Week*, January 7, 1983, p. 128.

Busch, David D. "Computerized Databases—Your Ticket to 1,001 Applications." *Interface Age*, July 1982, p. 66.

"A Buyer's Guide to Communications Software." *Personal Software*, June 1984, p. 121.

Cavuoto, Jim. "Previewing the Information Era—a Look at Four Commercial Information Services." *Interface Age*, December 1982, p. 120.

Davis, Dwight B. "U.S. Businesses Targeted as Major Videotex Market." *Mini-Micro Systems*, September 1982, p. 145.

"Electronic Publishing Moves off the Drawing Boards." *Business Week*, August 8, 1983, p. 54.

Emmett, Arielle. "Telecommuting: the Home-to-Office Link." *Personal Computing*, April 1984, p. 77.

Farkas, David L. "Knowledge Services—Opens the Door to Information." *Modern Office Technology*, October 1983, p. 70.

Ferrarini, Elizabeth. "All the Data You Will Ever Need." *Business Computer Systems*, October 1983, p. 51.

— — —. "Bypassing the Company Library" [NewsNet]. *Business Computer Systems*, January 1983, p. 21.

— — —. "Doing Research with an Online Library" [Dialog]. *Business Computer Systems,* February 1983, p. 39.

— — —. "Facts and Figures for Penny-wise Night Owls" [BRS/After Dark]. *Business Computer Systems*, June 1983, p. 43.

— — —. "Good-bye Travel Agents." *Business Computer Systems*, November 1983, p. 38.

— — —. "The Latest from Information Utilities." *Business Computer Systems*, March 1983, p. 33.

— — —. "An On-Line Dialogue for Small Investors." *Business Computer Systems*, September 1983, p. 25.

Gabel, David. "Modem Mistakes You Don't Have to Make." *Personal Computing*, June 1984, p. 120.

Gerber, Carole Houze. "Electronic Publishing: On-line Knowledge of the World." *Today—the Videotext/Computer Magazine* [CompuServe], August 1983, p. 14.

Goodman, Danny. "Information Power to the People." *PC Magazine*, January 1983, p. 207.

Greer, Tom. "Bank at Home Completes First Year—Offers New Dimensions to Convenience." *Mid-Continent Banker*, March 1982, p. 50.

Grosswirth, Marvin. "Getting the Best from Data Banks." *Personal Computing*, May 1983, p. 111.

Hewes, Jeremy Joan. "Dialog: the Ultimate On-line Library." *PC World*, August 1983, p. 74.

James, David. "Data Bases Fullfill Needs on Demand." *Personal Computing*, July 1982, p. 32.

Karten, Howard A. "In Search of a Significant Dialog" [In-Search software]. *PC Magazine*, August 21, 1984, p. 265.

Keichel, Walter III. "Everything You Ever Wanted to Know May Soon Be Available On-line." *Fortune*, May 5, 1980, p. 226.

Krajewski, Richard. "On-line Data Bases for Personal Applications." *Interface Age*, March 1983, p. 136.

Lanson, Gerald. "Information Please—a Consumer Guide to Electronic Libraries—or What to Hitch Your Apple to." *Science*, April 1982, p. 38.

Levy, Joann. "Flying High with the OAG." *Softalk*, August 1983, p. 133.

— — —. "How Travel Planning by Modem Can Work for You." *Softalk*, August 1983, p. 179.

Levy, Steven. "Cutting On-Line Costs." *Popular Computing*, October 1983, p. 71.

Lewis, Geoff. "The Rush to Serve up Instant Data." *Venture,* March 1982, p. 70.

Magid, Lawrence J. "Battle of the Networks: The Source vs. CompuServe." *PC Magazine*, January 1983, p. 41.

Markoff, John. "In Focus: Personal Computers Communicate." *InfoWorld*, November 1, 1982, p. 21.

— — —. "The On-Line Society." *ComputerWorld OA*, August 17, 1983, p. 75.

— — — and Tom Shea. "Information Utilities." *InfoWorld,* March 28, 1983, p. 41.

Miastkowski, Stan. "Information Unlimited: the Dialog Information Retrieval Service." *Byte*, June 1981, p. 88.

Owen, Robert and Eugene Doroniuk. "Computer Communications Using the Telephone Network." *Interface Age*, July 1982, p. 71.

Pearlman, Dara. "The Joy of Telecomputing." *Popular Computing*, July 1984, p. 107.

Pomerantz, David. "Electronic Mail: a New Medium for the Message." *Today's Office*, August 1982, p. 41.

Post, Dan W. "Online Information Industry's Influence Begins to Spread." *Interface Age*, February 1983, p. 22.

Powell, David B. "Buyer's Guide to Communications Software." *Popular Computing,* July 1984, p. 121.

— — —. "Buyer's Guide to Modems." *Popular Computing,* July 1984, p. 111.

"Re-Inventing the Post Office." *Dowline*, no. 7, p. 11.

Roberts, Steven K. "Database Downloading." *Today—the Videotex/Computer Magazine* [CompuServe], August 1983, p. 27.

— — —. "Information Brokers: the Online Free-Lancers." *Online Today*, March 1984, p. 28.

— — —. "On-Line Information Retrieval: A New Business Tool." *Today—the Videotex/Computer Magazine* [CompuServe], October 1983, p. 14.

— — —. "Online Information Retrieval—Promise and Pitfalls." *Byte*, December 1981, p. 452.

— — —. "Online: a Smorgasbord of Services." *Today—the Videotex/Computer Magazine* [CompuServe], November 1983, p. 24.

Rothfeder, Jeffrey. "Electronic Mail Delivers the Executive Message." *PC Magazine,* January 1983, p. 53.

Rubin, Charles. "Touring the On-Line Databases." *Personal Computing*, January 1984, p. 82.

Russell, Judith C. "All the Info, All the Time—Online." *Data Management,* February 1983, p. 41.

Sandler, Corey. "Electronic Mail—the Paperless Revolution." *PC Magazine*, January 1983, p. 53.

Scholl, Jaye. "The Videotex Revolution—Its Impact Will Be Felt Far and Wide." *Barron's*, August 1982, p. 1.

Seger, Katie. "Let Your PC Do the Walking." *PC Magazine*, January 1983, p. 198.

Seymour, Jim. "Videotex...Finally!" *Today's Office*, October 1983, p. 37.

Shea, Tom. "High-tech Librarian Tracks Down Facts with Modem." *InfoWorld*, December 5, 1983, p. 49.

Solomon, Abby. "Executive Micro: Loading the Bases." *Inc.*, December 1983, p. 211.

Steck, Richard. "The ASCII Agreement—an Introduction to the Codes and Methods That Allow Your PC to Talk to Other Computers." *PC Magazine,* January 1983, p. 79.

Stevens, Lawrence. "Doing Business from The Source." *Personal Computing*, April 1983, p. 72.

Stone, M. David. "Extending the Reach of Your PC." *PC Magazine*, February 7, 1984, p. 401.

Taylor, Carol. "Keeping Track of AT&T Alternatives." *Data Communications*, August 1982, p. 75.

White, Ron and Stevanne Ruth Lehrman. "Three Ways to Say Hello" (evaluation of three communications software programs). *Popular Computing*, July 1984, p. 174.

"Windows on the World—the Home Information Revolution." *Business Week*, June 29, 1981, p. 74.

Woodwell, Don. "Planning Your Portfolio Personally." *Personal Computing*, May 1982, p. 62.

Zander, Ben. "Commodities Trading—the Computer Exchange." *Personal Computing,* May 1982, p. 82.

Zarley, Craig. "Dialing into Data Bases," *Personal Computing*, December 1983, p. 135.

BOOKS

Bates, William. "Online Services." In *The Computer Cookbook*, Englewood Cliffs, NJ: Prentice-Hall, Inc., 1983. (Also online via NewsNet.)

Eliason, Alan L. *Online Business Computer Applications*. Chicago: Science Research Associates, 1983.

Fenichel, Carol and Thomas Hogan. *Online Searching: a Primer*. Medford, NJ: Learned Information, Inc., 1982.

Glossbrenner, Alfred. *The Complete Handbook of Personal Computer Communications*. New York: St. Martin's Press, Inc., 1983.

Hoover, Ryan E., ed. *The Library and Information Manager's Guide to Online Services*. White Plains, NY: Knowledge Industry Publications, Inc., 1980.

— — —. *Online Search Strategies.* White Plains, NY: Knowledge Industry Publications, Inc., 1982.

Knight, Timothy Orr. *The World Connection*. Indianapolis, IN: Howard W. Sams & Co., Inc., 1983.

Meadow, Charles T. and Pauline Cochrane. *Basics of Online Searching*. New York: John Wiley & Sons, Inc., 1981.

Naisbitt, John, "Industrial Society —> Information Society." In *Megatrends*. New York: Warner Books, Inc., 1983.

Raitt, David, ed. *Introduction to Online Information Systems*. Oxford, England: Learned Information, Ltd., 1982.

Roberts, Steven K., Doran Howitt and Marvin Weinberger. *Inc. Magazine's Databasics: Your Guide to On-Line Business Services*. New York: Garland Publishing, Inc., 1983.

Spigai, Frances and Peter Sommer. *Guide to Electronic Publishing: Opportunities in Online and Viewdata Services*. White Plains, NY: Knowledge Industry Publications, Inc., 1982.

DIRECTORIES

Data Base Directory. White Plains, NY: Knowledge Industry Publications, Inc., fall 1984. To be updated annually. (See also *Data Base User Service*, below.)

Datapro Directory of On-Line Services. Delran, NJ: Datapro Research Corp. Looseleaf, updated monthly.

Directory of Online Databases. Santa Monica, CA: Cuadra Associates, Inc. Updated quarterly.

Edelhart, Mike and Owen Davies. *OMNI On-Line Database Directory*. New York: Macmillan Publishing Co., Inc., 1983.

Guide to Online Databases. Boca Raton, FL: Newsletter Management Corp., 1983.

Mayros, Van and D. Michael Werner. *Data Bases for Business: Profiles and Applications*. Radnor, PA: Chilton Book Co., 1982.

Williams, Martha E. *Computer-Readable Databases: A Directory and Data Sourcebook*. Chicago: American Library Association, scheduled late 1984.

JOURNALS, MAGAZINES AND NEWSLETTERS

Computer Data Report. Potomac, MD: Information USA. Quarterly newsletter.

Data Base Alert. White Plains, NY: Knowledge Industry Publications, Inc. Monthly newsletter. (See also *Data Base User Service*, below).

Database. Weston, CT: Online, Inc. Quarterly magazine.

Database Update. Boca Raton, FL: Newsletter Management Corp. Monthly newsletter.

Electronic Publishing Review. Oxford, England: Learned Information, Ltd. Quarterly journal.

IDP Report. White Plains, NY: Knowledge Industry Publications, Inc. Biweekly newsletter.

Information Intelligence Online Hotline. Phoenix, AZ: Information Intelligence, Inc. Semimonthly newsletter.

Information Today: the Newspaper for Users and Producers of Electronic Information Services. Medford, NJ: Learned Information, Inc. Monthly.

International Videotex/Teletext News. Bethesda, MD: Arlen Communications, Inc. Monthly newsletter.

Link-Up: Communications and the Small Computer. Minneapolis, MN: On-Line Communications. Monthly magazine.

Monitor. Oxford, England: Learned Information, Ltd. Monthly newsletter.

Online. Weston, CT: Online, Inc. Bimonthly magazine.

Online Database Report. New York: Link Resources Corp. Monthly newletter.

Online Review. Oxford, England: Learned Information, Ltd. Monthly journal.

Videotex/Teletext. Bethesda, MD: Arlen Communications, Inc. Monthly newsletter.

Video Print. Norwalk, CT: International Resource Development. Biweekly newsletter.

View Text. Bethesda, MD: Phillips Publishing, Inc. Monthly newsletter. (Also online via NewsNet.)

ONLINE DATABASES

(The online databases listed here contain numerous references to publications about online services or deal exclusively with online services.)

ABI/Inform (Abstracted Business Information). Louisville, KY: Data Courier, Inc. A bibliographic database available on BRS, BRS/After Dark, Dialog, Knowledge Index and SDC Orbit Search Service.

The Computer Cookbook. New York: William Bates. A full-text encyclopedia available on NewsNet.

The Computer Database. Chicago: Management Contents, Inc. A bibliographic database available on Dialog and Knowledge Index.

Data Base Directory Online. White Plains, NY: Knowledge Industry Publications, Inc. A reference database available through Telenet. (See also *Data Base User Service*, below.)

DISC (Data Processing & Information Science Contents). Latham, NY: Bibliographic Retrieval Services, Inc. A bibliographic database available on BRS and BRS/After Dark.

Information Science Abstracts. Arlington, VA: IFI/Plenum Data Co. A bibliographic database available on Dialog.

Microcomputer Index. Santa Clara, CA: Microcomputer Information Services. A bibliographic database available on Dialog and Knowledge Index.

On-Line Computer Telephone Directory. Kansas City, MO: J.A. Cambron Co., Inc. A directory of free online bulletin boards available on NewsNet.

Online Database Report. New York: Link Resources. A monthly full-text newsletter available on NewsNet.

Online Hotline. Phoenix, AZ: Information Intelligence, Inc. A full-text newsletter available by direct dial only.

Viewtext. Brookline, MA: Information Gatekeepers, Inc. A full-text newsletter available on NewsNet.

Worldwide Videotex Update. Boston, MA: Worldwide Videotex. A full-text newsletter available on NewsNet.

MULTIMEDIA SERVICES

Data Base User Service. White Plains, NY: Knowledge Industry Publications, Inc. Includes *Data Base Directory* (see Directories), *Data Base Alert* (see Journals, Magazines and Newsletters), access to *Data Base Hotline* (a telephone hotline giving you the latest information on online databases and services) and online access to *Data Base Directory Online.*

CONFERENCES AND TRADE SHOWS

(These annual meetings deal exclusively with online information services and related new electronic media.)

International Online Meeting. Oxford, England: Learned Information, Ltd. December, London.

National Online Meeting. Medford, NJ: Learned Information, Inc. March-April, New York.

Online '84-. Weston, CT: Online, Inc. October-November, location varies.

Viodeotex '84-. Middlesex, England: Online Publications, Ltd. June-July, New York.

Appendix C: Directory of Services

ONLINE INFORMATION SERVICES

ADP Network Services, Inc.
175 Jackson Plaza
Ann Arbor, MI 48106
313-995-6400

Bibliographic Retrieval Services, Inc. (BRS)
1200 Route 7
Latham, NY 12110
518-783-1161 or 800-833-4707
(BRS/After Dark, BRS/Medical Colleague)

Chase Econometrics
486 Totten Pond Rd.
Waltham, MA 02154
617-890-1234

Chemical Abstracts Service
P.O. Box 3012
Columbus, OH 43210
614-421-3600 or 800-848-6533

Comp-U-Card of America, Inc.
777 Summer St.
Stamford, CT 06901
203-324-9261 or 800-843-7777

CompuServe, Inc.
5000 Arlington Centre Blvd.
Columbus, OH 43220
614-457-8600 or 800-848-4455
(Executive Information Service)

Control Data Corp.
Business Information Services
500 West Putnam Ave.
P.O. Box 7100
Greenwich, CT 06836
203-622-2000

Data Resources, Inc.
Data Products Division Headquarters
1750 K St. NW, Suite 1060
Washington, DC 20006
202-862-3760

Dialog Information Services, Inc.
3460 Hillview Ave.
Palo Alto, CA 94304
415-858-3785 or 800-227-1927
(Knowledge Index)

Dow Jones & Company, Inc.
P.O. Box 300
Princeton, NJ 08540
609-452-2000 or 800-257-5114
(Dow Jones News/Retrieval Service)

Dun & Bradstreet, Inc.
99 Church St.
New York, NY 10007
212-285-7669

Info Globe
The Globe and Mail
444 Front St. W.
Toronto, Ontario, Canada MSV 259
416-585-5250

I.P. Sharp Associates
Box 418, Exchange Tower
2 First Canadian Place
Toronto, Ontario, Canada M5X 1E3
416-364-5361
(Infomagic)

Interactive Market Systems, Inc.
19 West 4th St.
New York, NY 10036
212-869-8810 or 800-223-7942

Mead Data Central
P.O. Box 933
Dayton, OH 45401
513-859-1611 or 800-227-4908
(Lexis, Nexis)

NewsNet, Inc.
945 Haverford Rd.
Bryn Mawr, PA 19010
215-527-8030 or 800-345-1301

Official Airline Guides, Inc.
2000 Clearwater Dr.
Oak Brook, IL 60521
312-654-6000 or 800-323-3537

Pergamon InfoLine
1340 Old Chain Bridge Rd.
McLean, VA 22101
703-442-0900 or 800-336-7575

SDC Information Services
2500 Colorado Ave.
Santa Monica, CA 90406
213-820-4111 or 800-421-7229
(SDC Orbit)

Source Telecomputing Corp.
1616 Anderson Rd.
McLean, VA 22102
703-734-7500, x546 or 800-336-3366

Vu/Text Information Services, Inc.
1211 Chestnut St.
Philadelphia, PA 19107
215-665-3300 or 800-258-8080

DATA COMMUNICATIONS NETWORKS

ADP Autonet
175 Jackson Plaza
Ann Arbor, MI 48106
313-769-6800

GTE Telenet Communications Corp.
8229 Boone Blvd.
Vienna, VA 22180
703-442-1000 or 800-835-3638

Tymnet, Inc.
2710 Orchard Parkway
San Jose, CA 95134
408-946-4900

Uninet, Inc.
P.O. Box 8551
Kansas City, MO 64114
913-341-9161

MAJOR INFORMATION BROKERS

Associated Information Consultants
P.O. Box 8030
Liberty Station
Ann Arbor, MI 48107
313-996-5553

Cibbarelli and Associates
18652 Florida St., Suite 245
Huntington Beach, CA 92648
714-842-6121

Find/SVP
500 5th Ave.
New York, NY 10110
212-354-2424 or 800-223-2054

Information Consulting Inc.
2584 Coventry Rd.
Columbus, OH 43221
614-486-1112

Information on Demand (IOD)
P.O. Box 9550
2112 Berkeley Way
Berkeley, CA 94709
415-841-1145

The Information Store
140 Second St.
San Francisco, CA 94105
415-543-4636
213-624-3865 (Los Angeles)
714-239-4649 (San Diego)

Info-Search
1520 N. Woodward, Suite 110
Bloomfield Hills, MI 48013
313-642-5446

Index

ABOUT THE AUTHOR

Ryan E. Hoover is president of Information Resource Management, a Dallas consulting firm specializing in the design of records management systems and databases for corporate and non-profit organizations. He was previously manager of online services with Insource Corp., manager of information with Belo Information Systems and manager of life sciences information services with SDC Orbit Search Service.

Mr. Hoover was editor of *The Library and Information Manager's Guide to Online Services* and *Online Search Strategies*, both published by Knowledge Industry Publications, Inc. His articles on online services have appeared in many professional journals. He holds a B.S. from Ohio State University and an M.L.S. from Case Western Reserve University.

Other Titles from
Knowledge Industry Publications...

The Word Processing Handbook: A Step-by-Step Guide to Automating Your Office
by Katherine Aschner
191 pages

hardcover	$32.95
softcover	$22.95

Options for Electronic Mail
by Libby Trudell
172 pages

hardcover	$32.95
softcover	$24.95

Office Automation: A Glossary and Guide
edited by Nancy MacLellan Edwards
275 pages

hardcover	$59.50

Information Technology : An Introduction
by Peter Zorkoczy
140 pages

hardcover	$29.95

The Future of Videotext
by Efrem Sigel, et al.
194 pages

hardcover	$34.95

Taking Control of Your Office Records: A Manager's Guide
edited by Katherine Aschner
264 pages

hardcover	$32.95
softcover	$22.95

Online Search Strategies
edited by Ryan E. Hoover
345 pages

hardcover	$37.50
softcover	$29.50

The Federal Role in Library and Information Services
by Marilyn Gell Masson
177 pages

hardcover	$34.50
softcover	$27.50

Data Base Directory
640 pages (approx.)

softcover	$120.00

Available from Knowledge Industry Publications, Inc. 701 Westchester Avenue White Plains, NY 10604.